1000 AE

Power in Organizations

PROCEEDINGS OF THE FIRST ANNUAL VANDERBILT SOCIOLOGY CONFERENCE

March 27–28, 1969
Vanderbilt University
Nashville, Tennessee

Power in Organizations

Edited by

MAYER N. ZALD

1970
Vanderbilt University
Press

Standard Book Number 8265-1147-3

Library of Congress Catalogue Card Number 71-91949

Printed in the United States of America by
The Parthenon Press, Nashville, Tennessee

Acknowledgments

This conference was made possible by a grant to the Department of Sociology and Anthropology, Vanderbilt University, from the National Science Foundation.

Financial support from Vanderbilt University and the Russell Sage Foundation is also acknowledged.

The Authors

FRED L. BATES — Professor of Sociology, University of Georgia, Athens, Georgia

PETER M. BLAU — Professor of Sociology, University of Chicago, Chicago, Illinois

DAVID W. BRITT — Assistant Professor of Sociology, Vanderbilt University, Nashville, Tennessee

RUE BUCHER — Associate Professor and Director, Division of Sociology, Department of Psychiatry, University of Illinois College of Medicine, Chicago, Illinois

FRED H. GOLDNER — Associate Professor, Graduate School of Business, Columbia University, New York, New York

RICHARD H. HALL — Associate Professor of Sociology, University of Minnesota, Minneapolis, Minnesota

EDWARD HARVEY — Assistant Professor of Sociology, University of Toronto, Toronto, Canada

RUSSELL MILLS — Graduate Student, Department of Sociology, Ontario Institute for Studies in Education, Toronto, Canada

CHARLES B. PERROW — Professor of Sociology, University of Wisconsin, Madison, Wisconsin

RICHARD A. PETERSON — Associate Professor of Sociology, Vanderbilt University, Nashville, Tennessee

LOUIS R. PONDY — Associate Professor of Business Administration and Community Health Sciences, Duke University, Durham, North Carolina

WILLIAM P. SMITH — Associate Professor of Psychology, Vanderbilt University, Nashville, Tennessee

WILLIAM H. STARBUCK — Professor of Business and Public Administration, Cornell University, Ithaca, New York

JAMES D. THOMPSON — Professor of Sociology, Vanderbilt University, Nashville, Tennessee

BENJAMIN WALTER — Associate Professor of Political Science, Vanderbilt University, Nashville, Tennessee

GARY L. WAMSLEY — Assistant Professor of Political Science, Vanderbilt University, Nashville, Tennessee

MAYER N. ZALD — Professor of Sociology, Vanderbilt University, Nashville, Tennessee

Contents

Conference Welcome

JAMES D. THOMPSON

On behalf of the Department of Sociology and Anthropology at Vanderbilt, welcome to this first annual conference. The series is designed to stimulate graduate and postgraduate education, especially, but not exclusively, in the Southeast. It is supported by a grant from the National Science Foundation, for which we are grateful.

Although I was not present at the time, I am certain that when this conference was first conceived it was not realized how timely the topic would be this spring. The attendance today testifies to the current interest. Many persons in and out of sociology are concerned about complex organizations in modern societies, about the depersonalization associated with them, about their unresponsiveness to social needs, and similar rhetoric. Many also are worried about power, its distribution and use in contemporary society.

Both topics seem worthy of *informed* concern, but, unfortunately, some of the most vociferous are the least informed. But I am not convinced that sociology has helped the situation, for on the topic of power our preoccupations have been on domination of one by another, or on prevention of action or freedom. Power has been cast by sociologists into terms of attainment of *my* will at *your expense.* We have been preoccupied with the *differential distribution* of power—hence the power to prevent things.

This preoccupation is clear in studies of community power structures, but also in work on complex organizations, where we still focus to a large extent on conflict between line and staff divisions or between hierarchical levels or functional departments.

There are legitimate questions, important questions, of power distribution in organizations; and if sociology is going to understand either power or organizations, we need to be tackling those questions.

But in our preoccupation with the negative, have we missed another reality? Who is going to study—if we students of organization do not— the processes by which a whole becomes more than the sum of its parts?

Organization can be creative power, or, better stated, organization creates power. This power can be used in "desirable" or "undesirable" ways, and its uses must be understood. But I feel that especially we students of organization must also be examining the creative processes by which organizations generate power.

If we cannot yet appreciate in America that the whole is greater than the sum of its parts (perhaps because we take that for granted), we cannot escape it when we consider those parts of the world where lack of organization leaves large populations unsheltered, weak, sometimes starving.

If interdependence is a central fact of social life, then sociology must understand interdependence. And this means organization. And this means power.

My personal hope is that this conference might help us turn a corner, shifting sociological preoccupation from negative power (a notion which leads the less informed to conclude that power is simply a destructive force) and help us become preoccupied instead with power as organized, creative, energizing force.

POWER IN ORGANIZATIONS

Social Process and Power
in a Medical School

RUE BUCHER

According to the [students'] statement, the [dean] asserted that "nobody in the university has the authority to negotiate with the students."

"Obviously, somebody in the university makes policy decisions," the statement said, "and until an official body comes forward, we consider the present situation a refusal to negotiate our demands."

Chicago *Sun-Times,* February 1, 1969

The above quotation reflects the plight of students and faculties throughout the nation during these times of student protest. It also cuts into the heart of our inquiry: what is the nature of power in an academic organization? Where is it located, how does it accrue, and how is it manifested? Above all, how are we to understand this apparently odd kind of formal organization? Student activists interpret as deviousness what is plain fact in many universities, namely that "nobody has the authority," while harassed administrators cast about for the proper organizational forms to meet the student onslaught. Indeed, students and faculty are beginning to pose to themselves the question which will be discussed in the following pages.

In the past few years, scholarly attention has been turned upon the American university, as witness the recent publications of Jacques Barzun (1968) and Jencks and Riesman (1968). Although there are some pungent observations in these works, the primary focus is upon the goals and values being served by the universities, and an assessment of the general forces pushing them in particular directions. Demerath, Stephens, and Taylor (1967) have done a more empirical and closer analysis of universities. Their work, too, was directed toward an important value question: what is the proper balance between the bureaucratic elements in a university, which heighten administrative efficiency, and the collegial elements, which heighten creativity of the faculty? There are a number of parallels between their empirical observations and my own, although my goal differs from theirs. My goal is to achieve an understanding of how this type of formal organization works. And not just how academic organization per se works, but upon academic organization as it sheds light upon other, related forms of organization, namely organizations which are dominated by groups of persons identified as professionals (Bucher and Stelling, 1969).[1] It is particularly important to understand these forms of organization if one believes that more and more sectors of institutions are becoming professional. It also appears, from the work of such investigators as Fred Goldner, Melville Dalton (1959), and Warren Bennis (1966), that there may not be much difference between professional organizations and some sectors of industrial organizations.

I frequently have the impression that students of medicine are second only to freshman psychology students in being objects of study by social scientists. But very little is known about the faculty who organize the curricula and teach medical students, or about the medical school as a form of organization. To my knowledge, one other investigator has extensively interviewed the faculty of a medical school. Unfortunately, the data have never been published because the situation was deemed too delicate. I share some of this trepidation and have long held back from public discussion of my data. In my view, it should be considered a tribute to those persons who provided the data that I am proceeding with publication.

The data on the particular medical school with which this essay is concerned were collected by a combination of interview and participant-

1. There is another ongoing study of a university which is quite relevant to this medical school study. It is being carried out as a doctoral dissertation by Bernard Sklar, Graduate School of Education, University of Chicago.

observation methods, together with examination of relevant documentary materials. The initial sampling strategy was to cover a few chosen departments among those teaching in various years of the medical curriculum, together with participant observation in a number of different faculty situations. The sampling objectives have now been widened. On the basis of preliminary analysis (Glaser and Strauss, 1967), data are being sought from areas of the organization which should provide test cases, so to speak, for emerging propositions. Although all the data are not yet in, I have considerable confidence in the observations which follow.

There are some things which are unique about medical schools as academic and professional organizations. In this essay I do not aim at satisfying either the reader's or my own curiosity about medical schools. The curiosity is sometimes irrepressible, but we must keep in mind that the object of these observations is to shed light, not specifically on how medical schools operate, but on what these organizations can teach us about formal organizations in general, particularly upon political processes and variants of power which may be more obvious in academic organizations than others.

WHAT MANNER OF ORGANIZATION IS THIS?

It makes a great deal of difference whether one approaches the study of an academic institution from the background and perspective of formal organizational theory, or from the background and perspective of the sociology of professions. In the first instance, one might ask questions about the structure of the organization, its goals, the roles it contains, the norms which bind them, and the integration of functions. Secondarily, one might note that the actors are professionals and look for the structural strains which are introduced by this fact. In the second approach, one would view the organization as a site where members of many different professions are at work. Then one would inquire how the persons composing these pockets of various professions delineate their fields of interest and competence, what activities they see as proper to their professional roles, and what relationships should obtain between them and their clients or other professionals. But if one goes on to ask how all these different professionals get along together, a whole new vista of problems emerges. These questions, I would contend, push the frontiers of organizational theory much farther than the first approach.

I began with the second approach, from an interest in professionals, but very early there arose the issue of what kind of organization results when a number of professionals are enjoined to work together or, at least, in some relationship to each other. With a considerable amount of data in the files, I went back to the literature of formal organizations and, after some agony, concluded that it did not offer much assistance. Many of the questions remained cogent, but it appeared that a new order of concepts was required, or at the least, that the older concepts needed further specification to fit the circumstances. I am still working at this task of conceptualization and fitting together a schema which describes the phenomena. As the task proceeds, I am gathering new data to test the fit of the concepts. In addition, a pool of data gathered over the years from other kinds of professional organizations is available for comparative analysis. Since most of the readers will have personal knowledge either of academic institutions or other professional organizations, they can check my observations against their own.

Regardless of the order by which the work proceeded, I am going to discuss the medical school as a formal organization first, briefly, because I suspect that some critical points need to be made at the beginning in order to enhance later observations. With the main outlines of the organization in mind, I will turn to the actors concerned and their professional values and interests. Then comes the major problem— putting these ingredients together: how does this system work?

The medical school that I am studying is a university medical school— a state university medical school. Indeed, in terms of student enrollment it is the second largest medical school in the nation. It is geographically separated from the main campus of the university, being situated in a large metropolitan area together with other health-professional schools in the university. The medical school has its own teaching and research hospital, on the premises, so to speak; but it also has affiliations with a number of other hospitals, public and private, three of which are within walking distance. It has a faculty of approximately 1400, most of whom are part-time or voluntary teachers.

Several major points must be made about the organization of the medical school before we can proceed to a processual analysis. The first is that it is totally misleading to approach this institution as if it were a variant of a bureaucracy. This is a blind alley, which leads the foolish tourist away from the stimulating and novel. To be sure, a formal organizational chart can be drawn, as in Chart I, and everybody in the institution will attest to its accuracy. Chart I depicts the following features: On each of the campuses of the university is a chancellor, the

CHART I

ORGANIZATIONAL CHART: THE PLACE OF THE MEDICAL
SCHOOL IN THE UNIVERSITY

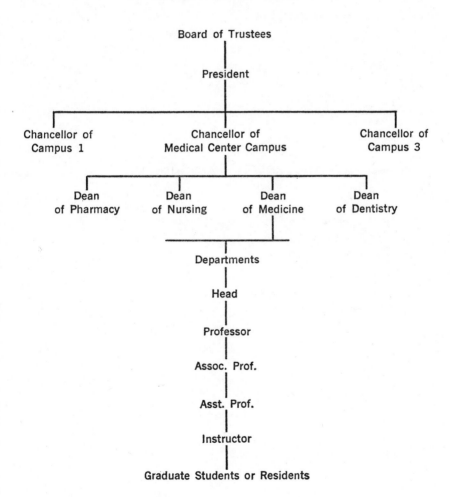

Board of Trustees

President

Chancellor of Campus 1   Chancellor of Medical Center Campus   Chancellor of Campus 3

Dean of Pharmacy   Dean of Nursing   Dean of Medicine   Dean of Dentistry

Departments

Head

Professor

Assoc. Prof.

Asst. Prof.

Instructor

Graduate Students or Residents

executive officer of the campus. Under him there is a series of discrete organizations. There are business offices, physical plant offices, personnel offices, etc., which might be designated as housekeeping sectors, rather than sectors directly concerned with academic affairs. These sectors are not depicted in Chart I, but they will come up again. Here we are concerned with the academic sectors of the university. On each campus there is a series of "colleges" or "schools," and, sometimes, "centers." Each of the colleges has its own dean and a series of divisions generally called "departments." Departments can be organized with some variations, but, since our focus is upon the medical school, the organization of its departments is shown here. These departments are organized "under a head," followed by the usual academic ranks of full professor down to instructor. Medical students are not in the bottom slot because of some novel features of schools of medicine, principally that medical students do not "belong" to departments; only graduate students and resident physicians belong to departments.

As mentioned above, the people who work in the institution would endorse this chart. But if they had any conception of how social scientists might proceed to interpret the chart, they would throw up their arms and shout, "No! that's not the way it is at all!" The issue is not that organizational charts are always idealized and therefore the organization does not conform to the chart; rather, the relationships between the elements depicted in the chart are not those usually read into such a chart. The point is that there is a hierarchy here, but it is a *nonbureaucratic hierarchy*.

This hierarchy is nonbureaucratic at all levels about which data are available. My direct interview and observational data stop at the dean's office. But it can be said that, so far as the faculty of the medical school is concerned, they carry on their business with no reference to events going on outside the school. They are aware that there are givens in their work situation which are consequences of policies made above them, and over which they have little or no control. Such givens include the number of students the college must educate, the degree of modernity of the physical plant, and the state of the library.

Faculty experience is that policies and plans go *up* the hierarchy, and sometimes sideways, rather than flowing down it. New curricula, appointments, and promotions are sent upward for approval by the president and board of trustees. Generally, the approval is routine. In five years, only one instance of blockage appears in the data, and that proposal was blocked at the level of state agencies outside the university. Conversely, there were only two instances of pressure for action originating above, and again the pressure was coming from state agencies other than the university. (It is a moot point to what extent the president capitalizes upon these stirrings from outside to present issues to the faculty as matters over which they can have no control. In other words, it is conceivable that higher administration can wave the state legislature above the faculty in order to gain compliance with policies which administration favors.)

Looking at the hierarchy within the medical school, one can find no bureaucratic elements. The dean does not issue policy statements or orders affecting those further down the hierarchy. Within the departments, full professors cannot, *as* full professors, issue directives to the associate and assistant professors. The position of department head is a peculiar one, which will occupy our attention at some length later on. Suffice it here to say that the head does not have *authority* over his staff, and he certainly is not an intermediary bureaucratic official, translating and relaying policy decisions from above into his department.

So we see that although there is a hierarchy in the school, it does not function as a bureaucratic hierarchy. Just what the hierarchy means, why it is there, and what it does are important questions for us.

Another major point about organization within the college is that more than one type of organization is operating in conjunction with it. There are coexisting forms of organization. A basic distinction that aids analysis here is whether the coexisting forms are located within the fabric of the academic organization, or outside of, and coterminous with, the academic organization. Early in this research, I found it useful to circumscribe my problem to academic organization, thereby separating out physical plant and maintenance, the business office, and other easily designated "nonacademic" areas. These sectors have their own forms of organization. The business office in particular is highly bureaucratized. Moreover, these sectors are relatively impervious to manipulation originating in the academic organization. The most common experience of faculty when they have occasion to interact with representatives from these nonacademic sectors is irritation and frustration: [2] these sectors have their own schedules and procedures, and neither part has any conception of the framework within which the other is operating. The relationship between academic and nonacademic sectors here suggests the abrasiveness between research and managerial sectors of industrial organizations that has been reported in the literature.[3]

There are two major types of coexisting or interlocking organizations within the academic organization. One of them is relevant mainly to the clinical departments, and the other to the basic-science faculty. Each of the clinical departments operates its own clinical services, both in-patient and out-patient services. The considerable variation among these services is a function of the nature of the specialty as represented in this institution and of departmental priorities. The faculty members of clinical departments are functioning within two frequently disparate hierarchies. A number of anomalies can and do result. A man who is an assistant professor with no influence outside the department, and little inside it, may be the chief of service and technically superordinate to an associate professor. Most of the full-time clinical faculty are constantly switching their hats, and literally their coats, during the day. A man may be making rounds with house staff at one point in the day, then running from the wards to a committee meeting concerned with matters far removed from the clinics.

The analogous duality for the basic-science faculty is the "graduate college." Unlike the clinics, the graduate college does not exist as a physical entity, but it is a social reality. Faculty have appointments in the college of medicine, but most of them also hold appointments in the graduate college, which allows them to educate graduate students in their own disciplines and participate in the making of policy and the institution of rituals regarding graduate education.

The clinical services run by the clinical departments constitute one of the attributes of a medical school which distinguish it from other

2. One would think that the extreme test of this proposition would be the ability of the dean to affect these sectors. I have two striking episodes in the data in which the dean was stopped cold in his attempts to expedite matters.

3. A good place to start an exploration of the literature on professionals is *Administrative Science Quarterly*, X, No. 1 (1965), which is completely devoted to the topic. Also, Bucher and Stelling (1969) review some of the literature.

academic organizations. The purveying of direct public services is built into the fabric of other professional schools, too, since students must have opportunities to practice. What is particularly striking about medical schools, though, is that academic departments undertake responsibility for extensive and complex physical plants, involving many different occupational groups and operating twenty-four hours a day.

One might expect that this interlocking of clinical responsibility with academic organization would have consequences for social processes within the clinical departments. However, one should be wary of the assumption that these departments have been formed by the *importation* and incorporation of a type of organization which is alien to traditional academic values, namely a rigid hierarchy acting under the orders of a "chief." The clinical departments differ from the basic-science departments in ways that reflect their clinical traditions and current responsibilities. But the difference is much more complex and variable than the simple incorporation or taking on of a traditional clinical system. The tradition of the "chief" has been modified by the incorporation, and it appears in different forms in different specialties.

Finally, let us turn to levels of organization within the system, and the major arenas in which action occurs. The vertical organization of faculty, department heads, and administration implies levels of organization. In fact, the level of a position does have consequences, mainly in terms of the other persons in the system with whom a given incumbent is likely to interact, and, more important, which other persons he *must* deal with in some fashion. For example, an assistant professor may interact with any of the faculty in his own department but have little contact with persons in other departments. From that position the dean is a remote figure. A department head will interact with his own faculty, but he also will have considerable contact with other department heads and the dean. These contacts are crucial for him and his department. Conversely, the dean has little direct contact with junior faculty and deals primarily with heads and other senior faculty. Here we have one of the consequences of the hierarchy in this institution: as one moves up, one's role-set alters and is likely to widen. This should be regarded as a tendency only. The numerous exceptions leave unanswered the question of conditions under which position in the hierarchy does widen role-set.

In addition to the level of organization in which action occurs, there are a number of *arenas* within which action proceeds. By arena we do not mean an actual physical site, although one can exist. Arenas are repetitive, focal situations in which the life of the institution proceeds.

Without a doubt, departments are the major arenas in the medical school. It is in and through the departments that most of the life of the institution is lived. Departments do occupy a physical site, providing faculty offices and research space, meeting rooms, and perhaps a departmental library. Departments vary enormously in numbers of faculty and the amount of space they command. The largest department had, at last count, a faculty of 271, the smallest 7. The departments are organized by *discipline*: that is, most of their members carry similar credentials; they have undergone some base of shared, prolonged, specialized socialization. There are in some departments people who represent other disciplines. Psychiatry has psychologists and sociologists, as does preventive medicine. Internal medicine has a biochemist, otolaryngology a neurophysiologist, etc. But generally the departments retain a basically disciplinary cast. This type of organization can be contrasted with, for example, that of a clinical service, which involves people of more than one occupational label and, usually, some division of labor along disciplinary lines.

The disciplines collected in the medical school are distinctive to that genre of academic organization. An important distinction is made between the basic-science departments—namely the departments which teach in the first two, nonclinical years of medical school—and the clinical departments. Some of the disciplines represented in the basic-science grouping, such as physiology and biochemistry, may be found on nonmedical campuses. But human gross anatomy and pathology are found in health-professional schools. The clinical departments represent local pockets of the specialties of medicine. Some specialties will be found as departments in any American school of medicine, while others may or may not have attained departmental status in any particular school. In this school, for example, urology and anesthesiology are sections of the department of surgery, rather than separate departments.

As mentioned previously, clinical departments are responsible for operating in-patient and out-patient facilities. These then are additional arenas in which clinical faculty participate. Similarly, basic-science and some clinical faculty may have appointments in the graduate college, so that its forums constitute arenas for these faculty. The extent of participation in these additional arenas is highly variable among faculty. Taking a clinical department first, a chief of clinical service may be in daily contact with that arena; while other of his colleagues may serve only one or two six-week stretches on the wards during the course of a year. Some members of the graduate college are deeply involved, serving on committees and participating in numerous doctoral oral examinations. Other basic-science faculty may have little to do with its forums.

A final major arena of action within the college exists within its committee structure. If departments are the sites where most of the work of the institution is carried out, committees are the major interdepartmental arenas. There are intradepartmental committees, but we shall be largely concerned with the interdepartmental committees. As any faculty member knows, to his sorrow, committees are ubiquitous in academic life. Who can appoint and dissolve a committee is of considerable importance. Another important distinction is the one between "standing" committees and, as one administrator put it, "hidden" committees. Standing committees are visible, their members and chairmen publicly available. They are appointed by a faculty committee on committees and approved (usually rubber-stamped) by the faculty at large. Committee chairmen can appoint subcommittees and ad hoc committees, which are less visible. Then there is a series of ad hoc, task-force, search committees, etc., which are appointed by the dean. The faculty has the statutory right to alter the structure of standing committees, a right exercised once in the past five years. How these committees work will be a principal concern as this description proceeds. It is sufficient for the moment to state that committees are the forums through which policy-making for the college as a whole occurs.

PROFESSIONAL IDENTITY, FACULTY PERSPECTIVES, AND ISSUES

One thing which the faculty of this college have in common is that they are the bearers of what we call a "professional identity." A professional identity involves the following components: (1) A definition of the field with which the professional (or scientist) is identified—its boundaries, what it encompasses, its major body of knowledge and associated methods; (2) A mission which the field serves—its place in a scheme of values; (3) The activities which are proper to the field; and (4) The relationships that should obtain both between members of the field, and with persons in other fields.

Two points about professional identity should be kept in mind. First, it cannot be assumed that all persons of a given occupation share a professional identity. Recent research has demonstrated that a number of segments may exist in a profession. In medicine, we have found that there are segments within specialties, like the differentiation between clinical and research-oriented pathologists and social, biological, or psychoanalytic psychiatrists (Bucher, 1962; Strauss *et al.,* 1964). When this kind of segmentalization exists, it is quite possible for persons of a given segment to have more in common with people in another speciality than with those in other segments of their own specialty. This is the case with social psychiatrists, many of whom are closer to social scientists than to other psychiatrists.

Second, a person can have multiple and overlapping professional identities. This is particularly evident with academic physicians, a number of whom can speak self-consciously about the various hats they wear and the circumstances under which they don them. For example, a man may feel like a scientist when he enters his laboratory, an internist when he makes rounds with residents in internal medicine, and a physician when he makes rounds with medical students. Particular situations call forth particular professional identities. This calling forth of different identities occurs with the basic scientists on the faculty also, but by and large they tend not to have the multiple professional identities that the physicians on the faculty have. In any case, it is necessary, when analyzing events in a complex organization like the medical school, to pose the question of which identity is being activated in particular situations.

In addition to possessing professional identities which guide their behavior, the basic scientists and physicians on the faculty share a rather basic assumption characteristic of professionals. As persons claiming expertise in particular areas of knowledge, they expect to be accorded the license to determine what should be done, how it should be done, and whether it is being done properly. In other words, they believe that they have the right to work autonomously. As we have seen, the type of hierarchy which is found in this institution is congruent with the value of autonomy. However, there are some differences between the basic scientists and physicians in the timing of acquiring autonomy, and in the areas in which autonomy is recognized. When a junior faculty member is hired in a basic-science department, the usual assumption is that he is ready to go—to organize his teaching and build his research program. Hiring junior faculty in clinical departments can be more complex. Some can be accorded full autonomy in clinical teaching areas but still be considered trainees in research. It is also usual in clinical settings for faculty to recognize the limitations of their own expertise and to defer to others who are more expert in particular areas. Thus, we can say that while autonomy is highly valued and carefully guarded in general, it is also situationally specific.[4]

There are some further implications of professional identity which suggest that it is inevitable that fundamental clashes of perspectives would occur in this kind of organization. To begin with, consider the individual member of the faculty. He needs the organization in order to accomplish the work which he has set for himself. Two phrases here are critical: "The work which he has set for himself," and "needs the organization." The organizational problem in the relationship between faculty member and college is not one of the faculty person pitted against an alien form of organization, such as a bureaucracy. The problem is one of the fit between the individual professional identity of the faculty member and the judgment of a body of colleagues (a collegial group) about the worth of his contribution to some collective value, plus the resources which they can bring to bear. The faculty member determines the work he wishes to do in terms of his professional identity. Whether or not he is able to do it depends upon the course of negotiations with specific others and the allocation of resources. He needs the organization because it provides the students he wishes to teach, the laboratory space he needs for his research, and the patients he needs for teaching and research. Thus, the faculty member's career is dependent, in a real sense, upon what the organization can offer. The courtship

---

4. In another paper with Joan Stelling, which is concerned with hospital wards, we analyze autonomy as *elastic*, as an attribute which can be expanded or contracted, depending upon judgments of competence.

involved in the hiring of a new faculty member is an elaborate rehearsal of what each can do for the other.

To the faculty member's dependence on the organization must be added another very important point: What faculty require from the organization differs in accordance with their professional identity. This is striking both within and between departments, both in how space is utilized and in how faculty organize their time. If a person with experience of medical schools were to get off the elevator absent-mindedly, without noticing the floor, he probably could determine which department he had landed in as soon as he turned a corner. Starting with basically the same physical plant, different departments remodel and arrange space to suit their specific needs. My experience as a researcher in the organization illustrates the differences in how faculty organize their time in relation to different places. In the basic-science departments, it is possible to drop into a person's laboratory and find him there or close by. If he is not in the midst of an experiment that compels his attention, or talking with a student, he can sit down and talk with you right there and then. Looking for a member of the internal medicine faculty is more complicated. The man may be in one of a number of locations, and you can get considerable exercise searching for him. When you find him, you can tag along and observe the proceedings, but he probably cannot stop to talk with you until a sequence of activities is completed. Trying to see a psychiatrist requires planning. Most psychiatrists' days are tightly scheduled with appointments, so you have to make an appointment also. If a psychiatrist is chairman of a committee, the meetings will be scheduled for one hour or some other specific length of time, and at the same hour each time. No matter what is happening in the meeting, the chairman leaves when the specified time is up.

These observations may seem trivial, but they are so basic that the actors take them thoroughly for granted—as applied to themselves. When they must interact with persons of different disciplines, though, they can be dumbfounded at just such actions—actions which flow from the other person's basic professional identity and which he also takes for granted. For example, the major criticism of psychiatry which I have heard in the school is about the difficulty that other faculty have getting in touch with the psychiatrists, and the semblance of being put off by them. They do not comprehend how psychiatrists organize their time.

When there is such diversity in the most basic grounds for behavior, it is not surprising that the presence of persons of differing professional identities can have consequences of far-reaching importance. Perhaps the most significant consequence for faculty politics has to do with how various faculty assess the implications of academic policies. Policies do not have the same consequences for all of the faculty. Insofar as people share a professional identity, they have a common fate; that is, events are likely to have the same impact upon them, and they are likely to define the same things as problems. This is certainly not the case with this faculty. Rather, segments of the faculty see different things as problems and wish to move the school in different directions.

As mentioned previously, the most pervasive segmentalization divides the clinical from the basic-science faculty. There are a few clinicians whose views are closer to the basic-science faculty than to those of their own clinical colleagues. Generally, though, there is little overlap in perspectives. Even the few faculty members in the basic-science departments who have the M.D. without the Ph.D. are more like their departmental colleagues. The fundamental clash of perspectives between these two groups can be summarized as follows.

The clinical faculty see the basic sciences in terms of their relationship to medicine, and that relationship is one of service to medicine on the part of the basic scientists. They are in the medical school to provide instruction to medical students and the latest information and techniques for the clinical faculty. The information provided students and faculty should be "clinically relevant," although a few of the more scientifically committed clinical faculty do not share this notion. The clinical perspective is symbolized in the clinicians' choice of language: They almost invariably refer to the faculty of the first two years as "preclinical," a term the basic scientists themselves rarely use. I am using the basic scientists' own language when I refer to them. The clinicians tend to take for granted a right to scrutinize what the basic scientists are doing and offer advice, for which the basic scientists surely will be grateful. When events suggest that the basic-science faculty do not share this view, the clinicians may very well ask, "What are they doing here then?" The academic physicians vary in the hauteur they express toward basic scientists. Particular basic-science faculty have reported instances in which the clinician, from the basic scientist's perspective, was downright arrogant. Others are usually respectful, but the assumption that basic scientists exist to serve medicine is quite general. From this assumption comes the general tendency to evaluate the work and attitudes of basic scientists in the institution in terms of the perceived consequences for medicine.[5]

The basic scientists, on the other hand, see their disciplines as having their own integrity—an existence and a mission separate from medicine. In this institution they accept the fact that they perform a service for medicine, namely teaching medical students. They stress, however, that they perform this service for other professions too. On this campus they also teach students in dentistry, nursing, and pharmacy. By no means, then, do they see themselves as "belonging" to medicine. Insofar as the work has applied value, it has this kind of value for many areas of human endeavor. To be sure, there are members of the basic-science faculty who say that they are here because their research interests are closer to medicine. But these people too, like the rest of the basic-science faculty, pick up the messages from the clinicians about the place they occupy in the physician's thinking, and they deeply resent it. They resent the implications of being "ancillary" to medicine. They maintain a posture of continual alertness against any maneuvers from the clinicians which could be interpreted as binding them more closely to the goals of medicine at the expense of their own goals.

These two perspectives clearly originate in deeply held aspects of professional identity which are shared by most clinicians on the one hand and by most basic scientists on the other hand. To the academic physician, medicine is the "queen of the professions," and there is no doubt of the primacy of its mission. Thus scientists are relegated into the position of servants. But the perspective of the basic scientists reflects their position as well as their professional identity. They gather that they are in a subordinate position, expected solely to serve. One respondent

---

5. The perceptive reader will have gathered that I am not unbiased in reporting these attitudes. My attitude should be taken as data also, indicating how basic scientists feel about their relations to clinicians. It is difficult for a Ph.D. to work for long in a medical school without being burned a few times. In my own case, derogatory comments about social sciences (which I expected) did not bother me, but instances when, from my point of view, clinicians made absolutely outrageous statements about Ph.Ds did rankle, particularly because they gave no indication of realizing how Ph.Ds might respond.

verbalized this position: "They always want something from you and give nothing in return." [6] They are a minority and consider themselves a beleaguered minority. Their fundamental strategy is to protect the integrity of their disciplines and their own right to self-determination. As a result, the basic-science faculty tends always to be on the defensive. As issues have been played out in the college, it has been the basic scientists who most often find themselves in the conservative, even reactionary, position.

These two basic perspectives came into play with reference to most of the major issues that have come before the faculty in the past five years. (An issue here is defined as any problem which has been taken up by some interested parties and enters the area of public discourse among the faculty; it also implies fairly wide faculty involvement.) Some issues are more or less perpetual; that is, they are not resolved, except temporarily, and come up recurrently. Two such issues—the area of medical education and the place and position of the graduate college on the campus, particularly with respect to the medical school—illustrate the way in which the fundamental split between the perspectives of clinical and basic-science faculty and the professional identities behind the perspectives influence their response to problems of the college.

Most educational establishments appear to go through periodic agonizing reappraisal of their curriculum and techniques. But there are several movements general to the profession of medicine which bring educational policies to the front rank of issues within this college. First, there is the accelerated pace of the development of new knowledge in medicine and the continual proliferation of specialties and subspecialties. The theme that there is too much to learn and it changes too quickly anyhow is constantly reiterated. A man can only expect to achieve mastery in a limited area. Now, presumably, the faculty of a medical school come as close as any physicians could to achieving mastery in limited areas. The problem that this raises, though, is what can medical students be expected to learn? How should the time in medical school be passed, and to what

6. It does appear to be true that the circumstances under which clinicians can do something for a basic scientist are very limited. The only one I can think of is when the scientist would like to have some human samples for his research. The question might be raised as to whether this state of affairs contradicts Blau's (1964) analysis of the origins of power, namely that power accrues to him who can dispense the most rewards.

should the students be exposed? Can one train students for general practice, and if so, how? Or, if one assumes that students will take specialty
training, what should they learn in medical school? These are the issues
that are being appraised and re-evaluated both on the national and
local levels.

Second, fundamental change in the staffing and organization of medical schools has been going on concomitantly with the above changes in
medicine. With a few conspicuous exceptions, the medical staffs of most
medical schools have consisted primarily of a large number of part-time
and voluntary teachers. The movement in recent years has been toward
replacing part-time staff with full-time academic physicians, or at least
creating a substantial core of full-time faculty, supplemented with part-
time faculty. This institution is participating in this movement; all of the
recent new department heads are moving toward building a core of full-
time faculty.

This movement may be bringing in faculty who are most aware of the
limitations of their own knowledge and therefore raise the most penetrat-
ing questions concerning the training of students. They are likely to
place most emphasis upon medical education as preparation for continuing learning and to insist that physicians must be scholars. They are
likely to be the people in medicine most involved in searching for new
ways of medical education. At the same time, a full-time faculty means
some persons are continually on the scene, taking responsibility and
evaluating the operation of the whole program.

Third, there is the professionalization of medical education—the
growth of a specialty or discipline of people whose job it is to concern
themselves with the goals and means of medical education. My data so
far indicate that clinicians are more receptive to medical educationists
than are the basic scientists. The clinicians are genuinely concerned and
bemused about what to do about medical students, and they accept their
own lack of competence in educational matters. They already have a
pattern of referral to experts, so when people who claim to be expert in
medical education appear on the scene, the clinicians are more willing
to accept these claims and be impressed by their expertness.

Most clinicians among the faculty have a very low opinion of the
traditional medical school curriculum and methods. One head of a major
department recalled that he very nearly dropped out of medical school

in his first year to go to graduate school because of the "rigidity" and rote-learning character of the experience. Such clinicians see the traditional format as stifling curiosity and the acquisition of critical thinking. It certainly is no preparation for modern medicine, which requires that physicians cultivate critical thinking and maintain the capacity to learn. Thus, what the clinical people want to see in the curriculum is greater freedom for the student to explore along lines of his own interest, and a more flexible, stimulating approach.

Accordingly, leading members of the clinical faculty launched a series of proposals intended to reform the curriculum in such a manner as to increase flexibility and place emphasis more upon learning than upon passing examinations. In drafting these proposals, they were assisted by a group of professional medical educators who had been invited to form an "Office of Research in Medical Education" in conjunction with the college of medicine. The attack, as it came to be perceived by the basic scientists, was three-pronged: It was aimed first at altering the examination system, second at reducing the number of hours which students spent in class and laboratories so as to provide more free time, and third at promoting elective opportunities so that students could begin, at least partially, to chart their own course through medical school.

These may seem perfectly reasonable proposals. However, the problem arose when the reformers defined the basic-science years as most in need of reform and the basic-science curriculum as most inflexible. Besides, since the student's first contact was with basic-science faculty, he picked up undesirable attitudes right away. Thus, the basic-science departments were pressured to make changes in two functions which were regarded as fundamental and, more important, as the proper prerogative of the departments concerned. They were asked (a) to scrap totally one system of evaluating students and substitute another and (b) to cut back significantly on scheduled, required teaching time, both in lectures and in the laboratory.

The basic-science faculty's response to the situation reflected several components of their professional identity. First, medical education is not their problem. While they exchange information on how to teach their disciplines with colleagues from other institutions, they do not have the identification and hence the concern about medical education that academic physicians do. Their major identification is with their graduate students and the perpetuation of their disciplines through graduate education. Thus, when the reforms became college-wide issues, many of the basic-science faculty began to resent the amount of time and emotional energy that they had to put into battles over matters that were not that important to them. As one man grumbled, "It's only medicine that gives us the trouble, not the other colleges."

Second, as the previous discussion implies, the basic-science faculty interpreted the situation as corroboration of their ideas about where they stood with relation to the clinical faculty. What they should be teaching and how were regarded as matters which only they had the professional competence to determine. The clinicians were seen as pushing them around. There even came to be paranoid elements in the response of some of the basic scientists: Some otherwise relatively innocent gestures and events were interpreted as "They're doing it to us again." Certainly, the climate of rancor between the two groups must have been heightened, but there are insufficient data to judge how much greater is the bitterness existing recently than that which existed before these events.

Third, the suggested reforms ran counter to the basic scientists' own implicit educational philosophy and the requirements of their own graduate-training programs. The notions which basic-science faculty have about education are derived primarily from their own graduate education and what they do with their graduate students. Added to that is the practice of using the basic course for medical students as the first course in the discipline for graduate students. The aim of these departments for their graduate students is to turn out productive scientists. They share with the clinicians the idea that it is ability to apply knowledge in new situations which counts, but they also hold strongly to the position that it is impossible to think critically about a subject unless one has the requisite knowledge about it. They therefore, in their basic course, aim at covering as much ground as possible. To the perennial issue of what to teach, the general response is to teach as much of the latest information as possible. To do otherwise is regarded as short-changing both the medical students and the graduate students—short-changing the medical students because no one can predict what physiology or biochemistry of today will be critical for medical practice in ten years; short-changing the graduate students because, if the amount of information being conveyed is significantly reduced, additional courses or exercises must be mounted by the departments. It is not just the amount of time for lectures that is important. The exercises provided by laboratory experiments and weekly quizzes are regarded as salutary, enabling both students and faculty to monitor the student's learning and providing additional time and forums for more intensive teaching.

The issue of the graduate college can be more succinctly presented than the more complex threads entering into the issue of medical education. It is a matter of direct, simple polarity of views, and the reader now has the information on professional identity and faculty perspectives to see the sources of the polarity. For the clinical faculty, the graduate college has negative value; for the basic-science faculty it has highly positive value. There has been little open discussion of these views— that is, discussions in which the opposing parties confront each other. The situation is mainly talked about with colleagues. But it is fairly pervasive among politically active faculty. If the graduate college barely qualifies as an issue, because of relative lack of openness, other attributes of the situation that occur around it make it interesting. Perhaps it should be categorized as a semi-underground issue.

One of the intriguing attributes is the way that people can talk about it, since it does not appear on the agenda of committees as a matter for discussion. They can say things they would not dream of saying in "public." The fact that there was something of importance at issue first came to my attention when a number of basic-science faculty had expressed the opinion that "The medical school does not want a strong dean of the graduate college." Questioned about the basis for this opinion, the typical answer directed me to look at who occupied that office. This still did not answer the question, but further probing elicited incredulity that I did not understand why medicine should have an interest in keeping the graduate college weak.

Then an event occurred which brought out the dimensions of the issue. In a committee meeting, one of the junior deans, a clinician, remarked that the graduate college was just an anachronism and that it should be abolished. A basic scientist who was present lost no time in circulating this story among his colleagues. (My impression is that rumors can circulate more quickly among the basic-science departments than among the clinical departments, because of their spatial proximity and the relative ease of reaching colleagues.) People were angry, but their manner suggested that they were surprised, not by the sentiments held by this clinician, but that he had expressed them in that situation. In any case, they were galvanized into their typical defensive fighting posture, but no fiery confrontations took place.

I proceeded to interview the dean concerned and brought up the topic in interviews and conversations with other significant figures among the clinicians. Thus my results do not indicate what proportions of clinical faculty hold anti-graduate-college sentiments. More important though, the results indicate what some of the most powerful figures among the clinicians think about this issue. Some of them were neutral or even sympathetic to the graduate college, but there were a few whose negativism was so strong that they became visibly agitated as they spoke to me about the graduate college. They derided the graduate college as an artificial creation that has neither a budget nor a spatial existence. Maybe it was necessary in the past to maintain standards, but not now; therefore it is an anachronism. These men were perfectly frank in bringing out what was really goading them on, namely that the graduate college symbolizes the true loyalties of the basic scientists. The basic scientists care more about their graduate students than medical students, they said, and this is not right. After all they are in the college of medicine and are being paid by the college of medicine. One man was toying with a proposal whereby medical students would be the only, or at least the main, graduate students.

These clinicians were perfectly correct that the graduate college has great symbolic value to the basic scientists. It symbolizes their independence from medicine. And in this we have the polarization of viewpoints. This appears to be a nonresolvable issue. Without major structural changes or major changes in faculty perspectives, there is nothing feasible either side can do to alter the situation.

The question might be raised as to how general this kind of cleavage between clinicians and basic scientists in medical schools is, and whether it is more evident here than other medical schools. I have seen the data gathered from faculty members of another medical school—the work referred to in the introduction—and the split was present in those data. My other source of information is not so reliable, but still suggestive. I began to ask faculty who had been at other medical schools to compare them to this one in terms of the clinical–basic-science split. The answers indicate that some such split exists generally. In some places, according to my respondents, the situation is not as bitter; in still others the situation was felt to be worse than this one.

A further question should be raised: Is this kind of cleavage between faculty groups unique to medical schools? I would think not. Similar partisanship appears on university campuses between say, liberal arts and sciences and the engineering school. However, there probably is something unique in the M.D.-Ph.D. confrontation. In a single sentence formulation of the underlying source of tension, I would say that the problem originates in the physicians' not according full acknowledgment of the basic scientists' professional identity. It is then compounded by the position of the basic scientists in the organization: They are a minority in an organization in which most of the faculty believe their purpose is to serve medicine.

I have discussed these two issues, medical education and the status of the graduate college, to illustrate the kinds of problems that arise when professionals of such diverse professional identities are gathered together. These two issues are extreme instances of problems faced by the organization—extreme because they reflect the strongest cleavage among the faculty. Other factions reflect other kinds of differences in professional identity, for instance the distinction between the full-time faculty and the part-time, voluntary faculty. Another distinction is between the research-minded M.Ds and the nonresearch-oriented physicians. These further kinds of distinctions result in particular faculty crossing back and forth, depending upon the specific issue under consideration.

FACULTY POLITICS AND POWER

Let us now confront the problem of how this organization runs. How the organization "runs" is essentially a process question, and we shall see that process and power are closely intertwined. In the following pages, I will attempt to demonstrate the utility of regarding this medical school as a *political* organization; in order to describe and understand the flow of events in the organization, it is necessary to use political concepts. Power is the most important such concept, but it also requires the use of related concepts, such as negotiation and persuasion. Authority as a concept has relatively little heuristic value in this setting.

Questions might be raised about the proper definition of the terms "power" and "authority." Many sagacious writers have attempted to clarify these two concepts, but when one comes to apply the various distinctions to this kind of organization, categorization becomes more clouded than clarified. My own approach has been to postpone sharp definitions of my terms and concentrate on the empirical situation in the expectation that definitions appropriate to the setting will emerge from analysis of the data.

Process and power will be examined at all levels and in the various arenas of the organization. I would like it understood that while the major focus is upon process, I am not saying that normative elements are of lesser importance. Quite the contrary. Concepts such as professional identity and faculty perspectives are normative in character; they constitute the givens of the situation at a point in time. There are other normative elements that have not yet been introduced but which will appear as we go into the analysis of the political process in the medical school—elements such as university statutes and proper manners, for example, gentlemanliness and ceremony. In any case, process and power operate differently in different arenas but can be discerned in all areas of institutional life.

The Department

A close analysis of the workings of a department within the medical school would recognize the series of arenas internal to the department and the numerous nonacademic personnel whose work is critical to the functioning of the department. For the purposes of this essay, however, I will confine discussion to the academic actors in the situation and touch upon some of the recurrent situations which bring them into political interaction.

Of the academic actors, the department head in his relations with faculty is of the greatest moment in our inquiry. Some faculty might maintain that the following excerpt is based upon their department.

When the collegiate type is fully developed, such bodies, in principle or in fiction, meet with the lord in the chair and all important matters are elucidated from all points of view in the papers of the respective experts and their assistants and by the reasoned votes of the other members. The matter is then settled by a resolution, which the lord will sanction or reject by an edict. This kind of collegiate body is the typical form in which the ruler, who increasingly turns into a "dilettante," at the same time exploits expert knowledge and—what frequently remains unnoticed—seeks to fend off the overpowering weight of expert knowledge and to maintain his dominant position in the face of experts. He keeps one expert in check by others and by such cumbersome procedures he seeks personally to gain a comprehensive picture as well as the certainty that nobody prompts him to arbitrary decisions (Gerth and Mills, 1958).

The university statutes define the responsibilities and prerogatives of department heads. Few of the faculty have consulted the statutes. In my data, covering a five-year period, the few instances in which the statutes were consulted were mainly situations in which dusting off the statutes served the argument of a party in a dispute. In two bristling instances, the problem was a conflict between the head of a department and his faculty, in which faculty were attempting to check arbitrary decision-making on the part of the head. It behooves us, thus, to consider what the statutes have to say.

In brief, the statutes state that the department head has the responsibility for determining the goals of the department and for seeing that they are achieved. In the same section is a paragraph which says that the department head cannot abridge the autonomy of faculty. (By not quoting, I am giving my own interpretation of these provisions.) These provisions give considerable latitude, and indeed, department heads play their roles with distinctive styles. However, there are some patterned differences between the clinical departments and the basic-science departments in the behavior of department heads and the response of their faculty.

The major difference between clinical and basic-science department heads is that the office of head has been admixed with the medical concept of "the chief" in the clinical departments. Authority appears in this organization only in those situations where some person defines himself as a chief, and he is so defined by others. The extent to which department heads are chiefs varies among the clinical departments. "Chiefmanship" is relatively weak in medicine and psychiatry and strongest in the surgical specialties. One can recognize that there is a chief in the background of the following vignette:

One of the full-time junior faculty in surgery was on rounds with medical students. The students questioned him about certain procedures being used for preparing patients for surgery. The faculty member acknowledged that there are different "philosophies" about pre-operative preparation but Dr. X says ———— and that's the way we do it in this department.

The chief is not a chief just because he occupies an office. On the basis of the data gathered so far, it appears that a person is accorded the appellation of chief because of his undisputed *clinical* competence. For example, one faculty member, a surgeon, proudly called his department head "an operating chief." A man of international research reputation, he was revered by this faculty member because he kept his hand in and was still able to help his staff when they ran into difficulties. In another telling instance, a new department head in one of the surgical specialties informed me that he had devoted his first two months in the department to proving that he was better than any of his staff. A chief, then, speaks with the weight of authority, an authority which seems closer to charismatic than any other type.

At one of the first meetings of the faculty of the college which I attended, an imposing senior faculty member of a clinical department rose and presented a discourse upon department heads as "robber barons" who divide up the spoils among themselves. The term "robber baron" has been repeated in other situations. It would appear safe for us to conclude that both heads and their faculties consider the position of department head a seat of power. Further evidence will suggest that they may be the most powerful figures in the organization.

Department heads are sitting upon several sources of power, sources which are critical to the careers of the faculty: (1) The head prepares the budget, which is submitted to the dean, and allocates the available funds within the department; (2) the head allocates the space of the department; and (3) the head recommends and supports faculty members for promotion. All the indications are that the heads zealously guard these prerogatives. For example, one head who was departing for a full year of sabbatical leave fully commended the affairs of the department to an acting head, but announced that he would return for the preparation of the departmental budget and the recommendation of promotions.

Some prerogatives of the head seem to be more zealously guarded than others, though. The data so far indicate that heads are particularly close-lipped, even secretive, about the departmental budget. It remains a task for further data-collecting to ascertain whether or not heads consult with any of their faculty on the budget. Faculty talk to the head about their own needs, but it appears that they have no idea of the eventual priorities built into the budget. By contrast, many heads do consult with their faculty about promotions. This is more general among the basic-science departments. Courtesy dictates that the head consult with those faculty at and above the level of a prospective promotion. The observance of this courtesy by clinical heads is more spotty.

Control of these three prerogatives would appear to make the head very powerful indeed, but there are a number of checks and balances in the system. To begin with, these prerogatives are not the only sources of power in the organization. I still have much to learn about this, but it appears clear to me now that the *assessed stature* of a man, whether head or faculty, is very important. Stature can cover a lot of qualities; nonetheless its very ambiguity makes it appropriate here because the faculty who are continuously assessing each other are usually not explicit or clear about what they are responding to when assigning a colleague to a given level or type of stature. From listening to a large number of assessments of each other on the part of faculty, I would say that any one or more of the following qualities may enter into an assessment: the quality of a person's research; whether or not he appears to be "smart," or clear-thinking; whether he is a decent human being (not just a "nice guy," which does not always procure respect); whether he has good judgment; and whether he "pulls his load." In addition, faculty take into account the reputations which colleagues have outside the department, either as researchers or effective participants in organization politics.

Any and all of the above qualities are quite fateful for the collegial group, particularly for the tenure faculty who have to live with each other for a long time. If a colleague fails to pull his load, someone else will have to pick it up. If his judgment is bad, he cannot be trusted to certain assignments for fear he will hurt the department. If he is an "operator" or vindictive, one must look to protecting himself. If he is stupid, the group must put up with a boor. If his research is mediocre or bad, he will not contribute to enhancing the reputation of the department or of his colleagues who are identified with the department. As we might expect, few faculty members are assessed as paragons of all the above virtues; however there are, unfortunately, those who are

assessed as "dead wood," virtually a total loss to the department. Most
people are judged as being good at some things and not so good at
others. Thus, there can be different types of stature, or a man can have
more stature in some situations than others. Stature is situationally
specific. Also, the assessments can change: Faculty members can come
to know each other better and decide that they were mistaken in their
earlier assessments. Faculty can be perceived as "developing," too,
with consequent reassessment of stature.

The major consequence of assessed stature is that it affects a person's
ability to negotiate and persuade successfully, and it is primarily through
negotiation and persuasion that the decisions that carry forward the
work of the organization are made. This is true both within departments and between departments. Before proceeding to examine how this
works within departments, though, we need another analytic distinction:
namely, whether or not faculty are negotiating individually or as part
of a coalition.

Some things are usually negotiated individually between faculty member and department head. These are precisely those things which are
usually connected to the head's sources of power: the salary of the
faculty member, the amount and quality of space he can command,
and his promotions. It may be that as long as a faculty member considers himself successful in negotiating these rewards, he will prefer to
keep the discourse on a one-to-one basis. It is to the head's interests to
keep these negotiations on an individual basis. In these negotiations,
both parties are operating on the basis of assessments of stature. The
head has his notions about the value of this faculty member, but he is
assessing how the faculty member assesses himself and how the faculty
member assesses his stature as head. The faculty member likewise has
his own self-assessment, an assessment of the head's stature, his perceptions of how the head regards him, and finally, judgments about
what the head is in a position to give him.

I will leave the reader to work out the likely consequences of variations in these complex mutual assessments. It should be added, though,
that this interaction can properly be called negotiation because what is
at issue is not just what will be given to the faculty member, but what he
is to give in return. This might be called the *academic bargain,* in
which the head undertakes to supply certain necessities (or luxuries,

depending upon point of view) in return for certain services. These services include the amount and kind of work which the faculty member will undertake for the department. They might also include the faculty member's avowal to publish more papers.

Another factor which enters into the negotiation between individual faculty member and head is how visible the consequences are to others in the department. Most visible to others are amount of space and other resources, amount of work they are performing for the department, and whether or not they are publishing. This places constraints upon both head and faculty member. The head has the problem of deciding how far he can support a "fair-haired boy" without bringing on a rebellion. He can also, though, negotiate with the rest of the faculty to attempt to gain their support for inequalities which might be demonstrated as in the department's best interests. This works in reverse when the head wishes to remove some "dead wood." He then has to ascertain whether or not his staff will fight for the principle of tenure or whether they will support him in cutting back the man's space or refusing a salary increase. The faculty member's problem is to avoid a miscalculation about how far the head will go. This could have disastrous results, such as forcing him to resign when he has had no intention of doing so. When the faculty member is not succeeding in improving his position with respect to the visible rewards, he has to face whether or not the embarrassment is sufficient to warrant his resignation.

Now let us examine the situation of collective negotiation within the department. I have already indicated that a group of colleagues can band together to confront the head on the behalf of one or more colleagues whom they deem are not receiving fair treatment. Most of the time the group becomes involved in negotiations around the more generalized aspects of the head's prerogatives, such as salary levels within the department and general priorities in the use of departmental space. There can also be general faculty discussion of criteria for promotion. These are major policy issues within the departments. Salary levels may be negotiable only within limits, limits which neither the head nor his faculty can much affect. Questions of criteria for promotion, though, touch upon such basic issues as the mission of the department and what kinds of persons they wish to attract and keep within the department. Questions of space-utilization equally involve issues of departmental mission and priorities. Faculty may not wish to discuss these things specifically with relation to themselves in the context of the collectivity, but the general policies which are derived from these areas have great consequences for the individual faculty members, who thus have considerable interest in the discussion of such issues.

An important point must be made here about which faculty are likely to engage in policy discussions with the head, either in a dyad or in the collegial group. The real questions are who are colleagues and who are valued advisors. The former of these questions takes on some unique properties in a medical school which has a large part-time and voluntary faculty in addition to a core of full-time faculty. The segmentalization between full-time and voluntary faculty is a major backdrop to the resolution of who participates in policy formation. For all the segmentalization that exists between departmental colleagues, between colleagues in different departments, and between the basic scientists and clinicians, one situation persistently unites them all: a confrontation between full-time faculty and part-time or voluntary faculty. In these situations it apparently comes home to the full-time faculty that they do share some basic values and would be equally vulnerable to the consequences should the local medical society prevail. (The town-and-gown conflict which characterizes the relations of academic physicians to those in private practice and represented by the AMA and local societies could be the subject for study in itself.)

The question which the full-time faculty members pose might be paraphrased as follows: Considering my stake in the institution, whom do I want to have any say in my fate? The answer is quite consistent. They do not wish those who do not have a similar stake to have anything to do with it. There are a few part-time men in clinical departments who are sufficiently esteemed by their full-time colleagues to be considered one of them when it comes to policy issues. (I have separated part-time and voluntary because there is considerable difference between the commitment of a man who devotes fifty or seventy percent of his time to the school for that percentage of a salary and one who voluntarily devotes two mornings for several months or even less.) Aside from excluding the nonfull-time faculty from policy, there is considerable variation among the departments in who, among the full-time faculty, constitute a collegium. However the lines are drawn in a department, though, the faculty in the inner circle tend to protect jealously each other's right to be there, whether or not they agree on issues or esteem one another.

At the same time it must be said that both heads and full-time faculty have their moments of guilt about the part-time and voluntary faculty. They need these people for the clinical teaching program, they use them with little or no monetary reward, and they occasionally call on them to come and vote at general faculty meetings for issues of import to the department. In the larger clinical departments it is patently impossible to carry out genuine committee-like deliberations in the context of a meeting of the full departmental faculty. The compromise which is usually taken is to hold an *affaire,* during which a report of what has been going on in the department is given and the nonfull-time faculty is given an opportunity to respond. Since the nonfull-time faculty have had no opportunity to organize among themselves in response to issues, these meetings have not produced any checking or reversal of the policies originating among the full-time faculty and the head.

The department head is enjoined by the statutes to listen to a departmental advisory group; he is not enjoined to follow their advice. It appears that department heads rarely proceed against faculty advice (a) when there is unity or near unity among the faculty, and (b) when the matter at issue is one about which the faculty have strong feelings. I witnessed a department meeting at which most of the faculty did not support the head in his intentions, but the problem under review was relatively remote from the department and did not threaten any vital interests of members of the department. Under these circumstances, the head announced that he would vote his own convictions at the executive committee of the college but would make it clear there that he was expressing his own opinions and not those of his department. In the instances in which faculty were attempting to check arbitrariness on the part of the head, there was a high degree of unity among the faculty and passionate feeling. Until further data prove me wrong, I would contend that a department head cannot, without grave consequences, engage in actions which his faculty considers an abuse of power. It seems that under those conditions the faculty unites quickly and pushes for a confrontation, which is successful.

Most of the time, though, the departmental faculty is not united but rather is divided into coalitions. Some coalitions persist through the years. The persistent coalitions reflect the continuing splits in professional identity within the department. They also tend to be activated around persisting, unresolved issues. For example, in one department meeting, a junior faculty member rose and asked about the current status of a proposal that would have involved a drastic reorganization of clinical services. The present organization of services reflects the professional identity of the head and a number of the senior faculty. A debate ensued, which the head concluded by saying that they had failed to convince him. They had also failed to convince a sufficient number of the senior faculty.

Most coalitions are shifting alliances, depending upon the issues. As issues come up, faculty within the department who are concerned shop around seeking out those who might be allies in relation to the particular issue. The most sought-after potential allies are those with the greatest assessed stature, since it is they who are most likely to persuade the department head and other faculty. It is quite possible that many issues are resolved without ever coming up for discussion at a meeting. One or more faculty may visit the head and succeed in persuading him to their point of view. Sometimes, after a number of faculty caucuses, a delegation may be sent. In any case, if the faculty are serious about an issue, they are likely to prepare carefully before a faculty meeting, lining up allies and strengthening their arguments through discussion in caucuses. If an issue is introduced into a meeting "cold," it is rare that any decision is taken. It either drops by the wayside or is postponed.

A strong coalition is one which includes some of the most esteemed faculty. Sheer superiority of numbers does not seem to have the same impact. Much depends upon who the members of a coalition are. If the coalition includes esteemed persons from more than one persistent coalition, it probably can carry the department. If different coalitions confront each other and neither succeeds in winning over additional strength, the debate remains inconclusive. The department head then can either attempt to persuade the parties into some measure of consensus, or he can simply proceed to act upon his own judgment.

I do not have sufficient data to construct any hypothesis about the conditions under which the allies in a losing faction become disaffected.

It may be so rare that I can never collect enough instances of it. If serious disaffection occurs only infrequently, it is probably because the tendency for coalitions to shift prevents lines from hardening unduly. It is my impression that disaffection is most often expressed by the junior faculty. In their case it tends to be explicitly tied to the fact that they have not had access to the councils in which decisions were made, or if they did they had no influence. In this sense there is a decided "establishment" phenomenon within departments of this medical school.

We have delineated a number of sources of power within departments of the medical school. We have seen that the exercise of power is a complex and fluid process, not solely located in the office of department head. Indeed, the preponderance of power at any one point in time may shift among the collectivity. Furthermore, power is exercised, not by the use of commands, but through the processes of persuasion and negotiation. Or, as one faculty member whose assessed stature is quite high put it, "If they want the faculty to do something, they have to convince them."

Interdepartmental Arenas and the Administrative Process

If department heads are robber barons who divide up the spoils, they do not all share equally. It is not just that smaller departments require fewer of the spoils. Some department heads are considerably more powerful than others. The size of the department, and the extent to which it is designated an important, or major, department, are clear contributors to the power of department heads. For reasons which doubtless have to do with deeply ingrained professional values in medicine, the chairman of the department of internal medicine tends to be among the most powerful, if not the most powerful, of heads in the school of medicine, followed by the head of the department of surgery. In this school, internal medicine is the largest department, and psychiatry, not surgery, is the next largest. I cannot judge now whether the head of psychiatry is more powerful than the head of surgery, but the power which the head of psychiatry has accrued is not a consequence of the size of his department, which is only grudgingly being acknowledged as a major department. He has achieved influence through the assessment which other department heads and administration have made of his performance. (As an interesting sidelight, the head of the department of medicine had been the chairman of the search committee that chose this head of psychiatry. The head of psychiatry is now chairman of the search committee that is seeking a replacement for the retiring head of medicine.) A newly appointed head of a major department can *ipso facto* expect that he will have the ear of the dean and the other department heads. However, he is being carefully observed, and a collective assessment of his stature begins to form.

The process of assessing the stature of a colleague is the same in interdepartmental arenas as within departments, except that there is some shift in the weight given to the various qualities attributed to the assessed one. The qualities which I summarize under the rubrics of "Is he a decent human being?" and "Does he have good judgment?" become further differentiated and come more to the forefront. A man can coast for some time on a brilliant research reputation, but if he comes to be assessed as a "bastard"—out to get all the spoils for himself and giving no one else any credit for claims to the spoils—his glamour pales; people may even begin to set up situations hoping to force the man into resigning. Or a potential Nobel Laureate may turn out to have no perceptiveness about other people and no political judgment. (The terms which are actually used are more pungent, but the reader can probably supply them for himself.)

The major point is that a department can—with whatever pain—accommodate the brilliant scientist who has no aptitude for handling the other aspects of academic life. But this combination of attributes is barely, if at all, tolerable with a department head in the interdepartmental arenas. It is not even much more tolerable from faculty members in committees. Department heads can probably become the victims of a bad assessment of stature outside the department more easily than their faculty, and then the department comes to suffer from this assessment too. I should hasten to add, though, that there does seem to be, in most situations, a genuine undercurrent of justice and good will on the academic scene, so that departments saddled with "difficult" heads do not suffer significant cuts in budget. (At least not in this school.) The price which departments pay for an ineffective head, then, is not so much that his budgets are cut, but that when he is speaking in an interdepartmental arena about issues which are of some interest to the department, his remarks may be discounted. This too should be qualified, again with a nod to the sense of collegial justice which usually prevails: If the head's remarks are interpreted as bearing directly upon what the department must have to carry on its work, people do listen carefully. After all, their aim is not to destroy Discipline X in the school.

There is, then, out of twenty heads of departments, a relatively small group of highly respected men who, when they rise to speak, are taken seriously. The men in this category who are heads of major departments are probably more influential, but there are also men who are heads of minor departments who have acquired considerable stature. In addition, there is an even smaller number of faculty members who receive an attentive audience. How this comes about will be discussed further on. Here let me just say that, over and above the virtues already discussed as entering into the assessment of a person's stature, there is the quality of articulateness. Articulateness is not often explicitly commended, but it seems to me that it is a sine qua non of effectiveness in interdepartmental arenas.

I have in effect been saying that the ability of those with high assessed stature to persuade and negotiate successfully is a form of power. Now is the time to take into consideration the relationship between extensiveness of role-set and assessed stature. There is the tendency of those higher up in the academic hierarchy to have a more extensive role-set, and department heads in particular tend to interact with a broad spectrum of persons within the organization. Does participation in an extensive network of relationships both inside and outside the departments constitute in itself a source of power? The data suggest that extensiveness of role-set is a necessary but not sufficient condition for power, and that assessed stature is the more critical variable. There are persons highly regarded within their departments, who thereby have an effect upon the formation of departmental policies; but however this may reverberate in interdepartmental politics, the direct influence of the particular man has been local. There are also faculty members of stature with extensive relations outside the department, and these tend to be among the powers of the institution. It is unlikely, except with department heads, that a person can have an extensive role-set without rating high in stature. The respective influence of these variables, assessed stature and role-set, is highlighted if one casts them into a fourfold table, as in Table I.

TABLE 1

The Relationship Between Extensiveness of Role-Set, Assessed
Stature, and Power

Role-Set	Assessed Stature	
	High	*Low*
Wide	Much and extensive power	Little or no power
Narrow	Narrow but effective power	Little or no power

Clearly, assessed stature is the most powerful variable, but its influence is limited by extensiveness of role-set. These variables are so
intertwined, however, that both are necessary conditions in the development of power. Participation in a number of arenas multiplies the
assessments being made of a person. If those assessments are positive,
a faculty power is in the making. If the assessments are negative, the
role-set of a person does not expand.

Turning now to deans, two contradictory attitudes about deans are
evident among the faculty. The first might be paraphrased: "Deans?
Who needs them?" This attitude relegates deans to a housekeeping
position: they certainly do not contribute anything of importance. The
second attitude may be evinced by the same person who expressed the
former: faculty tend to attribute more power to the dean than he possesses. The question of just how much power the dean actually possesses
may be unanswerable; however, this probably is the wrong way to ask
the question. Does he possess as much power as the faculty thinks he
has, or does he possess the power which he thinks is his? I am not being
facetious. We could pose the same questions of any of the offices that
have been scrutinized in this essay. The outer boundaries of prerogatives and potential influence melt away at the edges, but this is particularly evident with so visible an office as the deanship.

A major problem of empirical study of high offices is the difficulty of
getting a sufficient sample for comparative study.[7] There are a lot more
department heads than deans, and in five years there has been oppor-

7. It is difficult to do so by the methods used in this study. Demerath, *et al.*
(1967) have studied university presidents by questionnaire and interview methods.

tunity to observe how more than one head has approached a particular department. In five years, there has been one turnover of the deanship, with the latest incumbent still new in office. It was abundantly clear, early in his incumbency, that his approach to the deanship is quite different from that of the former incumbent. The previous dean indicated in all of his public behavior that he regarded himself as a mediator, a servant of the faculty. He was esteemed for his zeal in protecting the academic rights of faculty, but at the same time, he apparently never saw himself as influencing the course of faculty opinion in the development of issues. The new incumbent has a far more active conception of the deanship.

One immediate and highly visible indication of the different conceptions of the office held by the former dean and those of the new dean is the sheer size of the administrative office. The previous dean got along with one associate and one assistant dean and a few secretaries. The present dean has an "executive associate" dean, an associate dean, two assistant deans, and an "assistant to" the dean. The latter office is beginning to shape into a combination of a "systems analysis" and business-manager position. Incumbents of these new offices have found themselves increasingly busy. It is not that they have unearthed business left untended in the previous administration, but that they are discovering things which they define as requiring attention that were not previously under consideration.

The dean himself has made some bold strokes, mainly in response to a major reorganization of the college, which is projected as a means of coping with a doubling of student enrollment. Otherwise, he is moving with some caution, probing the potentialities of the office. One of his problems was that he was an internal candidate and assumed office already having some enemies, so that he has to be particularly careful in some areas while moving ahead in others. I have no doubt that he will be much more interested than I in discovering the type and range of power which he can command. Questioned about it, he agrees with me that the faculty tend to attribute greater power to him than he thinks he possesses. But then he proceeds to list his sources of power, which are much like those of the department head. He controls the budget of the college, he can allocate space among contending claims, and he has certain powers of appointment. (These were not listed by him in this interview situation but were discovered in other interview and observational situations.) The dean appoints the search committees which recommend candidates for headships. He can also appoint various ad hoc and "task force" committees charged with formulating policy to come back into the administrative structure. He also, in the semifarcical mode in which people will toy with the fringes of the expected, pointed out that the institution would grind to a halt if he stopped signing forms. This, it appears to me, highlights the problems surrounding the structural sources of power in this kind of organization. Department heads, too, could grind many things to a halt if they chose not to sign forms. But both heads and the dean rarely balk at affixing their signatures. It is a power which must be very carefully exercised. Whether it is signing forms or allocating space and budgets, flagrant abuse of power can have disastrous repercussions for the institution—and the persons concerned.

Perhaps the greatest potential source of power which the dean has flows from the expansion of the office which he has instituted. Department heads and faculty who are active in interdepartmental arenas chalk up two additional sources of power, namely knowledge about what is going on elsewhere in the institution and contacts with people in other arenas. The dean has the greatest potentiality of being "on top" of things, particularly utilizing his expanded administrative officers. He is in a better position than others in the institution to (a) spot problems, and (b) gather information upon which to base policy. It is the business of those in the dean's office to concern themselves with a variety of institutional problems, while others on the faculty concern themselves only with selected problems.

The dean does not proceed in policy areas without advice. There is an institutionalized forum which he does utilize. The executive committee of the college elects a subcommittee to serve as the dean's advisory committee. He also utilizes his own associate and assistant deans separately and in a forum. In addition, there appears to be a select group of heads and faculty who may be consulted. My information is understandably limited in these areas, but my impression is that these groups are used not so much for communication, but as testing boards—although it is difficult to draw a line between these functions. There is no doubt, however, that the dean's actions are influenced by these sources. What action is available for him is another question. A lot of problems can be handled by a phone call or luncheon with the right people, but for important policy issues, the dean is constrained to go through channels, and those channels are the committee structure of the college.

I have previously made a distinction between "standing committees" of the college and various ad hoc–type committees appointed by the dean. Chart II is provided to give the reader a visual guide to the committee structure of this institution. The "executive" committee of the college is a standing committee, but its membership is not derived through the same processes as other standing committees. Department heads are automatically members of the executive committee, deans are automatically ex officio members unless elected by faculty, and there are sixteen members elected at large from and by the faculty at annual meetings of the whole faculty. The executive committee is the channel through which the recommendations of other committees, both standing and ad hoc committees, are funneled before the recommendations go to the faculty for approval. Policy issues may originate in any of the

CHART II

THE MEDICAL SCHOOL COMMITTEE STRUCTURE*

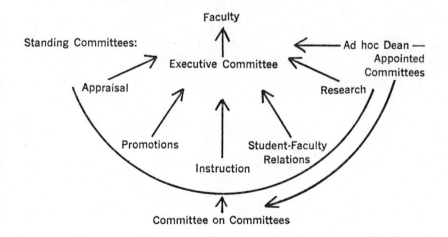

*Not all of the standing committees are included here. The object is to portray the relationships and flow of policy among the various types of committees.

standing or ad hoc committees. They may be placed before a committee by faculty or administration. It should be noted that the recommendations of the dean-appointed ad hoc committees can go directly to the executive committee for action, bypassing the standing committees. Decisions taken at the executive committee meetings are presented to the faculty either at regular, twice-a-year, general faculty meetings, or general faculty meetings called for special, more urgent problems.

Faculty members have told me that their department heads influence committee appointments. It may be that department heads can influence the dean's appointments to the ad hoc committees. Indeed, the dean may solicit advice from both heads and faculty concerning the appropriate makeup of a committee. However, I have not yet found any solid evidence that department heads influence the committee on committees' nominations to the standing committees. To the contrary, nominations of faculty to major committees flow from collective assessments of the stature of particular faculty members on the part of the members of the committee on committees.

The major evidence I have consists of an examination of who among the faculty has served on standing committees over a period of time. So far I have accumulated these data over a four-year period and can extend them for another four years with additional effort. I have not yet done all the possible permutations with these data that might be revealing. A relatively superficial screening seems to reveal quite enough. There is a definite "establishment" phenomenon. The same names appear again and again among the rosters of committee appointees. To analyze this phenomenon further, however, some additional distinctions are in order.

One distinction is whether the committee is charged with what are regarded as major issues. The "instruction" committee, charged with educational policy, is clearly a major committee. There are other major committees which carry on functions deemed highly significant but which are not the major seats of policy decisions affecting their activities. Then there are, overlapping with the last category, committees which are "working" committees, like the admissions committee, the committee which administers examinations, etc. Working committees do really put in a great amount of time on nonpolicy tasks, although their work is supposed to implement policies.

When one examines the roster of committee memberships, it is immediately obvious that junior faculty are underrepresented. Not only that, but with several conspicuous exceptions assistant professors are found only in the "working" committees. Looking at those persons who were members of three or more committees of the college, there are twenty people, twelve of whom are heads of departments. Focusing upon the major policy-making committees, aside from the executive committee of which department heads are automatically members, twenty-five names appear throughout the four-year period, nine of them department heads, sixteen general faculty members. So, again, we come down to a small number of persons who are participating in the making of policy. An important comparative point here is that these persons do not, as in governmental politics, depend upon their constituents for re-election. It is as if the members of Congress determine whether or not their colleagues will return.

While these facts might serve to give the lie to the value of collegial democracy in academic institutions, I would like to point out that the same processes of assessment of stature are operating in the committee arena as anywhere else. What is added particularly in this arena is a "willingness to serve." There is a decided process of induction of faculty members into positions of responsibility. If they have proven themselves in lesser assignments, they are made chairmen of minor committees and given assignments to major committees. There is no evidence that an establishment orientation—devotion to the status quo—is a prerequisite for rising in the committee structure. Quite the opposite. Those younger faculty members who have risen most quickly into major committee responsibilities have all been fervently outspoken and highly critical of the status quo. Persons with demonstrated courage and conviction tend to be snapped up quickly. In addition, if a man is known to feel strongly for or against something, the usual practice is to appoint him to the committee that will primarily deliberate the issue, so that his viewpoint will be expressed.

I would like to underscore that I do not believe that there is anything devious or deliberate in terms of power moves entailed in appointment to these standing committees. I am convinced that the appointments are a function of (a) a person's demonstrable willingness to serve, and (b) the emerging collective assessment of his stature, as he serves in various capacities. The faculty members concerned feel caught up in a system. There is, simply, a lot of work to be done. The issue is who is willing to do it, and how adequate is he? How persons perform in the lesser committee roles become grounds for considering them for more important assignments.

The various ad hoc committees appointed by the dean are even more "establishment" composed than others. It is a "blue ribbon" system. Persons are appointed who not only have proved themselves to be judicious but who have a constituency: faculty members in general will regard them as representing a viewpoint. Again, it is the same small group of people, reshuffled to meet another task. But it serves, for the most part. The work gets done, and, in the case of a well-chosen committee, faculty members can heave a sigh of satisfaction that someone will be representing their interests.

One might expect that the persons who go the whole road and enter into the smaller circle which is deliberating policy might be those whose professional identity comes to be predominantly associated with the school—the cosmopolitans-*versus*-locals hypothesis. That hypothesis does not hold in this institution. It should not be assumed that department heads are "locals." They differ in their readiness to move to other, greener, or more challenging pastures. Faculty members who move into the interdepartmental arenas also differ in their "local" orientation. Some of the most respected persons in the committee arena are also acknowledged as having cosmopolitan reputations. The dour evaluation of some of the leading faculty members in the institution is that the "good people are bled dry."

While the committee structure provides the forums through which the decision-making process is enacted, committee meetings are not the only place in which important discussions take place. When there are issues defined by the participants as important, a lively political process can go on outside of meetings. As in the departments, people seek out allies. In particular, department heads call upon other heads and sound them out on the issue, looking for support in the executive committee. It may even be that the head who initiates the call is really interested in reaching a faculty member in the other's department; or he may be interested in ascertaining whether the position taken by a faculty member in a committee reflects the ideas of others in the department, with the head being considered most important. Faculty members on a committee also may caucus, attempting to hew out a recommendation acceptable to those present and constructing arguments which may bring in additional support at the meetings.

Faculty members who have been caught up in the committee structure tend to become quite impatient about it. To them, the life and guts of the institution are in the work that they are autonomously carrying out in the departmental arenas. But grumble as they will, they miss a committee meeting with some trepidation: you never know what might come up. The significance of committees comes through in the following vignette, which I have abstracted from more detailed notes.

I was having lunch with a relatively new department head. He had succeeded in recruiting a number of bright new men only to see them being swallowed up in the committee system. "That isn't what I brought them here for," says he. I ask, naively, but can't you use some of the part-time people for this committee work? "God no! They don't have to live with what they do!"

I have placed such stress upon the committee arena because once a recommendation has survived the committee structure and is placed before the faculty, it almost always gains faculty approval. One reason for this is that by the time a recommendation reaches the general faculty, the rough edges have usually been smoothed. It is quite unusual for a proposal to emerge from a committee over the strong opposition of some of its members. A majority vote is not enough. In the two conspicuous instances in my data in which a proposal was pushed through the proposal had to go back to the relevant committees for compromise later.[8] Thus, most of the opposition to an idea is worked through in the committee forums, or else the proposal dies.

The other reason that faculty approval looks like rubber-stamping is that it takes considerable prior organization of a determined opposition to stop a proposal in a general faculty meeting. Over the years, I had asked faculty if they could remember any cases of a proposal's being defeated in a general faculty meeting. No such data came forth. It

8. Using cross-cultural data, F. G. Bailey (1965) discusses this phenomenon of committees which strive for consensus. He proposes some hypotheses to account for why some types of committees will push for unanimity while others will accept a majority vote. My own hypotheses differ from his. I think a majority vote is not enough because (a) faculty have to live with the decisions, and (b) the object of the game is to avoid damaging any sectors of the organization.

clearly is a rare phenomenon, but just last year it happened, and I was a very unhappy participant-observer in the controversy—a really blazing controversy. Normally, faculty meetings bring out one- to two-hundred people. In this instance, at least one third of the faculty—400 to 500 people—appeared. The departments were bringing in every body they could. There had been extensive discussion throughout the school, and several people came with prepared counterproposals which had already been shown to colleagues. By a close vote, the opposition succeeded in blocking the proposal. In "rehashes" after this stormy session, some persons who were in favor of the defeated motion expressed the notion that it would have been worse for the school if it had been a close vote in the other direction.

I have been analyzing a highly complex nonbureaucratic organization, namely the academic organization of a medical school. Perhaps its most distinctive feature is that all of its offices are occupied by professionals, and most important of all, a diverse collection of professionals. It is this latter attribute, the diversity of professionals, which gives rise to another major feature of the organization—the inevitability of conflict—as persons of differing professional identities define differing lines of policy as desirable or undesirable. As decision-making proceeds in this organization, it has seemed most appropriate to analyze it as a political organization.

Going back to the questions about power which were raised earlier, it does appear as if power is a far more meaningful concept than authority in this type of organization. If one takes authority to apply to those situations in which the subordinates experience an *obligation* to obey, on whatever basis, traces of authority were found only in some of the clinical departments, mainly surgery departments. In those instances, the type of authority manifested was closer to charismatic authority than any other.

Sources of power in this organization for the most part are familiar from studies of other organizations. Control of necessities for the advancement of a professional's career—such as salary, space, and promotions—were lodged in the offices of department heads and the dean. Insofar as we define power as involving the actual or potential use of negative sanctions, these were the *offices* in which power is located.

However, one other potent source of power was discovered, namely *assessed stature*. Assessed stature works independently of office. Persons who are not department heads or deans can have great influence by virtue of the stature attributed to them by colleagues. Conversely, the powers that office conveys to heads and deans can be eroded by a collective low assessment of the incumbent's stature.

It is important that, although there were offices in this organization which offered the possibilities of invoking negative sanctions, they were rarely invoked and probably not often threatened. Instead, persons of power proceeded to manifest their power through processes of persuasion and negotiation. In this sense there is very little difference between the influence of particularly highly esteemed faculty members and heads of departments in the power arenas.

The major contribution of this study to an understanding of power in organizations is to direct attention to situations in which power is not securely located in particular offices. Power is diffuse, but the locus and balance of power shift. The balance shifts, not just with the incumbents of offices, but as power blocs among faculty are activated and dispersed.

In this organization, then, it can be concluded that the balance of power shifts in response to (a) the flow of issues to which faculty differentially respond, and (b) the flow of different kinds of professionals through the organization.

REFERENCES

Bailey, F. J.
    1965 "Decisions by Consensus in Councils and Committees." In Political Systems and the Distribution of Power. New York: Oxford University Press.
Barzun, Jacques.
    1968 The American University. New York: Harper and Row.
Bennis, Warren G.
    1966 Changing Organizations. New York: McGraw-Hill Book Company.
Blau, Peter M.
    1964 Exchange and Power in Social Life. New York: John Wiley and Sons, Inc.
Bucher, Rue.
    1962 "Pathology: A Study of Social Movements in a Profession." Social Problems 10:40–51.

Bucher, Rue, and Joan Stelling.
  1969 "Characteristics of Professional Organizations." Journal of Health and Social Behavior 10(March):3–15.
Dalton, Melville.
  1959 Men Who Manage. New York: John Wiley.
Demerath, Nicholas J., Richard W. Stephens, and R. Robb Taylor.
  1967 Power, Presidents, and Professors. New York: Basic Books, Inc.
Gerth, H. H., and C. Wright Mills (trans. & eds.).
  1958 From Max Weber: Essays in Sociology. New York: Oxford University Press (Galaxy).
Glaser, Barney G., and Anselm Strauss.
  1967 The Discovery of Grounded Theory. Ch. III. Chicago: The Aldine Publishing Company.
Jencks, Christopher, and David Riesman.
  1968 The Academic Revolution. Garden City, New York: Doubleday and Co., Inc.
Strauss, Anselm L., Leonard Schatzman, Rue Bucher, Danuta Ehrlich, and Melvin Sabshin.
  1964 Psychiatric Ideologies and Institutions. New York: The Free Press of Glencoe.

Power in an Academic Setting

RICHARD H. HALL

The issue of power in the academic setting is both a great practical and immediate issue and a fascinating area for scholarly research. The students at the University of Minnesota refer to the university as the great marshmallow—implying that things are sort of absorbed without ever coming into contact with anything hard or firm. At the same time, hard and firm decisions and policies are made regarding such far-ranging issues as graduation requirements, curricular changes, and faculty personnel policies.

The issue of power in the academic setting really is based around three questions—how much power is there in the system, who has it, and under what circumstances is it exercised? The first question seems to be answered by the idea that there are varying amounts of power in the system. It is *not* a zero-sum game. The power seems to come and go as issues arise, not unlike the political scientists' appraisals of the situations in communities.

The question of who has the power is a more difficult issue. Rather clearly it resides in informal or unofficial systems within and between departments. There seems to be a definite "establishment" that rests on perceived professional competence. This would be true both intra- and interdepartmentally. It would be interesting to examine other bases of power groupings or cliques, such as age or subspecialty within a discipline. These power cliques seem to arise on the basis of issues, with the establishment being a rather continuous system.

The power differential between the clinical and the basic-science departments is not unlike that between liberal arts departments and professional schools such as education or social work. These professional schools generally have less power and are thus in the same position as the basic sciences in the medical school setting. The power here

seems to rest on the basis of the centrality of the operation. From observations at a number of universities, it seems to me that power is
distributed on the basis of the functional theory of stratification. That is,
the centrality of the operation and the scarcity of personnel are major
determinants of the power of a particular organizational unit. Like the
broader functional theory, this approach has the problem of the difficulty in determining centrality (functional importance), but Bucher's
data lend support for this interpretation. This power differential between departments, like that between individuals or positions in the
society, can be an important source of intraorganizational conflict.

Comment

Power and the Crisis of the Universities

GARY L. WAMSLEY

Dispersed Power and the Problem of Change

Bucher's paper is a fascinating one that could scarcely be more
timely. Antagonists and defenders of the university characterize it in
contrasting ways: as the personnel agency for the Establishment or a
training ground for radicals; as the critic of society's values or their
reinforcer and inculcator; as the ladder by which lower-class individuals
may rise in socio-economic status or a roadblock to their rise; as a
source of expertise in solving urban problems or a slum landlord and
an evictor of poverty-stricken tenants; as the source of advance in
science, art, and humanities or a backwater of irrelevancy where nothing significant develops. None of these characterizations can be said to
be wholly inaccurate. Bucher's analysis suggests to me that the reason
the university is perceived in such dichotomous ways is not only because
it has multiple and diverse goals but also because of the peculiar way

its power is structured in pursuit of those goals. Power in a university is dispersed and fragmented.

The scene evoked by the opening quotation of the paper captures all the frustration, drama, and even comedy inherent in the nature of the power structure of a university. The beleaguered administrator declaring that "nobody in the university has the authority to negotiate with the students," and the outraged and disbelieving students replying that "obviously, somebody in the university makes policy decisions," are *both* right, and therein lies the reason for the dichotomous characterizations. In the fact that they are both right lies the ability of universities to maintain relative freedom of inquiry throughout the ages while making such great contributions to civilization and also their inability to reform structures and processes that are essentially medieval.

The fragmented and dispersed power structure is a source of bewilderment and frustration not only to students but to faculty and administrators as well. Jacques Barzun, former dean and provost at Columbia, says (1968):

Indeed, the place is not always clearly seen by those within, so diverse are its activities and changeable its conditions of life. The internal stresses and strains are of course matters of gossip on the campus, but their cause is often a puzzle: Why do we do *this?*—is it the trustees? Why can't we do *that?*—doesn't the administration understand? Why weren't we told?—after all, *we* are the university. Faculty, student body, administration all suffer from a lack of mutual comprehension—and there are times when the lack seems irremediable.

While Barzun attributes the lack of mutual comprehension to "diverse activities and changeable conditions of life," it is noteworthy that the questions posed by his puzzled rhetorical questions grow out of power relationships—"why do we do this?"; "why can't we do that?"; "why weren't we told?"; "*we* are the university."

I sometimes find it possible to sympathize with student rebellion, not on any particular issue or ideological grounds, but simply because it is often difficult to see how anything short of the crisis-creating tactics of the students can wrench this peculiarly organized institution of dispersed power into new directions. Whether the student rebels know what they are doing or not and irrespective of the moral defensibility of their actions, I wonder sometimes if changes in universities can be wrought only by their successfully "shutting down" such an institution as California or Columbia.

The alleged ills of higher education have been thoroughly explored and discussed in the last few years. Discussion and debate have sifted down from the "intelligentsia media" to *Life* magazine and the *Reader's Digest*. Problems receiving discussion that widespread usually become the object of reform efforts. Yet remedies seem as far away as ever for such ills as pressures on faculty to publish, swollen classes, student alienation, the problems of the grantsmanship game, exploitation of graduate students for research and teaching purposes, poor teaching, lack of innovation in teaching techniques, and a host of other difficulties.

Bucher's analysis leads me to the conclusion that much of the reason for the lack of change in the face of such thorough and unrefuted criticism is the dispersed pattern of power in the university; it also causes me to wonder uncomfortably if the crisis tactics of the students may not be the only stimulus capable of causing change. Can anyone say with confidence that the crisis tactics of student rebels had nothing to do with the adoption of Black Studies programs? And now that mighty Harvard has adopted such a program will it not be far easier and more respectable for any other university to do so?

Bucher has pointed out that one of the criteria for power-measurements in interpersonal relations within academe is "assessed stature." But does not assessed stature operate at the institutional level also? Will not assessed stature among universities work to the advantage of militant student radicals? If the high-stature schools adopt a Black Studies Program, abolish R.O.T.C., place students on committees, lower entrance standards for lower-class students or perhaps develop two types of Ph.D.'s, one for teaching and one for research, will it not be acceptable for all others to do so?

The point of all this near-digression is to ask a question that Bucher's excellent analysis implies. Given the diffuse nature of power in the organizations we call universities, can anything but crisis bring about appreciable change? Her analysis is disturbing and leaves one feeling that to understand the nature and distribution of power in a university is to despair of changing their structure and processes through "normal" channels.

Is Power as Bucher Found it Peculiar to Academe?

If one draws a continuum with organizations resembling Weber's ideal-type bureaucracy at one end, universities would have to be located at the opposite end. At the bureaucratic end power or authority [1] would tend to be hierarchic: each level would have just that amount of power necessary to carry out its responsibilities; ascendant levels in the hierarchy would have increasing power based on broader knowledge about the organization and/or greater task expertise; the apex of the pyramidal structure would use its broader knowledge to reconcile "distinct tasks in accomplishing over-all goals and would thus have 'final' power over operations and behavior of lower echelons" (Burns and Stalker, 1961:120).[2]

At the university end of the continuum, power is as Bucher found it: variable; situationally or issue specific; surrounded by checks and balances; an interdependent relationship, often employing negotiation and persuasion and often found in changing coalitions.

This description of power structure shows considerable correspondence to Burns and Stalker's (1961:121–122) more broadly descriptive organismic model which is characterized by: (1) The wide dispersion of the special knowledge and experience necessary to accomplish the task of the organization with the location of knowledge becoming the ad hoc center of control and communication in given situations; (2) The individual task being seen as set by the total situation of the organization; (3) "The shedding of 'responsibility' as a limited field of rights, obligations and methods"; (4) A power arrangement that is network in nature rather than hierarchical; (5) "Adjustment and continual redefinition of individual tasks by interaction with others"; (6) Lateral rather than hierarchical communications; more consultation than command; information-advice rather than instructions-decisions; (7) Commitment to task and general societal welfare valued over mere obedience to superiors; (8) Status and prestige derived in part from sources outside the organization;

Bucher is describing power arrangements or structure, as are Burns and Stalker. It is another matter to discuss the *nature* of power apart

1. I agree with Bucher that for our purposes here they are interchangeable.
2. I am extracting power considerations from Burns and Stalker's more elaborate mechanistic model.

from its structure in organizations. At the risk of being presumptuous, I would like to do so briefly. I feel that to do so may make it clearer that the differences in power relations from one setting to another is one of degree rather than kind, and that the structure of power as Bucher found it is a reflection of certain aspects of the nature of *all* power relationships. Other power structures in other settings may obscure these characteristics, but they exist nonetheless.

The most widely used definition of power in Political Science is Robert Dahl's (1957:202–203)—"A has power over B to the extent that he can get B to do something B would not otherwise do." In this instance conciseness may not be a virtue if the definition implies a mere two-step process in which A commands and B responds. The crucial factors in any power relationship are B's decision to respond positively and the crucial variables considered in deciding to comply. A does not merely have some material and nonmaterial resources he manipulates to elicit the response he desires from B. B has to (1) perceive that A has such resources, (2) see the command as legitimate, and (3) calculate his response by assessing the congruity of the command with his values, his own self-interest, and the resources of A and his willingness to use them. Bucher's analysis of this particular organization highlights characteristics of power like these, but they exist to some degree in every setting (Schiltz, 1969; Keefe, 1969).

Our conceptions of power are protean, perhaps of necessity, for power is a relationship that depends upon perceptions and behavior that are mutual and reciprocal. It will also vary with situations and issues, and the authority of the superior is seldom if ever without checks.

The problems are formidable in a complete operationalizing of the concept of power outlined above. It would seem to require (Schiltz, 1969:8): (1) A specific situation, since one can speak of an actor's over-all power only generally or in terms of ranges and types of situations; (2) Knowing what A's intentions are; (3) Knowing what action B would take if it were not for A; (4) Determining whether B can comply with A; (5) Knowing what would be necessary or sufficient for B to see that self-interest dictates compliance; (6) Determining B's assessment of A's resources and willingness to use them; (7) Assigning a value to A's power with respect to B in the given situation; (8) Making similar determinations and assigning values to the power of other potential power-exerters over B; (9) Ranking competing power-exerters and thus determining which has power over B and thus how B will behave.

We can scarcely wait till we can operationalize power in this manner before we study it in organizations. Fortunately we can look for common situations. Also, many situations are so clear and unambiguous as to make full operationalization and measurement absurd.

At the risk of restating the obvious, let me assert again that the structure of power as Bucher found it possessed some distinctive qualities as an *arrangement* of power, but there is nothing unique (nor did Bucher claim there was) about the *nature* of power as found there. Power is always a complex relationship that is at least two-way in nature.

Political Science's Pluralist Model and the Power Structure of Universities

Political scientists interested in organizations are sometimes bemused by the extreme self-consciousness with which sociologists and social psychologists approach the question of politics or power in organizations. Bucher, for example, boldly announces that she "will attempt to demonstrate the utility of regarding this medical school as a *political* organization; in order to describe and understand the flow of events in the organization, it is necessary to use political concepts." A political scientist can scarcely perceive of an organization as anything but political, as anything but a set of power relationships. To a political scientist the power pattern of universities is familiar. A power structure in which the power of actors is variable, situation and issue specific, surrounded by checks and balances, and which often lies in changing coalitions—is our implicit and explicit model of American democracy, the pluralist political system. Some of us have been busy trying to apply organizational theory and concepts to the American polity. Perhaps we should have been trying the reverse.

The pluralist political system is one of countervailing power—A Madisonian concept of conflicting but counterbalancing groups that comprise shifting coalitions in different situations and on different issues. Robert Dahl (1967:455), one of the model's principal explicators, states

In the U.S., any group of people who have virtually the same views on political questions, the same political loyalties and identifications, is certain to be a minority. . . . every aggregate of American citizens large enough to constitute a majority of voters is necessarily a rather heterogeneous collection of individuals and groups who may agree on some matters but are sure to disagree on others.

To be sure, it can develop and pursue some common (if vague) goals; but doing so necessitates constant conflict, conciliation, compromise, negotiation, and bargaining.

Dispersed Power and the Problem of Order

The pluralist model is under constant criticism and refinement, but it remains widely accepted as a useful conceptual framework for describing and analyzing the American political system.[3] The basis of a pluralist political system is freedom of association, free speech, and the right to pursue self-interest. These key characteristics make it possible for a polity to be the antithesis of a hierarchical bureaucracy.[4] In Bucher's medical school the analogous key components are the professionals' belief in the right to work autonomously and in the differing needs of professional identity. These attributes of the organization mean that segments of the faculty see different things as problems and attempt to move the school in different directions.

In both the pluralist polity and the university, there is a crucial dependence on all participants' abiding by "the rules of the game" while reconciling the interests of the individual with those of the collectivity. As Bucher says, the faculty member must strike a bargain—a fit must be obtained between the professional identity of each faculty member and the judgment of a body of colleagues about the

3. Most of the debate has centered upon the question of elitism which is a matter outside our concern here. The pluralist model does assume a primary role for political activists whom some people insist upon referring to as elites. See Bachrach (1967) and Walker (1966). There is a rejoinder by Robert Dahl in American Political Science Review LX (1966).

4. For an interesting discussion of the nation-state viewed as an organization see Heaphey (1966). Heaphey is perhaps too rigid in setting up two bases for a polity. One is an "administrative concept which sees the nation-state as an organization oriented toward solving the problems faced by that organization." The other is a "political concept based on a vision of interests in conflict, and on the problem of reconciling diverse interests." The conception of a scale between a bureaucratic and pluralistic model might have been more realistic; nonetheless his point is close to the one I am seeking to make here.

worth of his contribution to some collective value, plus the resources which they can bring to bear.

So it is with a pluralist political system. Participants must above all be committed to "the rules of the game"—to the norm that everyone (at least theoretically) may freely participate—on the assumption that no single group or interest can win national elections, only a heterogeneous combination of groups which are willing to compromise demands. When too many groups reject the norms and assumptions, there is general dislocation.

Just as the pluralist polity finds it difficult to respond to the political expression in the form of an urban riot without overreacting and imperiling the "rules of the game," so the university finds it difficult to cope with violence and the physical expression of demands. As Robert Nisbet (1969:3) says, "The university is the institution that is by its delicate balance of function, authority and liberty, and its normal absence of power, the least able of all institutions to withstand the fury of revolutionary force and violence." If we forgive Nisbet the gaffe of assuming the "normal absence of power" (evidence again of the failure to understand the nature of power or the error of equating it with force or bureaucratic structure), he has stated an important truth about the university.

The structure of power in universities has everything to do with their current crises. The peculiar structure of power found in such organizations (not really so peculiar as it is merely a clearer manifestation of certain attributes of the nature of power) inhibits change at a time when change is being demanded in violent fashion. Understandably then, both the American political system and the universities are up against crises of historic importance. Both suffer from "constitutional fragility," to use Nisbet's phrase. It may not be a gross exaggeration to say that if both are to survive they must solve the problems inherent in a dispersed structure of power.

REFERENCES

Bachrach, Peter.
1967 The Theory of Democratic Elitism. Boston: Little, Brown and Co.
Barzun, Jacques.
1968 The American University. New York: Harper & Row.

Burns, Tom, and G. M. Stalker.
  1961 The Management of Innovation. London: Tavistock Publications.
Dahl, Robert.
  1957 "The Concept of Power." Behavioral Science, 2.
  1967 Pluralist Democracy in the United States. Chicago: Rand McNally.
Heaphey, James.
  1966 "The Organization of Egypt: Inadequacies of a Non-political Model
        for Nation-Building." World Politics XVII No. 2 (January).
Keefe, Robert.
  1969 "The Place of Power in Structural Functionalism." Unpublished
        paper, Vanderbilt University, Nashville, Tennessee.
Nisbet, Robert.
  1969 "The Twilight of Authority." The Public Interest, 15.
Schiltz, Timothy.
  1969 "Notes on Power." Unpublished paper, Vanderbilt University, Nash-
        ville, Tennessee.
Walker, Jack.
  1966 "A Critique of Elitist Theory of Democracy." American Political
        Science Review LX.

2

Departmental Power and Perspectives in Industrial Firms

CHARLES PERROW

It is my impression that for all the discussion and research regarding power in organizations, the preoccupation with interpersonal power has led us to neglect one of the most obvious aspects of this subject: in complex organizations, tasks are divided up between a few major departments or subunits, and all of these subunits are not likely to be equally powerful. In industrial firms, the subject of this paper, there are fairly clear divisions between the basic units of sales, production, research and development (or engineering), and finance and accounting. Equality of these groups is hardly insured by the fact that there is at least one person, the president, who stands above all these functional groups, and by the fact that each department is stratified into roughly equal levels of authority—each will have a vice-president and department heads, etc. Yet, presidents and top management in general are reluctant to recognize differences in power between the groups. When

Karl Magnusen not only organized much of the data for this paper and served as a resourceful research assistant and critic on the project, but criticized the initial draft of this paper constructively. Financial support for the research was provided by grant GS-742 from the National Science Foundation, and funds from the Center for Studies in Vocational and Technical Education at the University of Wisconsin, which is funded by the Ford Foundation. I am particularly indebted to Gerald Somers for the latter support.

asked which group has the most power—sales, production, R&D or finance—they generally say they are all equal, since they are all important. Presumably they would not exist if they were not important, but this hardly insures equality. If pressed further, top management is likely to invoke a distinction used by social scientists and say, in effect that their scope differs and finance and accounting, for example, is the most powerful in one area and production in another. We can believe it, yet it, too, hardly assures us that scopes are of equal importance or are seen as of equal importance.

Top management, like social scientists, like to avoid issues of power such as this and deal instead with individual, or face-to-face, power. The literature on power in organizations is generally, though not always, preoccupied with interpersonal or intragroup phenomena (see Kahn and Boulding, 1964), or else it takes as the major dimension of power the relative and absolute power of levels in the hierarchy, as in the literature on the control graph (see Tannenbaum, 1968). There has been some discussion and empirical research on the power of different departments in noneconomic firms (Zald, 1962; Perrow, 1963; Woodward, 1965), but I recall only one survey concerning economic organizations, and the question apparently only deals with the issue of product-innovation (Lawrence and Lorsch, 1967:111, 127, 262).

The question of which group dominates in industrial firms, then, will be the subject of this paper, and we will also discuss the perspectives of the four groups regarding the power of each other, and the degree to which they criticize each other. We shall raise some questions about what determines the pattern of group dominance and group perspectives, but we shall not be able to answer them all. The data come from a study of a dozen or so firms where power and perspectives were incidental and dependent variables, so we do not have as much information as we would like on these matters. Futhermore, since the data analysis has only begun, we will use only crude analysis techniques, but at the least this will open up a neglected topic in organizational research.

THE FIRMS

Our sample of companies drew from two long-established industrial areas in two different parts of the country. We approached companies that had at least 1000 employees, and we tried to cover a wide range of manufacturing technologies. The rejection rate was high, and there is no pretense at a representative sample here. The firms covered several industrial classifications but were all manufacturing firms. Some were producing quite sophisticated new products; others were not. Interviews in the firms ranged from a dozen or so to three dozen; at the least, three interviewers spent three days in a firm. After the interviews a forced-choice questionnaire was distributed to all salaried-exempt personnel—that is, everyone from foreman on up except clerical workers. The response rate was an incredible 93 percent, and the total number of respondents was 2633.

Though we will speak of 12 firms in the first part of this paper, we do not have 12 independent firms. Strictly speaking, only six of the 12 firms are autonomous companies where similar or related products were produced by all the facilities, except for a small acquisition or sideline here or there which we did not include in our study. Another firm had acquired some very small unrelated companies, and it in turn had been acquired by a large conglomerate. We studied only the original facilities of that firm, which were substantial in size. Two additional firms were quite autonomous (and quite different) divisions of a giant corporation. We studied no part of the corporation head-quarters itself. Two other firms were the fairly autonomous and quite different divisions of a moderate-sized corporation (the only two divisions of the corporation). In this case we also studied the corporate headquarters, but we will not count it as a firm; therefore its respondents are not represented in the first part of this paper. Finally, we have excluded from our sample of firms the field-sales, installation, and service unit of another firm. It was quite autonomous, large and powerful, run almost like a separate company doing business with the parent company. The parent company, which we include as a firm, also had a sales staff.

One reason I burden you with this detail is to indicate that the acquisition and merger patterns, as well as the various organizational devices, of U.S. companies are so complex and rapidly changing that it is hard to find many "companies" that produce one major line of products. During the year of research we witnessed the selling-off of divisions, the acquisition of new companies, attempted recombination of divisions, mergers, and merger attempts in virtually all of the firms. Indeed, one of the most frequent reasons given for not participating in the study was that a company was "undergoing a major reorganization" at the time, which would make the findings difficult to interpret and also upset the employees.

One other technical matter: We deal with three departments (or groups) and one residual group. The three departments are sales (or marketing), production (or manufacturing), and research and development (R&D). R&D includes those parts of engineering that are not under production or merely service production. The pattern in firms varied greatly, so that in some firms quality control is included with production and in others it is a part of R&D. In some firms what we have classified as R&D includes more personnel in such activities as plant engineering or electrical engineering than personnel who would be strictly speaking classified as engaged in research or development; yet, in these firms, these personnel did perform development services and even research services of a very limited sort. There was no "basic" research in any of our firms, though some designated small groups in this manner.

The residual group is labeled staff services. In order of roughly decreasing size this group includes finance and accounting, personnel and industrial relations, the corporate planning staff, the legal staff, the president, executive vice-president, and presidential assistants.

COMPANY ANALYSIS

Our question on which of the four groups has the most power is a ranking question; respondents ranked each of the four groups from 1 (most power) to 4 (least power). (All questions referred to in this paper appear in the Appendix. See Appendix, Part I, question 3.) We used this form to minimize the tendency to say that all groups are equal. If all groups were truly equal, the choice would presumably be random, and the mean ratings for all groups would be 2.5. To the extent that there is consensus that one group dominates, that group would have an average ranking of close to 1. Thus, technically, the question only measures consensus on power, not the extent or magnitude of power. All might agree that production has a little more power than sales, and in our measure production would be close to 1, and sales close to 2, but the absolute differences in them might be small. Nevertheless, all other evidence suggests that we can treat the scores as rough indications of magnitude as well as rank; those firms that appear as clearly sales-dominated from interview material show up as such on our measure.

We are also treating power as a zero-sum gain by this measure. Respondents are not able to qualify their answer by saying, for example, "Sales is the most powerful, but all groups are very powerful"; or "Sales is the most powerful, but no one really has much power." We are aware that this can be the case; but we believe that, generally, in matters of this sort, power is more of a zero-sum gain than a variable-sum gain.[1]

Finally, we are quite aware that a question which simply asks "who has the most power?" does not reflect the complexity of the concept, or the time dimension. Do we mean actual or potential power, power derived from internal workings of the firm or the market place, power based upon the force of personalities or the logic of group functions, power today or power in the next quarter, and so on? More important, what did the respondents mean when they answered? The resources of the study were not devoted to these issues, and thus many questions remain unanswered. Yet the differences among the organizations, and the internal consistency of subgroup perspectives, suggests that the bald term "power" does have some consistent meaning.

Figure 1 reports the response to the question, "Which group has the most power?" It is clear that sales dominates in 11 of the 12 firms. (The sales-service unit and the corporate headquarters unit are included in the chart, but ignored in our discussion.) We have used the mean of functional group means here because of the tendency of each group to minimize its own power as compared to other groups. Were we to use the grand mean for each firm, rather than correcting for the varying sizes of the groups, the dominance of sales would be even greater: production is the largest group in size, and it generally gives sales a

1. Our fear that only a ranking question would insure that people would discriminate among groups should not have prevented us from also asking respondents to place each of the four groups on a scale from, say, one to seven. This would have given us something comparable to a control graph, only for functional groups rather than levels, and, I now suspect, would have generated fairly reliable data, especially if respondents had already committed themselves to a ranking.

FIGURE 1. OVER-ALL POWER OF DEPARTMENTS IN INDUSTRIAL FIRMS

(Means of Departmental Means)

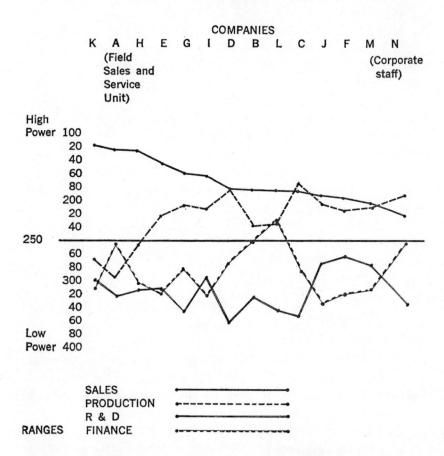

higher power-rating than do the other three groups. The range of responses is given to the right of the figure, and reflects the over-all ranking of the groups, with R&D last. The ranges are substantial, so there is a good deal of variability among companies. But before we examine that, let us explore the power of sales. We suspect that our data reflect the situation in most industrial firms in the United States. If this is so, why would sales be so powerful?

The Basis of Sales-Domination

In a market economy such as that of the United States, customers determine the cost, quality, and type of goods that will be produced and distributed. Customer selection thus determines organizational success. All groups—sales, production, R&D, finance and accounting—contribute to satisfying customer demand, of course, or there would be no need for them to exist. But sales is the main gate between the organization and the customer. As gatekeeper, it determines how important will be prompt delivery, quality, product-improvement, or new products, and the cost at which goods can be sold. Sales determines the relative importance of these variables for the other groups and indicates the values which these variables will take. It has the ability, in addition, of changing the values of these variables, since it sets pricing (and in most firms adjusts it temporarily to meet changes in opportunity and competition), determines which markets will be utilized, the services that will be provided, and the changes in products that must be made. As the link between the customer and the producer, it absorbs most of the uncertainty about the diffuse and changing environment of customers. As March and Simon (1958:165) have argued, the function of "uncertainty absorption" (the reduction and editing of information to the point where it can guide policy) is a key one in organizations and gives the group that performs it unusual power to define situations and control events. Sales performs more of this in more critical areas than other groups.

As a result of this strategic position, sales is in a position either to exploit present company capabilities or force a change in these capabilities. The consequences for the other groups are manifold, but sales—with few sunk costs (capital investment) and little interdependence with other functions that would require major changes in its own structure and operating procedures—is capable of more flexibility. Even if a change in capabilities is not called for, a shift in market-performance affects the other groups more severely than sales. A decline in sales calls for a demand for greater effort on the part of sales personnel, but also substantial cost-reduction in production. The latter, because of fixed costs and capital investment, is harder to achieve than the former, which involves only more personal effort. On the other hand, an increase in sales may tax the sales personnel somewhat—though generally it makes their life easier—but it taxes production a great deal.

Power and Technology

We had expected sales to be more dominant in firms where respondents described their tasks as fairly routine—that is, where they indicated that they infrequently came across problems that required a good deal of thinking-through for a substantial amount of time, and where they only rarely could not predict the outcome of techniques that they utilized. If things are fairly predictable and analyzable, it would appear that success for the firm would depend upon the sales force more than ever because the competition would be making similar products just as easily. On the other hand, if respondents described their tasks as fairly nonroutine—indicating frequent problems requiring analysis and uncertainty about the outcomes of their efforts—then there would be little edge for sales. (See Appendix, Part II, for questions.) Production and R&D would also be quite important in such a firm, with quality and innovativeness contributing heavily to the marketability of the product, and there would be a more even distribution of power.

We were wrong. There was no direct association between routineness of technology and sales-domination. In fact, try as we might, we could find *no* variable that could explain the ranking of firms in Figure 1. We examined such things as technological sophistication of the product, size of product, rate of unit production, rough industry classifications, size of firm, and so on to no effect. Knowing the firms, we could sometimes say "This should not be a sales-dominated company in view of its market and technology, but it is family-owned and the route to the top was established by the previous generation and the present son has followed it." Or, "This should be a sales-dominated company, but the president and the vice-president of production are very close, and neither likes the vice-president of sales, so sales has little to say." It is fascinating gossip but poor science.

Generally, I take the view that the most critical function tends to have the most power. I once explored this (1963) in the half-century history of a voluntary general hospital, relating the dominance of trustees, doctors, and administrators to the changing environment. Crozier (1964) has explored it in a cigarette factory, where the highly automated work left most of the uncertainty in the hands of the maintenance people. However, neither of these analyses sufficiently takes into account the ability of those who once gain power to manipulate the source of uncertainty, at least over a span of, say, ten or fifteen years. The maintenance people in Crozier's study augmented their power by removing information from the files that might make their performance more predictable and less uncertain, and by keeping information secret from machine operators and other engineers. Similarly, I think that sales, or production, or R&D can use their power to maintain either a fiction of uncertainty, or to steer the organization into areas where the uncertainty will be in their hands. If production dominates because of logistic problems created by customer demands for tailormade variations on the basic product, it may seek to reduce the complexity of this problem, but only in a way that production itself can control. In the one production-dominated firm in our sample, production, which had always been strong, got control of the computer and inventory and purchasing, and thus was in a position to tell sales what was and was not possible. Sales, without access to this information, was relatively powerless. In a firm making a product with similar problems, the finance and accounting department handled these services, and fed the information to sales (which had always been strong), arming them with unassailable facts with which they could call the tune for production. Thus, the area and degree of uncertainty did not follow the "natural" or "technological" pattern, but was manipulated. This is an explanation for the lack of fit between the logical and observed pattern that is at least somewhat better than gossip about personalities, but at the present time there are no empirical data available that would allow us to test it, or others to replicate it.

There are some data that do speak to the "distortion" thesis in general, however. If historical or personal factors distorted the expected relationship between sales-domination and technology, and if personnel had any sense of what the proper relationship should be, we would expect them to desire to correct the balance by desiring a decrease in the power of sales where it is too high, and increasing it where it is too low. We asked respondents whether sales should have more power than it does, about as much as it does, or less than it does. (See Appendix, Part I, question 3.) The midpoint of the scale is 3.0; only three firms

TABLE 1
Actual Power of Sales and Desired Change

	A All firms Sales-Domination		B Routine Sales-Domination		C Nonroutine Sales-Domination	
	Little or none	High	Little or none	High	Little or none	High
Some increase in sales power	4	2	3	2	1	
Little or no increase in sales power	2	4		1	2	3

went above that, indicating a desire to reduce the power of sales. The other nine wanted at least some increase. We can dichotomize the distribution into those that wanted "some" increase in sales power, and those that wanted "little or no" increase. Table 1, panel A, indicates the cross-classification of this dichotomy with that of high sales-domination and little or no sales-domination. Firms with high sales-domination are more likely to desire little or no increase in sales-domination. But more important are panels B and C, where we separate out the routine and nonroutine firms. Routine firms generally want more of an increase in the power of sales than nonroutine firms, but this is especially the case for those three "inconsistent" firms with routine technologies but little or no sales-domination. Nonroutine firms generally want less of an increase in the power of sales, and this is especially the case with those three inconsistent firms which have nonroutine technologies and high sales-domination.

Thus the data indicate a tendency on the part of firms to "correct" for the degree of sales-domination and bring it in line with their technology. High sales-domination is appropriate for some firms and not appropriate for others, we would argue. But power in a firm is a valuable good; it is sought after by many groups, and once gained, it is used to insure its retention. Thus, historical, personal, and other factors will affect its distribution independent of technology.

Other Variables

The sales-domination measure, however, does not reflect another aspect of domination that is of interest—the degree to which the group with the highest power (generally sales) shares power with the next-highest group (generally production). We devised a crude measure of "over-all power-sharing" to reflect this. (Actually, it measures the lack of consensus about the rankings of two units.) While it is closely related to sales-domination per se, it does take into account the relative degree of power of the next most powerful group.

A third measure of power we call subordinate power. We asked respondents to rate the degree of power that the middle management of each group had, and the power that lower management of each group had. (See Appendix, Part I, questions 1 and 2.) We then totaled these eight scores (four groups, two levels) for each company. This is a variable-sum measure; a firm could say that production, sales, R&D, and finance all had high power in middle management, for example, or that all were low, or some were high and some low. (Over-all, middle management received a substantially higher rating than lower management. Production was rated as the highest in both middle and lower management power, with sales next, and then R&D and finance tied for third place.) We also examined the extent to which subordinate power was *shared* among the groups, and the ranking is identical with total subordinate power. That is, if a firm is high on subordinate power, two or three of the four groups are also high; if it is low, at least three of the groups are low.

A number of other variables that were important for the larger study were constructed from questionnaire items. These are the extent to which the company and the respondent's tasks are well structured (task structure); the degree of discretion respondents feel they have; the degree of influence they feel they have; whether co-ordination is through feedback (on-the-spot, mutual adjustment) or through advanced planning (programmed co-ordination); and the amount of criticism directed at the four groups. (See Appendix, Part III.) The departmental-criticism item is based on responses to three typical criticisms made of each of the departments in industrial organizations; the extent to which each of the 12 items is true is summed to obtain the score of the organization. All variables except over-all power and over-all power-sharing are based on company means, rather than the mean of department means. The interrelationship of these and other variables is presented in Table 2. They will be discussed in two connections: first, an attempt to get at the

TABLE 2

Interrelationship of Variables for 12 Firms, Based upon Rank Data

	I Technology (Routine to nonroutine)		II Sales Domination			III Over-all Power Sharing			IV Subordinate Power			V Discretion			VI Structure			VII Influence			VIII Co-ordination	
	Rt	NR	Lo	M	Hi	Lo	M	Hi	Lo	M	Hi	Lo	M	Hi	Lo	M	Hi	Lo	M	Hi	Pl	Fb
1. Sales-Domination Lo	2	1																				
M	2	1																				
Hi	1	2																				
2. Over-all Power-Sharing Lo	2	1	1	1	3																	
M	1	2	1	3	1																	
Hi	1	2	3	1	1																	
3. Subordinate Power Lo	2	2	1	1	2	2		2														
M	1	2	2	2		1	3															
Hi	3	1	3	1		1	1	2														
4. Discretion Lo	1	2	1	1	2	2	1	1	2	2												
M	2	2	2	2		1	2	1	2	2												
Hi	1	2	3	1		1	1	2			4											
5. Structure Lo	1	3	2	1	1	2	2		2	1	1	1	1	2								
M	2	1	1	2	1	1	1	2	2	1	1	2	1	1								
Hi	3	1	1	1	2	3	1	1	2	1	1	1	2	1								
6. Influence Lo	2	2	1	1	2	1	1	2	3	1		2	2		1	2	1					
M	1	3	1	2	1	1	2	1	3	1		2	1	1	2	1	1					
Hi	2	1	2	1	1	2	1	1	1		3	1	1	3	1	1	2					
7. Co-ordination (Planned to Feedback) Pl	2	2	2		2	3		1	3	1		2	1	1	2	1	1	2	2			
Fb	1	3	3	1	1	1	1	2	1	3		1	3		2	2		2	2			
8. Departmental Criticisms Lo	3	1	2	1	1	2	1	1	2	1	1	1	1	2	2	2		2	2		2	1
M	2	1	1	2	1	1	1	2	1	1	2	1	2	1	1	1	2	1	2	1	2	1
Hi	1	3	1	2	1	2	1		2	1	1	2	1	1	3	1		1	2	1	2	2

matter of centralization of power and power-sharing, and second, the interrelation of the variables in an attempt to understand the lack of direct connection between technology and sales-domination (over-all power).

Centralized and Power-Sharing Firms

If we dichotomize sales-domination and subordinate power, the firms are distributed as in Table 3. Cell 2, where sales-domination is high and subordinate power is low, is perhaps representative of a centralized firm, and indeed, three of the four firms fall into the upper third of the task structure scores. Cell 4, where sales domination is low and subordinate power is high, might be described as power-sharing firms, where power is high. (Three of the four have structure scores in the lower third of the distribution, and these are three of the four most nonroutine firms.) Cell 1, with little sales-domination and also little subordinate power, contains two firms with moderate structure scores, both of which lack strong leadership and are particularly subject to internal power struggles in top management. They might be described as low-power companies. Cell 3, with high sales-domination and also high subordinate power, contains two interesting firms. One firm, whose manufacturing technology could rather easily be made more routine, had an executive whose management philosophy was to allow as little formal structure as possible, while at the same time subtly keeping personal control over most aspects of the firm. The result was a con-

TABLE 3

SALES-DOMINATION AND SUBORDINATE POWER

Sales–Domination

		Low	High
		C,F	D,H E,K
	Low	1	2
Subordinate Power	High	4	3
		B,J L,M	G,I

fusing perception of moderately high subordinate power, but low discretion; low structure, but very low perceptions of influence. The other firm had a legacy of sales-domination which appeared to be declining with a change in product lines; meanwhile, it had high discretion and influence, co-ordination by feedback, and an intermediate structure score. The coexistence of two product lines, one stable and routine, the other a new line, growing in importance, unstable and nonroutine, made analysis difficult.

Thus, the two "inconsistent" cells, 1 and 3, have few firms, and we can adduce some special considerations to help explain them (though special considerations can always be found to explain most anything in entities as complex as these). The other cells are suggestive of centralized firms, and of power-sharing firms. But we are not inclined to pronounce the distribution in Table 3 as "significant." Perhaps the relationships between the variables would have been stronger in a larger sample of firms, or using better measures, but perhaps not. The exceptions are many, and we are trying to link complex variables which are influenced by things for which we have no measure.

Technology, Intermediate Variables, and Sales-Domination

Ideally, we had hoped to show that the relationship between technology and over-all power was the result of a series of intermediate variables dealing with aspects of organizational structure other than simply over-all power. Technology shapes the structure of tasks and thus the nature of co-ordination. These two affect discretion and influence, and thus the degree of subordinate power. This in turn affects the over-all power structure. Many of these variables would also be directly related to the degree of departmental criticism. For example, routine firms require a high degree of task structure and co-ordination through advanced planning; this means that discretion and influence are likely to be low. Subordinate power will also be low, and because all these variables routinize internal processes, sales power will be high because dealing with customers becomes the most critical task. With routine internal processes, little uncertainty in tasks, little discretion and influence, but a centralized source of decision-making (in sales), departmental conflict should be low. The opposite values would be attached to these variables in nonroutine firms. (The theory from which all this is derived [Perrow, 1967] made more complex predictions for two additional types of firms, craft and engineering firms, as well as routine and nonroutine ones. While our sample of firms discriminated well on the routine-nonroutine dimension, there was less variance on the other dimension of craft and engineering. Thus, at least in this preliminary report, we have ignored the more complex model and restricted ourselves to analysis of only one of the two dimensions of technology.)

However, if we examine the strong and moderately strong relationships in Table 2 and lay them out in a manner suggested by William Starbuck during a coffee break at the conference—a suggestion for which I am very grateful—the best we can do is presented in Figure 2. There are two clusters: technology and structure, and power and discretion (and influence).

FIGURE 2

RELATIONSHIPS AMONG VARIABLES

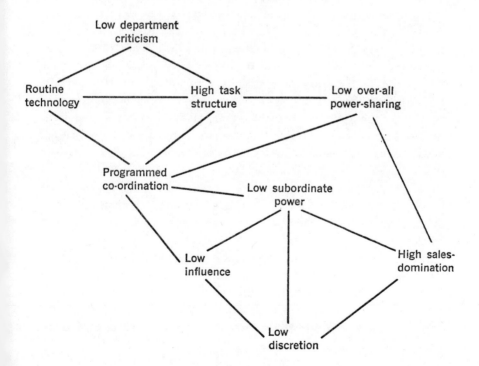

Technology is indeed well related to task structure and also related to co-ordination. But it is not related directly to the power-and-discretion cluster. Departmental criticism is only related to the first cluster, not the second. All the relationships in Table 2 of moderate strength are indicated here, and it is important to note that none of them go in the wrong direction.

The figure suggests that technology will only be correlated with over-all power in the predicted fashion if all the intervening variables (co-ordination, subordinate power, etc.) are also related in the predicted fashion. This is only roughly the case. In some cases the predicted relationship between technology and over-all power exists despite the lack of relationships among intervening variables. In some cases the relationships among the intervening variables are correct, but the relationship between the independent and dependent variables does not exist.

The most useful point to make about all this is that as one moves from the left of the figure to the right, the opportunity for the entrance of exogenous, unmeasured, and uncontrolled factors increases greatly. Thus, market, history, and personality factors can have a great deal of influence upon the relationship between subordinate power and over-all power (at the far right), but would be likely to have less influence upon the relationship between co-ordination and subordinate power (middle), and little on the relationship between technology and co-ordination (far left). Table 4 illustrates the decomposition of the effect of technology as one moves from co-ordination to subordinate power to over-all power. Note that the relationships between co-ordination, subordinate power, and over-all power are maintained, but there is "turnover" in the cells. It is not always the same four organizations that appear in the upper left-hand cell of the three panels showing the relationships of these three variables. There are just too many other variables at work here.

It is now time for another urgent caution. The analysis of the data at this point is highly preliminary. For one thing we are not sure that we have selected the best questionnaire items for some of our variables. Rank-order correlations will be a more appropriate statistic than contingency tables. And most important, there are only 12 organizations. Using a slightly different ranking of the organizations as produced by

TABLE 4

THE DECOMPOSITION OF CORRELATIONS

	Routine firms	Nonroutine firms	Programmed Co-ordination	Feedback Co-ordination	High Subordinate Power	Low Subordinate Power
Programmed Co-ordination	5	1				
Feedback Co-ordination	1	5				
Low Subordinate-Power	4	2	4	2		
High Subordinate Power	2	4	2	4		
High Sales-domination	3	3	4	2	4	2
Low Sales-domination	3	3	2	4	2	4

the over-all power-sharing variable from the one that obtains when using the over-all power variable (sales-domination) produces quite different relationships, as is clear from Figure 2.

Nevertheless, as far as sales-domination goes, I think the broad outline will remain. It is associated with certain things such as subordinate power and discretion, but we can only speculate on what brings it about. To paraphrase a remark by Richard Peterson at the conference, we are searching for variance here among static variables; the true action may lie with that neglected variable in organizational analysis, history, and, we might add with James Thompson, the environment. Yet internal, static variables are better than none, and it is at least a place to start.

ANALYSIS OF GROUP PERSPECTIVES

From now on we will ignore firms and deal with groups in the total sample, including those respondents in the field sales and service unit of one firm, and the corporate headquarters group of another firm. In order to correct for the varying sizes of companies and the varying sizes of groups within companies—both the four functional groups of sales, production, R&D, and finance, and four levels of management—we use the mean of group means in the analysis. When we speak of production's view of sales, we thus give equal weight to production people in all the companies. Furthermore, we are usually not concerned with absolute responses, but with the responses of a group relative to the responses of the other three groups. For example, almost all groups rate R&D as the least powerful group in the company. But we are interested in which of the four groups rates R&D the highest. Finally, we shall treat the staff-services group as the spokesman for finance and accounting, since finance people are the largest single unit in this category.

Self-Serving Perspectives

First, regarding over-all power, one might expect each group to see itself as having more power than the other groups see it as having. The opposite is the case. With the single exception of R&D, which rates itself as third-lowest rather than fourth, all the other groups rate their own power lower than any other group rates it.

Are these groups being modest? Hardly, as we shall see. Are they perhaps more accurate judges of their own power than the other groups? It seems quite unlikely. What does appear to be the case is that each group suffers from a case of "sour grapes"; they do not feel that their reward in terms of over-all power is commensurate with their contribution.

We asked whether each of the four groups should have more power, less, or about "as is." The consensus was that R&D was the group that should have the most additional power, production was next, then sales, and finally, finance tipped slightly towards the less powerful side of the distribution. But, in all cases except one, each group thought that its own group should have more additional power than any other group thought it should have. The exception is the staff-services group, which gave R&D a slight edge over finance. Generally, then, each group minimizes its actual over-all power, and maximizes the degree to which this should be corrected.

Without exception, each group rates the power of its middle management higher than do the other groups, and the power of its lower management higher than do the other groups. Each group, then, feels that it is stronger at the middle and lower management levels than others feel it is. We should be cautious here, though, and note that both R&D and finance, while giving themselves higher power-ratings for middle and lower management than other groups give them, do feel that both production and sales have more powerful middle and lower managements than they have.

Why, even in sales-dominated firms, is the power of middle and lower management of production rated higher than that of sales? It may be a factor of sheer size at this level; production is larger than sales; R&D is next in size; then finance; and that is the way they rank in subordinate power. Or it may be that the power of sales resides in its upper management—but not in its middle-management marketing personnel, district sales managers, product sales managers, and so on— much less than in its lower management group. The power of middle and lower management rests upon a different base than the over-all power of the departments.

Finally, as might be expected, each group attributes less justifiable criticism of its own performance than other groups attribute to it. Over-all, sales received the most criticism by far, perhaps reflecting its superior position in these firms, followed by the most busybody group, finance and accounting, with production and R&D in a tie for third place.

In sum, then, with only a couple of minor exceptions, groups minimize the over-all power they have, maximize the amount they should have, see their middle and lower management groups as more powerful than others see them, and minimize the extent to which they should be justly criticized. So far, all we have demonstrated is that perspectives are quite self-serving; each group magnified its virtues, its resources (if we can treat middle and lower management power as such), its needs, and the injustice of its position.

Intergroup Perspectives and Conflict

The importance of these data, however, lies in the patterns of intergroup perspectives. We have four variables to work with: over-all power—which is a dubious compliment for a group to receive, as we have seen; the extent to which over-all power should be increased or reduced; the power of middle and of lower management; and the extent of criticism of a group. Without exception, sales singles out production for the most negative rating on each of these four variables; and production returns the compliment by singling out sales for the most negative rating on each. Each gives the other higher over-all ratings of power than do other groups, recommends greater reductions in power, thinks the least of the power of middle and lower management, and is more critical of the other than of other groups. The consistency and magnitude of these perceptions are striking. The folklore of industry is confirmed; sales and production are natural enemies.

Somewhat more surprising, though, is the virulence of production's attitude toward R&D. Of course, R&D makes problems for production in countless ways—changes in manufacturing design, new products that cannot really be made, little attention to the problems of long-run production, and an attitude of superiority and reluctance to provide help with production problems. Sales has its grievances against R&D and vice versa, but apparently they are not as great. In the (by now) familiar pattern, production rates the over-all power of R&D higher than other groups rate it, would like to see it reduced more than other groups, and (along with sales) downgrades the power of both middle and lower management in R&D and, of course, is the most critical of R&D. R&D does not return the attitude; it is the most critical of all groups but spreads its criticism evenly, rates the over-all power of other groups fairly evenly (in comparison with the other groups), and generally ranks high in wanting the power of other groups reduced. R&D is even-handed in its grievances and putdowns.

The enemies of finance are the most diffuse. R&D is most critical of its performance; sales attributes the most power to it and would most like to see it reduced; production denigrates the power of its middle and lower management the most. Recall that finance is the group that receives the highest rating for having its power reduced; its middle and lower management gets the lowest power-ratings; it is the third least powerful group over-all; but is only the second most criticized group. We can infer something of this nature: finance is a centralized group with power residing at the top; it does its job fairly well; it does not have as much power as sales and production; but what it does have interferes with the other groups and so should be reduced.

Management Levels

We divided the respondents from each company into four levels— upper management, which includes the top officers at the presidential and vice-presidential level and the heads of major departments below the vice-president of each department; middle management, which includes the heads of minor departments or subdepartments of the larger ones (e.g., production control manager, quality control manager) and assistants to the heads of major departments; lower middle management, which includes general foremen and higher-level technicians (e.g., systems analyst, associate project engineer, industrial engineer); and lower management, which includes foremen, technicians, and most salesmen.

The division is annoyingly inexact. We have been amazed at the nonchalance with which most researchers make their unexplained divisions of levels and can confidently report that one organization has five, whereas another has six or four. We discussed problems of ranking at length with personnel officers and top management in the companies, without much confidence that they used any systematic criteria. In some organizations we puzzled over charts drawn up by department heads for their own use and then made our own master chart because the organization had none, or at least none that they would show us. We then asked a top officer to make any corrections which he saw fit. In one case the personnel officer eagerly joined us in the conference with the effective head of the organization (not the president), because he himself was *forbidden* to draw up an organization chart and wanted to know what the verdict was on the placement of personnel.

All criteria—charts, formal or informal; salary data, where we could get it; official level-designations by the organization; observations of department heads; our own observations; or a ranking performed by one official—had grave disadvantages. We tried to get as many as possible and use them to check each other, but we have little assurance that our ranks are both internally consistent and consistent across organizations (a well nigh impossible achievement). Just trying to fit the ranking of nonproduction departments such as sales and R&D (however that might have been obtained) with that of production departments proved to be a trying assignment. But, all things considered, we are confident that vice-presidents are higher than foremen, and that everything in between makes at least some sense from some point of view. But we do not think we can assert confidently from these data whether one company was more centralized, or hierarchically differentiated, or more complex.

Management levels, obviously, do not have the homogeneity that departmental groups have. Therefore, we would not expect the clear patterns we found in the last section to appear here. Each level contains representatives of all functional groups, and our questions on power and criticism deal with functional groups. However, this at least minimizes the role of self-serving perspectives. The differences between the group means to be reported are much smaller than those reported in the last section, and sometimes quite small indeed. But, some consistent patterns did appear that bear upon our general topic. Let us first look at upper management.

If any level should have a balanced picture of the power and performance of the various groups, it should be that which sees the farthest and uses the widest context—upper management. But upper management rates the power of production higher than other levels rate it, rates the power of sales lower than other groups rate it. It is the group that would most like to see the power of sales increased, and the group most likely to feel a decrease in the power of production is necessary. It sees the power of both middle and lower management in sales as higher than do other groups (though it does not see the power of these groups in production as the lowest; that is reserved for the middle management level). And, finally, it is the group most critical of production and the least critical of sales.

Thus, upper management is the most partisan of the four levels in the struggle between sales and production. Not surprisingly, in these predominantly sales-dominated companies, it sides with sales. It does not logically follow that while it is for sales, it has to be against production, but it is, more so than any other level. This pattern, then, is one more confirmation of the sales-dominated character of our firms: those with the most power to determine the character of these companies put down production and applaud sales more than do those levels with less power.

Middle management shares some of these views. It ranks second in its perception of production's having high over-all power, and is next to lowest in feeling that sales does not. After upper management, it is the group most likely to call for a reduction in the power of production (though not the next most likely to increase the power of sales). It has the least respect of any of the levels for the power of middle and lower management in production. It is the second-most critical of production (after upper management) and second-least critical of sales (after upper management). So, in general, the attitudes of top management are shared by middle management with regard to the relationships between production and sales, though they are not as extreme.

But the real preoccupation of middle management is not with production but with finance. Middle management is the level that perceives the power of finance to be the greatest and the most needing of reduction in power. It thinks the least of the power of middle and lower management in finance, and it is also the most critical of finance. We have no direct evidence as to why middle mangement would single out finance. We suspect, however, that it is at the middle management level that the imperfections of financial control are most apparent (resulting in high criticism) and at the same time the power of finance is most felt. In some companies we know that middle management is impatient with the discrepancy between the help that fiscal controls could give and what they in fact do (which is to clog the decision channels with irrelevant and imprecise criteria and information).

In addition to its negative view of finance, the middle management group also thinks little of the power of lower management in R&D and is the level that would most like to see R&D's power reduced. All in all, it is the most critical of the four levels.

Lower middle management has a more diffuse perspective on the four groups. Lower management, however, which has a disproportionate number of production personnel in it, is preoccupied with sales. It rates sales as the highest in power, is second (after lower middle management) in wanting to reduce it, thinks least of the power of middle and lower management in sales, and is the most critical of sales.

In our sample of industrial firms, management respondents in 11 of the 12 firms considered sales the most powerful of four groups. Production came next, followed by finance and accounting, and then Research and Development (which included engineering). We argued that the power of sales in a market economy rests primarily with its strategic position with respect to the environment. The firms varied considerably in the degree of sales-domination, and this was the major dependent variable in the analysis of the first half of the paper. We had conjectured that sales-domination would be greatest in firms with routine management technologies but there was no direct link between technology and sales-domination (or "over-all power," as we labeled the variable). We then examined intervening variables that dealt with various aspects of organizational structure, such as the definition of tasks, co-ordination, influence, discretion, and the power of middle and lower management. The relationship between technology and task-related aspects of structure was high, but the relationship between technology and subordinate power, influence and discretion was attenuated. Apparently, considerations of organizational history and leadership variables, which were not measured, played an increasing role here. The power and discretion variables were related to sales-domination, but by the time this part of the assumed causal chain was reached, technology had no independent influence.

Some data indicated that firms with an "inappropriate" fit between technology and sales-domination sought to redress the relationship to make it appropriate. Our data also indicated that the greater the structure of a firm, the less the four departments criticize one another. Since the more highly organized firms were also those with the most routine management technologies, we find some support for the observation of Burns and Stalker (1961) that conflict is higher in "organic" than in "mechanistic" firms, and some agreement with the finding of Zald (1962) that intergroup tensions are higher in treatment-oriented institutions than in custodial ones.

In the second part of the paper we explored the perspectives of each group regarding the other groups in the total sample, ignoring differences between companies. Here it was apparent that sales and production were the "natural enemies" of each other; that production was also highly critical of R&D; that upper management favored sales and was critical of production; that middle management was close to upper management in this regard but also leveled criticism at finance and accounting; and that lower management was the level most critical of sales.

Among the many deficiencies of this preliminary analysis of the survey data is the lack of a clear concept of power. The resources of the study were directed toward measuring technology and relating it to structure and to goals. Thus, in the questionnaire no attempt was made to distinquish types of power; furthermore, no attempt has been made in the analysis to clarify what the respondents "really" meant when they answered questions using the bald term "power."

These and other issues are raised in the pointed and thoughtful commentary by James Thompson. I regret to say that I have no way of answering them directly from the data, and I cannot respond to them adequately on a conceptual level. But, in conclusion, let me make a few statements, some of them reckless.

Power is a preoccupation of the managers in the firms, as evidenced by interview data, and most had no trouble identifying sales, for example, as dominant over-all. Thus, I do not think the question was an "unfamiliar" one, in this sense.

Given the nature of the concept and the "reality," I am not disturbed that the term "power" has different meanings in different contexts of the paper, nor even that what I may offer as an explanation of the power of sales may be different from the criteria that respondents utilize to judge the power of sales. (Nor am I very concerned about using a reputational measure of power, a point raised by Richard Peterson. There was simply no alternative, and I do not think the "reality" that we observed was distorted by this measure.)

A single, consistent meaning of power, or decomposition of the concept into various types, might be preferable, but I doubt it. The annual production of new typologies and distinctions in the sociological journals has been intellectually stimulating, but operationally a nightmare. The latest published attempt to make a complex typology operational strikes me as unconvincing and not illuminating. On the other hand, to tie respondents to only one meaning would violate their own perceptions of the complexity, as well as the reality, of power.

Part of the problem, I suspect, stems from the persistent attempt to define power in terms of individuals and as a social-psychological phenomenon. Organizations are viewed as co-operative systems and power as a "problem" of interpersonal relations. Even sociological studies tend to measure power by asking about an individual or a role-occupant (wing-commander; head of social service; dean). I am not at all clear about the matter, but I think the term takes on different meanings when the unit, or power-holder, is a *formal group* in an *open system* with *multiple goals,* and the system is assumed to reflect a political-domination model of organization, rather than only a co-operative model.[2] Some meanings of the term that come from an interpersonal viewpoint are irrelevant in this case; others are magnified.

The fact that after a cursory search I can find only a single study that asks survey questions regarding the power of functional *groups* strikes me as odd. Have we conceptualized power in such a way as to exclude this well-known phenomenon? Or, perhaps, have we been so paralyzed by the operational and theoretical problems of different meanings and concepts that we dare not do such research? I suspect the former, but it is only a suspicion.

Obviously, I am not pleading that we all use a bull-in-the-china-shop approach, neglecting the painstaking attempt to clarify the con-

2. For an extended discussion of the significance of different models of organizations, including the co-operative system model, the bureaucratic (domination) model, and the political science (power) model, see Perrow (forthcoming).

cept. I am arguing that we give functional group power (a lateral dimension) its due and separate this aspect of power from hierarchical or "levels" power (as in the control graph), and from interpersonal power. Then we might make more progress in clarifying the term. My own bull-in-the-china-shop approach at least raised these issues for me, as well as generating some interesting and possibly unique data on functional group power in industrial firms.

REFERENCES

Burns, Tom, and G. Stalker.
1961 The Management of Innovation. London: Tavistock Publications.
Crozier, Michel.
1964 The Bureaucratic Phenomenon. Chicago: University of Chicago Press.
Kahn, Robert L., and Elise Boulding (eds.).
1964 Power and Conflict in Organizations. New York: Basic Books.
Lawrence, Paul R., and J. W. Lorsch.
1968 Organization and Environment. Cambridge, Mass.: Harvard University Press.
March, James, and Herbert Simon.
1958 Organizations. New York: John Wiley and Sons.
Perrow, Charles.
1963 "Goals and Authority Structure: A Historical Case Study." In Eliot Freidson (ed.), The Hospital in Modern Society. New York: The Free Press.
1967 "A Framework for the Comparative Analysis of Organizations." American Sociological Review 32:2(April)194–208.
Complex Organizations. Glenview, Illinois: Scott Foresman, forthcoming.
Tannenbaum, Arnold S.
1968 Control in Organizations. New York: McGraw-Hill Book Company.
Woodward, Joan.
1965 Industrial Organization. London: Oxford University Press.
Zald, Mayer N.
1962 "Power Balance and Staff Conflict in Correctional Institutions." Administrative Science Quarterly 7(June):22–49.

APPENDIX

Part I

Four questions regarding power were asked in sequence. All are given below.

(1) Think of the salaried, nonclerical people in the company as divided into three groups—top management, middle management, and lower management:

How much power does *middle* management have in each of the following areas? (You may not know a great deal about all the areas, but we are still interested in your impressions.)

	Middle management has very little power					Middle management has a great deal of power
a) Production	1	2	3	4	5	6 7
b) Sales and marketing	1	2	3	4	5	6 7
c) Research and development	1	2	3	4	5	6 7
d) Finance and accounting	1	2	3	4	5	6 7

(2) How much power does *lower* management have in each of the following areas?

	Lower management has very little power					Lower management has a great deal of power
a) Production	1	2	3	4	5	6 7
b) Sales and marketing	1	2	3	4	5	6 7
c) Research and development	1	2	3	4	5	6 7
d) Finance and accounting	1	2	3	4	5	6 7

(3) Sales, manufacturing, research, and finance and accounting are likely to have different degrees of power within a firm. Right now, how would you rank the power of these four groups?

Write in an "A" for Sales and Marketing   Most powerful ＿＿1
            "B" for Manufacturing   ＿＿2
            "C" for Research and Development   ＿＿3
            "D" for Finance and Accounting Least powerful ＿＿4

Regardless of whether you think the *ranking* should change or not, should any of these groups have more power, or have less power, than they do now?

	Much more power	Somewhat more power	As is	Somewhat less power	Much less power
a) Sales and marketing should have	＿＿	＿＿	＿＿	＿＿	＿＿
b) Manufacturing should have	＿＿	＿＿	＿＿	＿＿	＿＿
c) Research and development should have	＿＿	＿＿	＿＿	＿＿	＿＿
d) Finance and accounting should have	＿＿	＿＿	＿＿	＿＿	＿＿

Part II

The technology variable was constructed using the following questions, which were weighted as follows: Q. 1, -1; Q. 2, $+1$; Q. 3, -2; Q. 4, $+2$.

1. During the course of your work, how often do you come across *specific but important problems* that you don't know how to solve, and you have to take some time to think them through by yourself or with others before you can take any action?
   1_____Daily
   2_____2-3 times a week
   3_____Once a week
   4_____2-3 times a month
   5_____Once a month or less often

2. Even though the problem may go unresolved for some time, how much actual "thinking" and/or discussion time do you usually spend trying to solve such specific problems?
   1_____ 5-15 minutes   4_____45-60 minutes
   2_____15-30 minutes   5_____1-2 hours
   3_____30-45 minutes   6_____2-4 hours
                                             7_____Over 4 hours

3. In some jobs, things are fairly predictable—if you do this, that will happen. In others, you often are not sure whether something will work or not. What percent of the time would you say that you are *not* sure whether something you do will work or not? (Please circle the number)
               10% 20% 30% 40% 50% 60% 70% 80% 90% or more

4. If there is something that you don't know how to handle in your work, can you go to someone else in the organization for an answer, or is it likely to be something that no one really knows about?
   Rarely will   Most of the time
   others know   1   2   3   4   5   6   7   others will know

Part III

Unless indicated otherwise, all questions had a format similar to that given in the fourth item in the technology variable (see Appendix, Part II) where the extreme values are specified and the respondent chooses a number ranging from one to seven. Here we will only give the content of the question, not the extreme values (which are such things as "definitely false" to "definitely true," or "very little" to "very much").

Discretion

Employees are often permitted to use their own judgment as to how to handle various problems.

Individual initiative (how much is this emphasized in this company?).

Some companies, aside from the secrecy necessary to keep things from competitors, are quite reluctant to let information circulate freely within the company; others are not reluctant. Which is true of this company?

Task Structure

How precisely defined are your duties?

How precisely defined is your authority?

Whatever situation arises, we have procedures to following in dealing with it.

The same procedures are to be followed in most situations.

Whenever we have a problem, we are supposed to go to the same person for an answer.

Influence

How much influence do you feel you really have within the company in areas that are important to your job?

How much influence do you feel you have with your superiors?

In the past year, have you ever participated in formulating long-range plans for at least a year in advance? (1—Never; 7—Over 10 times in the past year. Intermediate values were specified.)

If you added up the time you spent in the last year on long-range planning, how much would it total? (1—Did not participate; 7—Over a month. Intermediate values were specified.)

Co-ordination

When the group you work with co-ordinates its activities with other groups that it deals with, is this generally done on a routine basis that is planned in advance, or is it primarily handled on the spot and on a case-by-case basis depending upon the problems at hand?

When you come up against a tough problem that might involve the concerns of another department, do you almost always check first with your superior before getting involved with the other department, or do you almost always go directly to people in the other department without checking first?

Group or committee decisions (How much is this emphasized?)

Interdepartmental teams (How much is this emphasized?)

Departmental Criticism

Here are some typical criticisms that are made of these groups in various companies. Please check how false or true they are in this company.

Sales is more interested in high sales figures and dollar volume than selling the most profitable items.

Sales presses manufacturing too hard on scheduling and delivery.

Sales too often insists on manufacturing trying something that manufacturing knows it can't make.

Manufacturing too interested in easy production runs rather than scheduling profitable items.

Manufacturing is unwilling to try to make products that are difficult to make.

Manufacturing is unresponsive to sale's delivery problems.

R & D comes up with fancy things that won't sell.

R & D is too conservative; not enough blue sky thinking about totally new products or processes.

R & D is not responsive to manufacturing's problems.

Finance and accounting doesn't supply the kind of information that would help departments.

Finance and accounting does not exercise proper controls over manufacturing and pricing.

Important policy decisions often have to be made on the basis of information from finance and accounting that is too misleading, inaccurate, or inadequate.

Power as Energy or Power as a Reflection of Things?

JAMES D. THOMPSON

I would like to consider briefly two questions about Professor Perrow's paper: What does this paper tell us about the state of the world "out there"? and what does it tell us about the state of its author? I will take them in reverse order.

It seems to me that the paper reflects Perrow's deep and recent immersion in this body of evidence. I can sympathize with Professor Perrow, trying to find patterns in a very complex phenomenon, as I think this paper reflects. But the fact does have one consequence for the paper, which I hope he will treat in later work: the data and interpretation are not placed in sociological perspective. I would like to know what we already knew about the topic—or thought we knew about it before Professor Perrow undertook his research.

The absence of such an anchor seems especially important in dealing with the complicated and messy aspects of an already messy world. The presence of such a sociological anchor might have helped the author maintain stability in wrestling with the data, for I find in the paper a tendency to conceive of power in several ways, which may or may not be consistent.

At several points, I gathered that Perrow approaches power in terms of constraints: "He who interferes with my autonomy has power over me." I find this somewhat congenial, although in my opinion the formulation of Richard Emerson which defines power in terms of dependence seems cleaner and more defensible.

But, in saying that each group feels that its *reward* in terms of over-all power is not commensurate with its contribution, Perrow seems to be defining power in terms of "sour grapes." This seems to me to be a different concept from one of power defined in terms of autonomy or dependence. This newer concept is one I would expect to find under the label of "equity" or "distributive justice."

Then he states that "each group feels it has less over-all power than it *deserves*," and deserves more because (1) its middle and lower management groups are strong, and (2) it does few things for which it might be criticized. Now this smacks strongly of "prestige" or "esteem," rather than what I have understood as power—or what Perrow offered as a concept of power.

Well, if power, equity, and esteem are slippery concepts for us social scientists, I wonder what was on the minds of Perrow's respondents! And we have some clues: First, it appears that they think of power in zero-sum terms and this suggests to me the possibility of conceiving of organizational power as a nonzero sum while admitting the possibility that the spheres of action created for different individuals within that organization are created in zero-sum terms.

But then I wonder whether Perrow's executives are reporting on power, or on something else. For we see that they are reluctant to recognize power, they minimize their *own* power, and *underrate* their own power. It seems plausible to me that they do not normally think in terms of power, but rather in terms of opportunities and constraints on their own spheres of action. We learn, for example, that R&D, which is a greater contingency for manufacturing than for other departments, is rated more powerful by manufacturing than by others. And we learn that sales and manufacturing are "natural enemies," which the contingency hypothesis would predict. We also are told that at the middle management level, finance is seen as having more power than is reported for finance at the top management level. This could be interpreted as reflecting greater cost-consciousness at the middle management level, hence greater constraints upon other departments by finance at the middle management level.

And we are told that the higher the structure, the less the discretion, and the more that co-ordination is achieved through advanced planning, then the less criticism of groups by each other. That could mean that the less they feel the others getting in their way, the less they criticize others. This interpretation is supported by the observation that low group criticism is associated with routine technology.

Now, if we interpret respondents' responses as reflecting felt constraints and contingencies, thus reduction of autonomy, then we would not need to be surprised as Perrow was, when he said that he found a rather remarkably consistent tendency for each of the groups to minimize its over-all power.

In short, I wonder if the respondents—forced to respond to unfamiliar "power" questions—were not also forced to respond by identifying power in negative terms—in terms of prevention of action.

Let me close by raising the question, not especially about Perrow's paper, but more generally about organizational sociology, of whether we are getting at power as energy, as the cause of things, or merely at power as a reflection of things.

Comment

Must the Quest after Variance End in History?

RICHARD A. PETERSON

Professor Perrow's candid style of presentation invites others to join the intellectual pursuit in which he is engaged. I would like to stir around in the "question of power" briefly with a footnote to Professor Thompson's discussion and then go on to examine an anomaly, suggested in the Perrow data, which may be symptomatic of the current state of the sociological enterprise.

The Reputational Study of Power

The data on which Professor Perrow's paper is based consists of *imputations* of relative power of corporate elements made by personnel in the organizations under study. He is able to make a very neat and sensible analysis of how these various organizational elements view power. It tells us much concerning beliefs about who holds and who should hold power.

At the same time, this study suffers the limitations of all "reputational" studies of power, be they in social class, the community, or the organization. Valuable as this tactic may be, *power* defined *reputationally* cannot be equated with *power* as observed in organizational *behavior*. Perrow is close to this error at several points. For example, in summarizing a set of findings, he concludes, "The folklore of industry is confirmed: sales and production are natural enemies." This statement seems illegitimate because it is precisely *folklore* which is being tapped in a reputational study. The author might do well to look at the consequences for research and theory-building of using reputational as over against other means of measuring power that have long been discussed in the areas of stratification and community. Certainly, it would be instructive to study the degree of fit between organizational power defined in reputational terms with power defined as decision-making or resource-allocation. My guess is that there is no simple correspondence. For example, as I read Professor Goldner's paper, I inferred that the Industrial Relations Department seeks to *hide* its power over Production Departments both because its power is not fully legitimate and because it does not want to incur the risks of responsibility for the exercise of power.

Whither Variance

Pitirim Sorokin has instructed us that there is a sharp distinction between an "individualizing" discipline, such as history, which seeks to explicate events in their uniqueness, and a "generalizing" discipline, such as biology, which seeks, by abstracting from the welter of unique events, to build general laws. Sorokin puts sociology in the latter group, and we might all point for proof to our ever more sophisticated, computer-based technology designed to facilitate generalization.

I am not convinced that the issue is all this simple, and a candid comment of Professor Perrow is symptomatic, I believe, of the dis-ease with current abstractions in sociology. Reviewing the generalizations he is able to formulate, Perrow cautions, "The exceptions are many, and one comes away from research such as this with the very strong impression that firms are more unique than they are alike, and the prospects for generalizations based upon complex variables such as these (which include power-sharing, co-ordination and the like) are not great."

To place this comment in a broader context, let me cite two studies in which sophisticated methods seem to produce "uniqueness." Some years ago, C. Wright Mills reported data on four cities showing that a diversity of employers in a community as against industrial concentration made for a more robust civic and cultural life. The implications for received theories about entrepreneurship and the concentration of power were obvious. Recently, Michael T. Aiken, suspicious of the facile generalization made in the early study, has been collecting data on a wide range of American cities in order to explain better the relationship between industrial concentration and civic life. His findings are most perplexing: each time he introduces another explanatory variable he finds variance explained by the interaction term. Thus, with each level of sophistication in the explanatory variables, he is pushed away from global explanations toward *unique* descriptions. For an example, a given variable might contribute to civic pluralism only in a special class of cities such as New England towns, founded on textile production between 1830 and 1845 and using English-speaking immigrant labor. Clearly, Aiken is only one or two steps away from descriptions which fit but one city uniquely.

My attention was first focused on the possibility that the pursuit of variance might lead to unique description by a study in which David Johnson and I are currently engaged. We have started from the coherent notion derived from Marx and others that the quality of life on the job will influence the workers' extra-job round of life. Using the One in a Thousand 1960 Census tape we identified 33 relatively specific work situations such as automobile production operatives, lumberjacks, newspaper craftsmen, and the likes. With a number of demographic controls in a multiple classification analysis we have tried to *explain* the variation in selected family life variables in terms of work situation. Yet the more variance that can be explained, the more "generalization" becomes unique to a specific work situation. Seemingly, we are moving back to the statements made a half-century ago on the order of "Miners are just different."

The irony suggested by all three studies and many others, I am sure, is that in the pursuit of generalization with sophisticated contemporary techniques we approach the detailing of unique circumstances. This irony exposed, I have no ready remedy. It may be that the variance model of explanation is not appropriate for social phenomena. It may be correct, as Mills says, that each era, and by extension each event, has its own unique explanation, so that we are fated to be social historians. Or it may be that Holmans is right, the inevitable direction that generalization of social phenomena must take is away from sociology and toward psychology.

I, for one, am not ready to give up faith of our forefathers that social phenomena are a level of organization *sui generis*. Many critics of the sociological enterprise have pointed to the time- and situation-bound nature of many of the concepts on which we try to hang theory. They would have us look for more analytic and content-free variables. This may indeed be necessary but it may not be the most important direction which reconceptualization could take in the next several decades. We may need to look at variables in a somewhat different light.

Recall that Perrow has told us "firms are more unique than they are alike." If this is a fair generalization from his data, a number of explanations are possible. Perhaps he has poor measures of the variables which express the concept of "firm" or perhaps "firm" is a poor basis for classifying the events under study; it may be that some firms are more like families and others are more like street-gangs and should be thus classified.

"Uniqueness" is often seen as a perplexity of *too many* independent variables. Perhaps lots of things *do* "make a difference" as Perrow suggests, but we may be wrong in treating them conceptually and statistically as if they all operated simultaneously. This notion of simultaneous variation is inherent in the current usage of the term "variable" and analytic induction as it is generally employed. Even our most sophisticated computer-dependent statistical techniques are nearly all based on multiple *co*-relations.

The outspoken critiques of this "opportunistic empiricism" would point us in the direction of historical specificity, but this is not, I believe, a necessary trip. Rather than seeing many variables as simultaneously influencing the outcomes in which we are interested, it might be more fruitful to study the various sorts of *conditions* in which given variables influence outcomes. This strategy focuses attention on a *system* of variables in interaction rather than on numerous variables considered additively.

The growing fascination with cybernetics, evolutionary functionalism, and economic models such as political economy with their focus on "sequence," "threshold," "elasticity," and the like, as well as the current proliferation of techniques such as multiple-classification analysis point in this direction. Arthur Stinchcombe's recent *Constructing Social Theories* is quite helpful in illustrating the fabrication of contextually contingent models.

Let us finish this commentary by recalling Perrow's discussion of "sales-domination" and the "exercise of power by subordinates" which evoked this critique. It is instructive to note that he presents intriguing evidence to explain the four cases which do not fit the model of linear association between these two variables. These explanations had to do with "lack of strong leadership," "management philosophy," and the "legacy of sales-domination." Within the received methodology of Robert Merton, which makes a sharp procedural distinction between theory generation and its testing, Perrow's comments would be defined as an inappropriate form of post facto explanation. Of course, logically all explanations come *after* some collection of facts. Rather than being embarrassed by engaging in post facto conjectures, he could reinterpret his exceptional cases in order to show the boundary conditions within which the variables under study operate. In this way we will be modeling our science more along the lines of contemporary biology and less along the lines of Newtonian physics. What is more, in this way we may more nearly approach a methodological sophistication adequate to match the theoretical richness of classical sociology.

3

The Division of Labor:
Process and Power

FRED H. GOLDNER

There are strong pressures within competitive industries for the continual increase of rationalization to meet organizational problems. No activities of the organization—at least none of those that "make a difference"—are left to chance. In fact, it is advantageous to an individual's career to find such activities if they are not already apparent. Thus, both problems of the organization and the motivation of individuals create pressures for the continuing division of labor in order to provide the specialization and differentiation necessary to reduce all areas of uncertainty.

The resultant proliferation of separate units greatly increases the complexity of intraorganizational relations, for it is impossible to create a clearcut division of labor. Most large organizations that are involved in process industries, or that have sophisticated technologies, or that produce many new products need to divide labor simultaneously by product, by time, by geographical area, and so on. Each unit is held responsible for an area in which another unit is also held responsible. The attempt by different units to secure control over what they see as their area of responsibility results in conflict and, hence, uncertainty.

What starts out as a search for ways to reduce problems and uncertainties in organizations leads, then, to the increase of other uncertainties.[1] Rationalization sows the seeds of increased complexity and hence of pressures for yet new forms of rationalization.[2]

Conflicts over control continue until an area is completely routinized, if ever. And if that happens, there will be new areas of conflict within the organization, at least so long as there are areas subject to further rationalization (see Ritti and Goldner, 1969). Changes in the environment will assure the existence of such areas. The inevitable conflicts are then resolved either through the relative power of the various parties or through accommodative mechanisms and tactics.

I hope to illustrate some of the processes involved by taking what is by now a fairly old division and showing how it complicates organizational relations and how power and ancillary processes are mobilized when units of management must deal with each other.

ROCK PRODUCTS COMPANY

This study is an analysis of the relationships among management units of Regional Industries,[3] a multicompany industrial corporation. More specifically, it is a study of the Industrial Relations (IR) unit of one of the companies—the Rock Products Company—and its relations with other management units. The study, conducted over a twelve-month period, consisted of interviews, observations of individuals, observations of meetings, and published material. The published material consisted of letters, memoranda, contracts, speeches, published departmental objectives, organizational charts, and job descriptions. Interviews, with over thirty people, ranged in time from one hour to three days. Observations of many more than that number were included. Much of the material was secured by accompanying different people for periods of from one day to three weeks, including whatever meetings they attended.[4]

1. For an abstract treatment of the relations between uncertainty and organizations, see Thompson (1967). For a more specific discussion, see White (1961).

2. The dialectical nature of organizational processes has, of course, been suggested by others. For example, Max Weber (1946:226) made the point that "democracy inevitably comes into conflict with the bureaucratic tendencies which . . . democracy has produced." See also Blau (1964:Chapter 12).

3. Pseudonyms for company names and for geographical locations are used throughout this study.

4. The data for this paper were originally obtained for appearance in different form in Goldner (1961).

Most of the day-to-day observations reported in this chapter were made at the main plant of the Rock Products Company, whose production consisted of a continuous "process" operation which converts raw material into a structural product. The company had three plants and a number of distribution facilities, as well as two small subsidiary companies which produce related products. Apart from these subsidiaries, the company employed over 1100 people about 750 of whom were at the main plant located at Woodside. Two of the plants had been added in the two years preceding the study, and a fourth was being built. The recent and continuing expansion had put the company on the *Fortune* list of the 500 largest industrials and had led to a boom atmosphere.

Rock Products was only one of a number of companies affiliated with the Regional Industries Corporation. The parent corporation either owned the affiliated companies outright or owned a substantial share of their stock. Rock Products fell in this latter category. The three top men in the corporation were on the board of each company and were the acknowledged leaders of all the companies.[5] Along with other top officials of the Regional Industries companies, they were located in the Regional Building in Elm City.

Industrial relations at Rock Products, as in all Regional companies, was headed by a vice-president of industrial relations who reported to the executive vice-president and/or the president of the company. A director of safety, a director of labor relations, and a director of personnel worked directly for the vice-president. There was an industrial relations superintendent at each of the three main plants of the company. Each superintendent was directly responsible for safety supervisors, wage-and-salary supervisors, clerks, and secretarial help.

Overlapping Responsibilities: IR and Production

Industrial Relations' most important tasks were those dealing with the unions: negotiating union-management agreements; handling

5. Regional Industries placed a strong emphasis on a common corporate identity despite the fact that the member companies were separately listed on the stock exchanges. Practically all the companies shared the name "Regional" in their title. Although Rock Products was not so titled at the time of the study, the name was subsequently added. Even then the company tried to play down the Regional part of their name.

worker grievances if they were turned down by, or were against, the foreman; and the day-to-day interpretation of all issues covered in the agreement. They additionally handled safety and wage-and-salary administration. But these areas were also the most important for those charged with the direct management of the hourly work force. This was especially true of the largest such unit—the operations (production) unit.

The front-line supervisor was the nominal authority figure for the hourly employee; any disturbance of that appearance of authority was keenly felt by the supervisor and his superiors. Not only was his authority challenged by the presence of a union, but direct dealings with the union were taken out of his hands and placed in those of an apparent third party.

A series of dialogues between an IR superintendent and members of Operations Management is presented below to illustrate the typical overlapping of responsibility and to illustrate a number of issues discussed later in the paper: IR's prerogative of "interpreting" the union contract; the use of the union and the threat of arbitration to bolster the IR position; IR's use of ameliorative tactics instead of head-on confrontations; and the bureaucratization of employee relations. Readers not interested in purely descriptive material may want to skip to the next section.

Superintendent O——, faced with the need of a layoff in his department, called IR to tell them of his desire to proceed with laying-off without regard to seniority. He was immediately informed that if the men could perform the job, he could only base the layoff on seniority and not on performance. The IR end of the phone conversation was as follows:

It's one or the other, O——. It's not half-way in between. I'll throw in with you on anything you want to do, but I want to let you know what we'll have to eat. Have they been warned? If you've talked to them and they haven't improved you've got a case. Layoffs are by seniority, and poor qualifications are by termination. All we're going to do is end up eating these guys if we don't have a firm case on them. We have the burden of proof.

I'll be glad to spend any amount of time on this and go over the names with you. This stuff is damned important. Any time we have a case, we ought to can them.

In an aside to another IR man: "I emphasized firing the guys so we are on the offensive instead of the defensive and telling them what not to do all the time."

IR also had to make clear to the supervisor the difference between discharge and layoff, for the supervisor had suggested that they lay the men off and put "do not rehire" on their records. A layoff, however, means that employees have recall rights. In fact, in this company, laid-off employees' seniority continues for a specified period so they are only "recalled" and in no sense "rehired." [6] Unlike discipline, layoffs are not negative sanctions employed for the purpose of control. They arise because of a lack of available work and are seen to be outside the control of the individual employee. Applied according to seniority, layoffs are standardized and predictable and thus outside the context of the authority relationship between supervisors and supervised.

Later that same day the IR representative went to the operating superintendent's office where the following conversation took place:

O——: The men involved have, on occasion, been jacked up for not doing their job. They are not as desirable as the others. We won't say they are such that we could just go out and fire them, but they are borderline—right on the line—quivering. The union contract says everything else being equal then seniority shall prevail. So why can't we let them go?

IR: If we took them out of seniority the burden is on us. If they are that bad why are we keeping them around?

O——: You're not telling me we have to let good men go and keep less-than-average guys.

IR: We shouldn't be keeping less-than-average guys anyway.

O——: I'm willing to do anything you guys say as long as we're all playing on the same team. You give me pause, however, in firing them. I'm afraid you'll get skittish.

IR: That's why we're here. To go through their records and see what we can do.

O——: But you're saying we can't lay them off.

IR: You can't mix when it's the company's fault for their getting laid off and when it's their fault for getting terminated.

O——: Can we fire them for not doing work?

IR: Let's play some roles. I'm the union. How come it took you ten months? Have they been talked to?

6. However, it should be pointed out that the unions were mostly connected to the construction industry, which generally does not make much distinction between layoff and discharge because laid-off employees seldom return to the same job. See Colean and Newcomb (1952:99, 325).

O——: They have been warned and are not as bad as they once were but still are not doing as much.

F—— (a foreman): You shouldn't have to tell them more than once.

IR: They may figure they are getting by if nothing's said.

O—— (directly to foreman): Better be sure they have been warned twice apiece and then tell them it's their last time.

F——: They won't last long—I'm not going to back down on them.

O——: They'll be out by Friday.

F——: Suppose we have to let more go. The next guy is the best laborer I have. Why should I have to let him go?

IR: If we let a man go who has been here a couple of years it makes us look like bad managers if we haven't warned him.

O—— (heatedly): When you let men go—you let the worst go—I don't care what the union says, men are different.

IR: If it goes to a third party, an arbitrator, it's how he rules. I think you guys have a good case if they've been warned a couple of times.

O——: It gets back to the same thing. If you have to cut, you never cut in terms of eenie-meenie-mo, not knowing which—you always have some worse than others. The "Agreement" says we are the sole judge of competence of people. They [the union] are always throwing the thing in our face and I'd like to throw it back in their faces.

The "Agreement" clause referred to above read as follows:

The Employers are to be the sole judges of the competency and fitness of prospective employees and the satisfactory performance of work by any employee and may discharge any employee whose work is unsatisfactory or who fails to observe the safety precautions or other rules or regulations prescribed by the Employers for the health, safety and protection of its employees.

Although this clause did not contain the usual "just cause" statement contained in most union-management contracts, it was interpreted as if it did. That is to say, the company recognized that it must have a just cause for disciplining an employee and further recognized the union's right to grievance in disciplinary action. The recognition of grievance rights meant that a disciplinary action might go to arbitration. Thus if IR, as experts on what arbitrators will hold, can cite arbitrators to justify IR's position, the operations supervisors are faced with the unpleasant possibility that a discharged man may be reinstated—a direct slap at supervisory authority.

We now turn back to the dialogue and IR's response to Superintendent O——'s last remark.

IR: The contract is how it's been interpreted and this is how it's been done for years.

O—— (turning to the author as an observer): Will you write an article on the plight of the poor supervisors for the benefit of IR?

IR (coming back at O—— rather heatedly): I'm with you—I'll go along and fire anybody you want.

O——: You might as well throw out the clause in the contract.

IR: We have used it consistently in promotions, and they would push for going the other way.

O——: In negotiations we ought to take care of this. I'd just as soon exercise the rights we have.

IR: Rights aren't just as it [the contract] looks. Suppose it was arbitrated. They would take into consideration the intent of the clause, how it has been practiced, other companies, etc., other awards. I know of cases where it come out almost opposite to what it reads. Clauses are like muscles. Got to flex them to keep them in shape.

O—— (to his subordinate superintendents, who had just come in): It turns out we should have fired them long ago. Now not even sure they have been warned twice. This should be a lesson to us—to get rid of this kind of guy early. Now F——'s in the position of having to let go one of his best people.

F——: How did this warning thing come up? When they hire out of the hall they should know enough to work and that it's expected of them. We shouldn't have to warn them.

O——: When it came up I told F——, take your six worst men and we'll try and sell it to IR, but we haven't had much help.

IR: I'll go along with you, O——, and we'll both watch them come back in.

After this interchange the IR man insisted that O——really knew what was going on and was "just playing a role to make it look like it's us. I was not about to let him get away with that. That's why I said I'd go along." IR meant that O—— was trying to show his subordinates that IR was to blame for operating's not being able to get rid of whomever they wished. The layoffs were finally done by seniority.

About five weeks later the superintendent called about some employees who had been absent. Again, IR took the line that operations could go ahead but would have to suffer the consequences:

IR: You can fire him—that's up to you. I'm just saying it won't stick. In absenteeism you're talking about the frequency too. It's no rule, but I think we have to be consistent.

Later in the day the IR representative went to see the operations superintendent.

O——: I'm ready to argue with you. Let me get my book. I usually don't win.

The IR man attempted to explain his opposition by maintaining, "If we are going to get into this, I am probably extreme because I'll have to defend it. The union always brings up what is the practice on absenteeism and we usually have had it 14–16 times in a six-month period." The superintendent asserted that they would "get" the employees if they were absent three times in a month. The IR man's reply attempted to be both sympathetic and assertive:

IR: That's all right with me. If we let some go with four days, better make sure we aren't keeping one with five or six days. I do agree that you are in a bind when men don't show up. The union often says what does it hurt . . . you're not paying him. Then we have to tell them how much it costs in money. Timing-wise now, we should make sure we have a case. They are still talking of C—— (an employee who had been reinstated through the grievance procedure). I'm not interested in defending any gray-area discharges cases. The head of one of the larger units of the union has been in on it. He ran into the IR Manager the other day and asked: What's all this rhubarb going on at Woodside?

Consideration of these discipline cases indicates the growing bureaucratization of this area: the attempt to standardize offenses such as attendance, the use of universalistic criteria, and the use of more written records to avoid question about past actions. As a result of a number of layoff-discharge incidents, the layoff clause in the union-management agreement was revised. The old clause provided that seniority would be the determining factor when such things as physical fitness, skill, experience, and ability to perform the work were equal. The clause was changed so as to make seniority the major factor.

Sources of Power

The major source of IR's power over specific plant-level issues was, as illustrated above, the use of the union as an outside threat.[7] Recogni-

7. While we have referred to the union as an outside unit, we do not mean that there are not many problems for which the union would be considered as part of the organization. Moore (1951:326), for example, maintains that "the union . . . is not simply an external element in industrial organization; to an increasing extent, it *permeates* it." (His italics.) This matter will differ according to the type of structure of the union. In industrial unions of unskilled and semiskilled workers where the local is coterminous with the plant, the local will be more a part of the organization than where there are skilled workers and the local is geographically based. So too with customers. The firm with a few major customers must consider them a part of the organization, while the retail store is less liable to this need.

tion that their nominal antagonists were the source of their internal power was even made explicit by one IR manager: "As I told one of the [other IR] guys who was damning the unions—Don't bite the hand that feeds you."

IR used the same source of power, at all organizational levels, to justify the structure of the entire IR organization. Thus, Industrial Relations was characterized throughout the Regional Corporation by a functional line of reporting. Each IR superintendent, in addition to reporting to a plant manager, was responsible for the performance of IR functions to a successive line of IR managers throughout each subdivision of the company on up to the top of the corporation.[8]

While labor relations required specialized skills, knowledge, and experience, specialization alone would not result in a functional line of reporting. The crucial difference was the need for a uniform industrial relations policy in the face of the union.

Such organizational arrangements run counter to the American industrial norm of decentralization (see Stryker, 1955:95). Centralization has to be continually justified. The union, through its threat of whipsawing tactics, legitimates this organizational arrangement. Given the complexity of union-management agreements, it is difficult to find an easy way to compare one agreement as a whole with another, thus permitting comparisons to be made on individual items. Whipsawing, hence, is the attempt to gain from one part of an organization what one has already gained from another. As one IR manager put it:

> There might be some [conflicts] when talking about a few dollars in Rock Products which will have a cost bearing on other plants, so that IR will resist. For example, time and a half for Saturday—some production people may say fine since they do not have Saturday work, while other units may have. And because of that responsibility, we get into changing line management more than in a [single-company] corporation.

Without co-ordination, management personnel representing one company might yield on a demand unimportant to them but vital to one of the other companies.

In order to sustain its position and increase its autonomy, IR never

8. For accounts indicating the extent of this in Industrial Relations and in Accounting see Baker and France (1954), and Simon, Guetzkow, Kozmersky, and Tyndall (1954).

lost an opportunity to push these arguments. In a number of booklets published to describe the areas under their responsibility, they constantly reiterated the theme of uniformity. These arguments also appeared in their year-end progress reports as well as in their "objectives" for the future.

IR consequently claimed to possess the "bigger picture." Disputes were centered over the question of the immediate interests of the operating units versus the "bigger picture" portrayed by IR. Actions within one unit had to be controlled in terms of their effect on other units and other plants.

There was constant joking about IR's having the "big picture." Managers frequently referred to IR as being "international" and resented their cosmopolitanism. As one IR man said: "There was general resistance to staff functions that cut across units since it is a symbol of general authority and lack of autonomy [on the part of operating units]."

During negotiations over new union contracts the perspectives of an IR unit were even more "international" than during day-to-day bargaining. Rock Products IR had its greatest degree of power in this area. Everyone had to rely on IR for estimates of what must be given in one area in order to obtain and maintain goals in other areas. Flexibility of bargaining was even greater at Woodside because the master agreement covered eleven unions. IR needed more room to maneuver and manipulate among the unions and had to be freer in its relationship to the rest of management.

During the negotiation period IR's power was further broadened. *Any* of the issues in a union-management relationship can influence contract negotiations. Hence, plant management "allowed" IR a freer hand in all matters during negotiations. As a plant manager put it:

During negotiations they [IR] consider themselves like ward-heelers during an election—anxious to give things away and do favors.

The complexity of union-management relations also resulted in other kinds of centralizing forces. In the words of one IR man: "When the union has experts at the table, we counter." Management had to organize a research unit to handle the complicated preparation for union bargaining. And to avoid duplication of effort it was necessary to centralize this research [9]—just as it was necessary to centralize a legal unit to prepare cases for arbitration:

> Where arbitration is not a way of life, it becomes a traumatic experience. The union takes it seriously. If a local IR man handled it, he would have to fight them in public and be an S.O.B. Hence, we have someone to be this S.O.B.

> [And] it has to be outside the legal department, as such. You can win an arbitration at the expense of "labor relations." Pure legal can't appreciate this.

Joint Bargaining

One of the most interesting results of the presence of unions is the corresponding unity among industrial competitors—a unity which, in turn, produces internal changes in the individual organizations. The presence of one large union throughout an industry pressures the otherwise competitive companies in that industry to "get together" for their bargaining.

Joint bargaining also puts IR in a centralized position, for such bargaining again requires co-ordination at the higher IR levels. Joint bargaining further requires the kinds of specialization, time-consumption, and contracts that may shut out general management. IR lost no chance to "push" this.

Our research shows that joint bargaining contributed to IR's freedom from other internal organizational controls, for they had to have some degree of freedom to bargain and to make commitments with the other companies.[10] The question of the autonomy of an IR unit was even an explicit factor in joint bargaining. One IR manager reported that bargainers tried to find out from the IR staff in the other companies

> about how much weight the department has in their company. This may be especially important to know if we are negotiating jointly. The important

9. See Harbison and Dubin (1947:185) for the assertion that "relationships between big unions and big industrial empires tend to pyramid the influence of top officials in both."

10. It is important to note that the kinds of professional identification that arise in joint bargaining are without power to influence internal organizational arrangements. For professional identification to be organizationally meaningful, the profession identified with must be a group with some power of its own within a society. The community of industrial relations specialists is significantly without this power. As an example of the strength of an independently based profession and its effect on the internal workings of an "organization" see Colvard (1959).

thing is, if someone is not so sharp, then it is important to know how much say-so he has.

Joint bargaining helped mitigate the strains which arose from the inadequate methods of measuring IR's achievements. IR's goal in labor relations was to obtain a committed labor force at the lowest possible cost. The indexes for this goal were at best not very good. The commitment of the labor force was measured by turnover, strikes or work stoppages, and something called "morale." IR's contribution could not be measured in terms of profit and loss or standards of engineering efficiency. As for lowest possible costs, it was impossible for the individual firm to equate wages to marginal productivity. The method used, then, was a comparison with the costs of one's competitors and even, more particularly, a comparison with his average wage rates.

Given the complexities of determining even such a seemingly simple measure as comparative wage costs, IR could fall back on the expedient of getting the same "bargain" as that obtained by the competitor, a bargain best achieved through joint bargaining—thus relieving IR of the pressure to produce, for then no single IR unit could be blamed for obtaining the "short end of the stick." One of the IR managers put it:

We are now interested in becoming as much like the rest of the industry as we can and hope to become exactly the same with respect to wages, pensions, and everything else in the way of costs. We want to be just like our competitors.

While joint bargaining appeared to increase the autonomy of the IR unit, in the longer run it threatened to bring about a decrease in power. Joint bargaining over time may mean that similar wage costs will be taken for granted; the work of IR may become more and more routine. And *the more routine the work of a unit, the less real power the unit will possess.*

HISTORY AND ORGANIZATIONAL ANALYSIS: THE OPERATIONS UNIT

While much of IR's internal power obviously came from its dealings with the union—an outside organization—it was also dependent on the relative position of the operations unit, with which it had most of its dealings. Consequently, it is necessary to understand the recent changes that had occurred in operations in order to understand the position of IR.

Organizations have histories. Consequently, what "is" at any moment is influenced by what "was" and by what "is becoming," as well as by what "will be"—for histories also imply the existence of a future. An examination of the operations unit points up this frequently overlooked historical aspect of organizational analysis.[11]

The dominant theme in the recent history of the operations unit has been its steady loss of power, which had accompanied the increased rationalization of the organization. Those in operations were subject to the effect of more extensive decision-making by others on matters that directly affected operations. They had lost autonomy and resented it. Their greatest losses appeared to be to the maintenance department and to the process engineers.

Operations vs. Maintenance

The maintenance superintendent at Woodside reported directly to the plant manager, although he had previously reported to an operations superintendent. The change, which had taken place three years before, was made because of the increasing importance of the maintenance function. First, there had always been the need for specialization. Maintenance required highly skilled craftsmen. Second, industrial and market competition had forced the company to compete on the basis of decreasing costs.

"Maintenance" was responsible for maintaining an inventory of very expensive parts. The parts, obtainable only on special order, had to be available to prevent long shutdowns. At the same time a large inventory of parts would have tied up a large amount of the company's capital funds. Therefore, the process had to be rationalized to the point where parts were stocked according to projections based on estimated life-periods of each piece of equipment as well as on estimates of delivery time for each piece. Planned or preventive maintenance programs were also set up to prevent equipment breakdowns. These standardized jobs then had to be continually co-ordinated with emergency repairs. These

---

11. Analysis of historical factors is more likely to occur in studies of organizational growth. For a comprehensive account of this phenomenon, including a valuable bibliography, see Starbuck (1965). Some economic historians have produced histories of individual companies, but little connection has been made between their efforts and those of sociologists. See, for example, Chandler (1962).

planning and rationalizing procedures required greater skills and more time than were available within operations management.

The operations superintendent no longer controlled maintenance, although it was crucial to continuing production in a process industry with large-scale machinery. As some of the operations superintendents said:

> The biggest and most general problem is getting maintenance at the right time. Not necessarily the problem of getting hold of maintenance people but of simply being able to do maintenance at the right time.

> Our main concern is maintenance. It is more of a problem than operations.

"Maintenance" had a good deal of power because of the importance of its high degree of rationalization. In other cases reported in the literature (see Crozier, 1964), "maintenance" held power because of lack of rationalization. In both situations, however, "maintenance" leaders held power because of their knowledge and control of information. In one instance these were based on experience, while in this case they were based on higher education and the utilization of new operations research techniques.

The organizational change that removed the maintenance superintendent from under the authority of the operations superintendent obviously decreased the responsibility of the latter. Evidently it was also an extremely unpleasant change for him; under direct questioning about past organizational arrangements, the operations superintendent denied that the maintenance department had ever been organized differently in the past. In his case, history was too painful to be acknowledged.

Operations vs. Process Engineers

As in many other plants, the greatest interunit difficulties at Rock Products were between operations and engineering. The skills of the engineering personnel had become increasingly important to the company. Although the basic process of producing the company's product had not changed over the past decades, many aspects of the process were constantly being improved—especially in the attempt to reduce costs. The final product was basically similar from one company to another; therefore competition took place in costs and in marketing. The industry also required constant innovation, not only in products but also in manufacturing processes. Both kinds of innovation required increased technical skill and had given the trained technician ever-increasing prestige.

The process engineering department at Rock Products had been formalized about three years back with seven persons and had grown to thirteen. The department was responsible for improvements in the processing of the product throughout the company, though all its work was done at the Woodside plant.

There was a great deal of conflict between the engineers and the operating personnel. The classic reasons for these conflicts were well expressed by one of the neutral officials at the plant:

> There are the usual conflicts between operations and engineers—operators trying to get out X number of units and engineers X number at such and such a cost.

The operations personnel appeared to be on the defensive when they discussed process engineers:

> An engineer is the smartest man going—just ask one.
> It's important to know what you don't know. For example, B——, who came over from process, could answer almost anything. Now he sees how much he didn't know. He was an authority on everything when in Process—writing editorials on "how to" without ever doing.

> They have never come up with anything; but a few of the things they have tried have given me some ideas for something else. . . . They just don't know as much as they think about this operation.

And the engineers, well aware of the hostility of operations, held them in disdain:

> We don't want our operational people experimenting around here—they are not capable of keeping data and measurements, so that their experiments are not "scientific" and can't use results since they are not controlled.

> The operating people do not call us in. They are afraid of intelligence coming in to show them up. They co-operate only to an extent. They assume they are operators par excellence, and when you see results you know they are not.

> Operations will generally resist because they do not understand it. So we attempt by various devious means and can succeed. We do get frustrated. It's not morale building to know how things could be improved.

As expected, the engineers saw their achievements in a different light:

> We have had a few successes that have saved a lot of money. We reduced fuel by devious means by six percent—that has amounted [to a lot of

money]. We also developed the method of transporting material in the plant. We also changed the process in the mills.

There was little doubt that the engineers had taken over many of the functions of operations. In their short existence they had started new practices and had assumed new functions that directly involved the work of the operators and further deflated the status of the operators. Although the plant had gone along without change for a long period, the area of innovation—an area that was the explicit responsibility of the engineers—was now accepted as vital to survival and growth. The engineers were also responsible for obtaining new products from the materials they used.

The operators, under these conditions, sensitive to anything that further reduced their status vis-à-vis the engineers, easily misinterpreted reality. At one point, one of the operations superintendents angrily came in to see another with the report, "They [the engineers] want me to pick up samples twice a shift and bring them to them. I'm not going to pick up samples, when *they* have sample men out there. They said they would bring it up with P—— [the plant manager]." The other superintendent replied, "Good. I just had a go-around with P—— over the phone and *we* are going to run the machines for the experiment." But he had not really been as firm as he tried to appear, nor was he really going to run the machines as this part of his phone conversation with the plant manager indicates:

I don't object to the study but I want it done right. They can't do it in the time they want, but we'll set it up and have it ready for them to come in and let us know what they want. I think we can get something out of this but only if it's done right. You should see the stuff they worked up on the mills . . . it's all off.

As in many organizations, disputes about goals or processes are ultimately fought out on the issue of the recruiting and promoting of key personnel. For example, the operators maintained that their field should still be the way to the top job: "It's a lot better for the people who work under him if the top man came up through operating." On the other hand, the engineers saw *their* department as now furnishing the leaders. They would not accept a move into operations as a promotion:

We're trying to build up out of this department the source for operations and managerial personnel. People from here could move to chief chemist, assistant plant superintendent, and above.

When an engineer moved into operations without making a substantial jump in salary he was seen as "going where the competition is not as tough."

The engineers (all college-trained) constantly referred to men by their IQs, while operations superintendents (none college-trained) judged a man by what he had learned from experience. For example, engineers with experience in operations were "OK" with operations people:

> G——, for example, can read the operating sheets. There are things there that don't mean anything except to an operator. Speaking strictly as a man in the field, he knows what I'm talking about.

The difference in education, however, was not nearly the whole explanation of the difference in judgment. IR personnel also had degrees and also were involved in an overlap of functions with operations, but the relationship was not marked by the same bitterness. Part of the explanation lay in the backgrounds of people involved and the types of skills required for their respective functions. The engineers with their technical training considered themselves holders of a professional expertise. They were impatient with what they considered to be a lack of intelligence. The specialty of Industrial Relations—or the IR expertise—was not in technical knowledge but in interpersonal competence.

Other members of management interceded to calm down these bitter relations. For example, one vice-president told operations to permit engineering to do some experiments but at the same time told them to make sure the engineers did no damage. In another instance, cited above, a plant manager reassured operators that they should be the ones to run the machines for an experiment. These remarks were meant as a "cool-out" in the now classical sense of that term (see Goffman, 1952). The engineers really lost little power to function and to carry out their responsibility, while the operators were left some "face." The engineers were considered strong enough not to be harmed by having an occasional decision go against them.

Management: A Shifting Distinction

The process which had been responsible for the demise and difficulties of the first-line supervisor has long since been documented.[12] The following quotation from a higher manager should indicate the position of the first-line supervisor in this company:

> I've seen them spend all their time on outside materials like watching sand come in. . . . The job is so routine they look for anything that is different or that they can supervise . . . like unloading.

The process which had reduced the status of the first-line supervisor had the same effect on the operations superintendents, who were all third-level managers.

Although the operations superintendents still considered themselves managers and were quite concerned with maintaining authority over hourly employees, they strangely disassociated themselves from the term "management." They, too, had become part of a work force, albeit a managerial work force. Management was something above them.

During the course of this study, these superintendents constantly referred to management as though this was a distinct stratum above them. Other managers at their level, mostly from the newer functions and units, referred to those above them with the qualifying and, hence, inclusive adjective such as "top" management. The following represent the phrases used by seven superintendents who had subordinate managers and hourly employees below them:

> I do what management says. It's up to them.
> We have had this problem for months, and it was only when the machinery in one of the units started to slow down that we started getting support from management.
> Management can't understand. They immediately yell money.
> In a phone conversation with another superintendent: I understand management, meaning Mr. G——(a VP), doesn't want to shut down.
> The management's really anxious about that. (In talking to an outside salesman.)
> We felt, rather *I* didn't feel—the management felt; they made the change.

In all these cases, the superintendents referred to those immediately above them as management. Five of them invariably used the unadorned term of "management," while two occasionally shifted. One of

---

12. For example, there have been a number of accounts which illustrate what happens to supervisors as work becomes automated. See Blau (1957), Faunce (1958), and Simpson (1959).

the two used the term "big brass" once but most of the time used "management"; another used both "management" and "top management" to refer to the same level above him. The former was one of the two college-educated superintendents and the latter was among the more recently appointed superintendents and also one of the few who ever wore a tie at work. Although he was the same age as the other six, the latter manager was part of a newer organizational generation. Although he was in the same position as the others, he had entered it at a significantly later date and had gone through different socialization processes.

In contrast, IR employees, if they used the term "management" to refer to anyone above them, used the adjective "top" or something similar. Usually, however, if they had to refer to those above them in the company, they used names and not categories—unless they were talking about a group.

Identification with management was also typical in the various other nonproduction units, where those higher were almost invariably referred to with some adjective in front of "management," indicating the speaker's identity with management. Those above him were simply "higher" management. For example:

General management does not realize what the functions of our unit can do.
Central management are not organizational conscious.
People on the topside have this feeling.
Once top management is sold, it's more routine.
Our function is strictly one of service to higher management.

Thus third-level superintendents in the historically defined, so-called line did not identify themselves as management. Superintendents in what are normally called staff units did so identify themselves.[13]

The larger the organization, the more difficult it is to obtain an identification with management on the part of those at the bottom and in the middle ranks of management. They have to be treated in more

13. The split in identification with management illustrates the fact that those occupations which have normally been considered part of the "line" may, in fact, belong less to any line that reaches the top of the organization than do those occupations and units which, again, have normally been considered "staff." We would also argue that this paper indicates the limitation of the model of line-staff relations presented by Dalton (1950; 1959).

universalistic terms, and they come closer to making the kinds of attachments peculiar to nonmanagerial personnel. This kind of growth into large-scale organization means that, like the employees, managers have become a work force and have to be thought of in terms of categories.

History as a Tactic

It is in the nature of history that acts taken to meet a problem may serve to justify subsequent and analogous acts. Knowledge of this possibility means that compromises made to meet present conflicts can also be used as tactics for future bargaining. The setting or the avoidance of a precedent becomes a possible ingredient in all union-management situations. It is not uncommon to find labor relations representatives maintaining or even creating an ambiguous situation in order to avoid precedent-setting acts. They may also carefully work to set up a series of small precedents, each one building on the previous one. A solution unacceptable at one point in time may become acceptable after the "ground work is laid" (see Goldner, 1967). Operations superintendents at Rock Products, not so involved in the same kind of legal structure, seemed to prefer firm settlements and complained about any ambiguity.

For example, one of the more common problems was that of classifying work as either construction or maintenance. Construction work carried a considerably higher rate of pay so that the designation could affect the decision to undertake certain kinds of work. Many of the unions performing maintenance work in the plant were building-trade unions and, hence, also had jurisdiction over construction work.[14] The union-management agreement had a clause which seemingly covered this issue:

For the purpose hereof, the term "construction" shall mean any work the cost of which under the United States Internal Revenue laws and regulations, is required to be capitalized by Employers on their books and amortized over a period of years. Work, the cost of which, under said laws and regulations, is permitted to be charged off as current operating expense, shall be considered to be "maintenance" under the terms of this Agreement.

14. Building trade unions claim that construction work is within their jurisdiction. If a plant is organized by other than building trade unions these internal unions perform maintenance work but may have to forego jurisdiction of work classified as construction. In that case jurisdictional fights over maintenance-construction classifications leave management caught between two different unions.

However, the contract clause became outmoded. The Internal Revenue department changed its methods so that some items that the parties had agreed as not being "construction" now had to be capitalized. It also had been decided that some items that were not capitalized would be "construction" if they were new. While there was an understanding of the general conditions, there no longer was an automatic method of determining "construction." IR now had to be consulted before work was begun, in order to determine whether or not the work was to be paid at the higher rate.

One such incident involved the construction of a new office in the plant, including, of course, lighting fixtures. About a week later management ordered the lights changed. While there was no question that the initial work was "construction," the union claimed that the change should also be paid at construction rates. The steward's position was that the change was "construction," since it involved alteration of fixtures included in the initial plans. The supervisor disagreed and asserted that as soon as office people started working in the office, any subsequent change would be "maintenance." The supervisor maintained that they had to draw the line somewhere or they would be fighting this issue all the time. His concern was that the union would claim that *any* change was one that was part of original plans.

In the course of the discussion, the IR man got an agreement from the steward that any office changes or shifts would be "maintenance" and only expanded office space would be considered new and, hence, "construction." The IR man felt that the acceptance of this point far outweighed the question in dispute. Glad to have won agreement on this principle, IR told the supervisor not to fight the battle only to lose the war.

It is important to note that the supervisor explicitly acknowledged that the decision-making power was in the hands of IR and that he, himself, was in an advisory capacity. At times during the discussion the supervisor would say, "It's your decision," but then would go on with his arguments. In fact, at one point the union steward interrupted the supervisor's argument with: "IR is here to decide this, so let them make the decision. I've taken their decision where I disagreed with them." Interestingly enough, the union steward saw IR as some kind of arbitrator performing an intermediary function between the union and

supervision. The IR man concluded by saying,"I'll take the responsibility, and I'm glad if we can get that agreement on new offices."

IR had a general policy of avoiding premature decisions, although
operations management chafed under uncertainty. In describing union-
management relations one IR informant pointed out:

> Things don't have to come to a final conclusion to be effective. Sometimes
> you'd rather not force a decision on them. Lots of times people agree but
> might not want to commit themselves. It [commitment] leaves no room
> for [the] future.

THE ORGANIZATION OF UNCERTAINTY

The conflicting pressures of maintaining a central labor relations
policy and of providing a fair degree of autonomy for the operating
heads at successive levels produced an organizational structure that
contained a good deal of uncertainty and conflict. Under these pressures
the IR plant superintendent inevitably ended up reporting to two bosses.
As noted above, while he worked for, and was paid by, the plant
manager, he was also held responsible by company and corporate level
IR for the implementation of IR policy.

The mere division of authority into direct and functional did not
suffice to define the situation for the participants. The relative power
of IR with other managements was not simply "determined" for any
point in time but was a moving relationship that varied depending on
the organizational forces that we have been discussing, plus the definitions that participants brought to each act. To say that on balance one
or the other had greater power provided no answer for what would
happen at a specific event.

There were no clear, formal definitions by which subordinates could
choose between conflicting frames of reference. Hence, the pressures
that helped create functional authority would seem to be the best guide
as to when the functional frame of reference supersedes the more usual
lines of authority. For example, it would be expected that the more a
subject was company-wide in scope the more the functional frame of
reference would take precedence. In one instance, the IR procedures
manual for the Regional Metal Company provided a listing of the line
of oral communications to be used when labor problems arose:

IR Representative, to Assistant Superintendent of IR, to Superintendent-IR, to Manager of Labor Relations, to Manager of IR, and then to the Vice-President and Assistant General Manager of the Company.

The main point is that the line of communication should not get jammed up where economic conditions are pending, such as pending strikes, walkouts, picketing, slowdowns, or similar activity because one of the persons involved cannot be contacted. Let's hear about it in [Elm City] just as fast as possible.

No mention was made of also informing management other than IR—except, as we see, after it had gone all the way up through the highest IR manager.

The handling of relations at the plant level between IR and plant management was a curious blend of accommodations. The IR personnel were mostly on their own, though they constantly "wired-in" plant management who, in turn, recognized that IR's responsibility extended beyond both the plant and the company. Each party possessed a fairly healthy respect for the other's position.

There was, however, a historically derived norm that a general manager at any level should be in total command. Alternative arrangements when compared to that norm produced frustration for plant management personnel and a feeling of defensiveness for IR. Specific objections to the arrangement were frequent:

IR might be an enclave. I like the decentralized approach. I would like to see more of it handled on our level.

The trouble of the central reporting of IR is they pay too much attention to what [Elm City] will think. The IR Superintendent constantly has his eye on [Elm City] and acts in terms of their approval.

IR acknowledged the norm by apologizing for the front they had to maintain:

We are a bunch of hypocrites in saying we work for [the plant manager]. Our functional boss is the IR Manager. In the final analysis it is him in terms of policy and staff assistance, et cetera. Placement-wise we are more centralized than the chart. Direction of incentive is to the functional boss. The plant manager naturally assumes I work for him. He is supposed to be the captain of his ship.

The ambivalence that characterized the whole relationship was indicated by the managers' inability to make flat declarative statements about power without immediately qualifying or even contradicting the statement. A plant manager, in contrasting the organization of IR with that of accounting, made the following successive series of statements:

> We don't have trouble with Accounting. The only place is with IR in the functional reporting. We really have no trouble with IR. They know they have to get along.

IR managers, for their part, found the same difficulty:

> We recommend and they pretty well follow. But it's their decision. They call the shots but pretty well leave it up to us.

It would be fairly safe to assume that dual lines of responsibility result in a lack of clarity about the powers of the respective parties whenever there is conflict between the interests represented by the two responsibilities. The organization structure itself—the very presence of this type of dual authority structure—helps to define the power situation for the participants. Open disputes become rare because most people involved develop "workable" perspectives over a period of time. However, new situations cause a recurrence of tension. Struggles may then have to be open if the structure is untested and undefined by previously unencountered situations. Once a perspective is upheld in a specific encounter, it then becomes part of the definition of the total relationship and serves to narrow the area for possible open clashes.

Salesmanship as an Accommodative Mechanism

The ambiguity and anxiety over the uncertainty present in the relationship between IR and other members of management were largely resolved by making the IR representative responsible for the resolution of this uncertainty. An informant from another function made the contrast: "We think more black and white than IR men can afford to think. We are more doctrinaire." Conduct and procedures, unstructured by the usual notions of authority, were not sharply defined. The existing ambiguity was resolved not just by organizational arrangements but by the ability of the IR personnel to resolve and contain this ambiguity within themselves.

The organizational emphasis was put on the relationship, as such, rather than on delimiting and defining the respective functions. The tension was shifted from between the two units to the person of the IR manager, who was then characterized by an ability to handle ambiguity.

One respondent described the desirable characteristics of a potential labor relations representative as "A dynamiter with diplomacy and tact—someone who will talk back and can talk his way out of hell."

The most important accommodative mechanism was the characterization of IR members as salesmen. IR personnel, in this as well as other corporations, were told they had to be salesmen; they had to sell their programs to the union and also to the rest of management. The burden of resolving the uncertainty was placed on their shoulders. It was part of their functional specialization, for they spent more of their time in such unstructured relationships than other members of management.

Given the norm of decentralization, there was a consequent attempt on the part of operating units to preserve as much of their autonomy as possible or at least to preserve the image of autonomy. For this reason, while IR men had to "put across" the IR goals, they were urged not to give the appearance of circumventing or directly contradicting operating management.

The IR man's skills in interpersonal relations were used to smooth over the opposition from operating units. His characterization as salesman provided a "face-saving" device for operations. It seemed to put those in other units in the position of buyer, with the buyer's prerogative of choosing whether or not to buy, and consequently enabled them to retain a self-image of importance. The IR representative was encouraged to practice salesmanship by defining others as his clients.

The characterization gives the impression that different perspectives can be resolved by convincing those with dissimilar views that it is in their best interest to follow IR policy. Otherwise, there would be open acknowledgment that there was a source of authority additional to the normal concentric form of organizational authority. There was less organizational conflict than if IR had tried to force policy upon others, regardless of how much power IR might have had.

The following incident may help to illustrate the "sales" relationship between IR and production supervision. An IR member was trying to persuade Superintendent B—— to accept a worker who had been under observation for mental trouble. Near the end of the conversation, the IR representative repeated the initial proposal and was met with this reply: "I don't want him. I'm not sure he's safe. I'll take him if you will sign an affidavit that any accident is not our fault and won't count as a lost time accident against us." The IR man replied, "I want him in the right situation and the right job; we have a moral obligation," while Superintendent B—— said, "I'm having trouble now with the guys on shift seniority. If you fellows want to take him and the manager's wired in, I'll take him." The conversation had gone on like this, going over and over the same points, for thirty minutes.

The IR representative thought he was "selling" something to production, but it appears it was something other than his salesmanship that mattered. In recounting the incident, the IR man told his IR superior and others that, while Superintendent B—— was reluctant, he had gotten the superintendent to accept the moral obligation. During the conversation, however, Superintendent B—— never gave any indication that he accepted any moral obligation but emphasized from the beginning that he did not want the worker and would take him only if IR insisted and if the plant manager did not object.

It was evident to this observer that the decision was made by IR with, as it were, the negative advice of the production superintendent. It was only his self-image as salesman that enabled the IR man to interpret the incident as he did and prevented the superintendent from simply being told to do it. In terms of the usual notions of seller and buyer in the competitive marker, the situation was actually reversed. The superintendent was trying to sell a rejection to the IR man; IR's only selling was an attempt to make the supervisor like what he *had* to do.

At the same time it should be clear that the salesman-characterization was inaccurate despite its accommodative function. The IR program had essentially been accepted by the top management of the corporation. IR had been made responsible for its implementation and was held accountable for its success. Nevertheless, the implementation of the policy involved the responsibilities of other units and consequently required some method of conflict resolution.

While the IR men many times assumed the posture of salesmen, their wares had to be bought, although there might be some legitimate stalling tactics. The proper use of the characterization of salesman does occur when one tries to sell a program to a superior. Consequently, in those areas of IR responsibility that did not deal with unions and would not otherwise require a functional line of reporting, the IR man did attempt to sell the program to the plant manager. In these areas, IR performed a service for plant management as does any subordinate to his superior.

IR successfully, though unintentionally, implemented what had been an explicit policy by which the British were able to rule West African colonies with a relatively few colonial administrators. The policy, called "Indirect Rule," consisted of making decisions "behind the scene" in order to permit already established African chiefs to maintain all the appearances of authority over their subjects.[15] The salesman-characterization thus provided a "face-saving" device for operations.

If it is true that decision-making by Industrial Relations tended to destroy the relations between operations supervisors and their subordinates, certain mechanisms existed to alleviate this disruption. The relations between IR and supervisors could be hidden from the subordinates. The "selling" notion helped to define the relationships, but it also hid or at least disguised some of the real power.

Union Bargaining: Training for Dealing with the Rest of Management

The experience that IR men received from bargaining with unions helped to provide them with the interpersonal skills so useful for internal accommodation.[16] Bargaining skills, in the course of their application, must answer the need to maintain peaceful relations with unions in order to prevent work stoppages. As a representative of the company in the role of boundary maintenance, the bargainer must prevent encroachment by the union on the boundary of the management organization.[17]

IR personnel at Rock Products were so involved in the bargaining process that they even came to value the bargaining experience for

15. For an interesting account of "indirect rule" see Lugard (1926). Baker and France (1954:180–181), make somewhat the same point: "There is considerable evidence that the appearance of authority along with the recognition of the plant manager's or supervisor's knowledge of local conditions is of more importance in its effect on intra-management relations than the actual degree of decision-making authority delegated and exercised."

16. For the reverse—the influence of internal affairs on the bargaining tasks of IR men—see Walton and McKersie (1965).

17. For a review of the literature on boundary roles and interorganizational analysis, see Guetzkow (1966).

itself. They consequently judged the respective participants on the basis of bargaining ability. At an extreme, this led IR representatives to seek out the more competent and stronger union officials despite the possibility of, thus, obtaining a less favorable union contract. For example, one IR man complained about the "real weak officials at this plant" and highly praised the "smart and aggressive" ones at another plant. He repeatedly referred to the negotiations with the latter group as a "real good bargaining session."

When the tasks of a position require the development of personal relationships, incumbents become more irreplaceable and more powerful. The signing of a contract between a Regional company and a union did not end their relationship. Day-to-day negotiations have to continue under the framework of a present contract, and there are always subsequent contracts to be negotiated. Therefore, the participants had to establish good relationships in order to deal with each other effectively. Indeed, this was an explicit tactic of IR units throughout the Regional companies. Prior to the contract-negotiating sessions, all the labor relations people were given orders to "get the lists of business agents you deal with and start taking them out to lunch so you will have contact before actual negotiations start." The IR manual listed under "union relations" a subsection entitled: "Respectful, friendly, and constructive relationships on and off the job between Labor Relations and Union Representatives."

The role of bargainer necessarily involves the ability to "take the role of the other" [18] in order to anticipate possible actions or reactions of one's "opponent." The necessity of so acting, and the ability apparent in the successful practitioner, combined to provide IR men with an invaluable "tool" for dealing with other management units. They were better equipped to win their point without incurring the wrath of others. In addition to their bargaining skills they had to learn to deal with union representatives who, like themselves, were both bargainers and representatives of an organization in which they also had internal re-

18. For a fuller explanation of this process of taking the role of the other, see Mead (1934). Surprisingly enough, there has not been much research on the variables associated with the different degrees of self-reflection and the differential incidence of the process of taking the role of another. It is apparent, for example, that "bargainers" are more adept in—and more involved with—this process than others in organizations.

lations. The IR staff, then, had to try to obtain contacts within the unions in order to find out what was going on in union meetings and internal discussions. They, thus, became further politically sophisticated about intraorganizational relations.

The peculiarities of these requirements—the strong emphasis on interpersonal relations and bargaining—bear a strong relation to the variables associated with personality. Personality is simply more pertinent to the tasks of labor relations than to other tasks in organizations.[19] For this reason, the labor relations staff members were identified in terms of personality much more than others:

> Line people are a little more crusty and don't have to deal with as wide groups of people and they are interested in "things." IR is everything to do with people—have to have a different sort of personality.

Evidence of the payoff of IR's training and experience was provided above where the IR personnel stood in contrast to the process engineers in the ability to "handle" operations managers. The latter resented IR's intrusion much less than they did that of the engineers. While they may have been recruited on the basis of their personality, the training and experience in bargaining furthered this ability to "handle" the rest of management.

The unique personality characteristics of labor relations men reduce the organizational strains brought about by the complex division of labor in the multi-unit industrial organization. *In this one important way personality contributes to the forming of the organization rather than merely being formed by it.* The resolution of interunit conflict is accomplished by the demands made on the personality of the incumbents of labor relations positions.

The Power of Marginality

The marginal position of the IR unit further enabled its incumbents

19. Work on the relationship of personality and organization has been done by Merton (1957) and Argyris (1957). Merton deals primarily with the effect of bureaucratic rules on personality, while Argyris has dealt with the limitations placed on personal growth by the organizational hierarchy and the narrowness of tasks. Merton does deal with the reverse effect back on the organization in what he calls a process of "displacement of rules." The view that relates to the necessary kind of interpersonal relations within the organization is dealt with in Whyte (1956).

to enjoy a good deal of organizational freedom and power along with the anxieties which accompany uncertainty. Their boundary-maintenance position left the organization dependent upon them for interpreting the outside. Their access to all levels of the organization made them sought after by all those who wished to bypass normal channels of organizational communication—in any direction. They could intercede for any one unit with any other. And, finally, they were able to help construct the measurement system by which they were evaluated.

The Control of Knowledge

Whatever power IR derived from its responsibility of dealing with an outside organization was augmented by IR's further responsibility of implementing the union-management agreement. IR was responsible for making specific what was general. A union-management agreement cannot possibly cover all eventualities—it must be interpreted daily. The IR administrators attempted to keep the agreement "secret" or, failing this, to make it vague. They continually stressed that a contract was not what it seemed and agreed to make it specific only under pressure.[20]

IR personnel were well aware of the benefits that accrue to a unit possessing some kind of exclusive knowledge. The more they kept all relations with the union to themselves, the more they were in a position to act without fear of contradiction. For example, IR did not encourage widespread distribution of the union-management agreement. As one IR man put it: "No, they [front line supervision] do not have contracts. It doesn't help them a bit and maybe even screws them up. There are only about a dozen in all the plant."

But mere possession of knowledge is not enough. It must be aug-

---

20. Even in Weber's account of bureaucratic legal authority (1947:339) there is a passage devoted to the benefits gained by "official secrets": "But in addition to this, bureaucratic organizations, or the holders of power who make use of them, have the tendency to increase their power still further by the knowledge growing out of experience in the service. For they acquire through the conduct of office a special knowledge of facts and have available a store of documentary material peculiar to themselves. While not peculiar to bureaucratic organizations, the concept of 'official secrets' is certainly typical of them. It stands in relation to technical knowledge in somewhat the same position as commercial secrets do to technological training. It is a product of the striving for power."

mented by control over the application of this knowledge. Time and again the IR personnel attempted to convince others that contract clauses were not to be taken literally. The union-management agreement had to be interpreted to be understood. More particularly, they insisted that it was important to know how the union or arbitrators would interpret the agreement, something only IR personnel were in a position to know. They asserted that, "You never go by the wording in contracts. You go by *the* interpretation." In the disputes over maintenance *vs.* construction rates, which we previously discussed, IR evinced no desire to change the appropriate agreement clause. The inapplicability of that clause placed more responsibility on IR for contract-interpretation and afforded less chance for others in management to understand or be aware of what the agreement contained.

Bypass Opportunities

IR was able to serve in a bypass capacity because of its position in the organization. It was outside the normal system of authority within the plant. IR personnel, as part of their job, regularly "toured" all plant facilities. Employees came to IR when they feared going directly to their own superiors. Attitudes were planted with IR in the hope that IR would pass them on. Men asked IR about merit raises instead of going directly to their superiors. Supervisors told IR about their problems with higher management, and so on, up each level of the organization.

IR was in a position to bypass communicatively every level of the organization below that of the top man for the whole corporation. The more a unit is in a pivotal position which enables it to obtain information not readily obtainable by others, the more powerful its position.

IR's bypass position was also employed by superordinates in their relations with subordinates. Nevertheless, plant management was ambivalent toward IR's bypass capacities, for while they wanted to use IR to control hierarchical problems with those below, they also resented IR's intrusion into matters defined as "line" management's concern.

Plant management, hence, in its concern with maintaining controls, frequently took contradictory positions. On the one hand, plant management argued that IR should not interfere with the supervisor's responsibility of running his crew: "IR should only hear of actions [like discharge] afterwards so that they will be prepared when they hear from the union, and they should only go out to there [the plant area] to get the facts so they can present a straight line." On the other hand, plant management also wished to limit the supervisors. In the same conversation the plant manager contradicted the above statement:

We are trying to lay down procedures for [the foremen] so things are uniform and they can easily tell what to do. We don't print up the union contract because there is so much that is not in the contract but is just a verbal understanding of supplemental agreement. Also, the foremen want things one way but then at another time want it another, since it is a friend of theirs or a relative.

The control function that plant management desired of IR can be illustrated further. In discussing the problem of absenteeism with plant management, IR was told to audit the superintendents:

On the point of consistency, I want to mention something to you. You're leaving it up to the superintendents. Why don't you set it up so you have it by name of all those that get reported? I'd think you'd be a little nervous about what's happened and set it up by employees [as opposed to the more gross filing by department]. With them doing it, you're not doing any auditing; there is no cross check. You are the one that has to inject consistency in this. All you have is their own records.

Bypass mechanisms enable individuals or groups to "negotiate" with each other without making commitments or setting precedents for either side. IR thus served as a channel of communication for those matters which one level or another thought it best not to discuss openly.[21] There are issues which are considered illegitimate for subordinates to complain about. Other issues, if put on an open agenda, would force participants to make commitments that none of them might desire.

IR as Intermediary

Wage-and-salary administration for the Woodside plant was handled by a special corporate IR unit called "Wage and Salary" and located in the corporate offices at Elm City. Woodside plant management naturally resented such split control.[22] Resentment of the division of authority was coupled with circumvention of it. Job duties were fre-

21. Barnard (1956) discusses the provision of channels for the communication of matters which cannot go direct.

22. For an account of the specific reasons for the centralization of a company wage program, see Steiber (1959:124–125, 321).

quently "glorified" by plant management in order to get a higher rate for the job. This was possible for slightly unusual jobs because there was little auditing of salaried jobs. The work load of Wage and Salary was such that audits were difficult to conduct; Wage and Salary was frequently kept busy with those wage rates that were included in union negotiations.

Plant IR personnel played a peculiar role when wages and salaries were handled at the corporate level; they became intermediaries between the plant manager and Wage and Salary.[23] When Wage and Salary was in a completely different IR unit, as was true at Woodside, then the IR plant personnel could maintain that they were without control over the wage-and-salary unit. But they did have a closer relationship with, and were more informed about, Wage and Salary than the plant manager. They were in a position to achieve some things he might not be able to achieve.

One incident illustrates the desire of IR to appear as such an intermediary. Plant management wanted to rate a new job as highly as possible in order to reward the incumbent for doing more work than his supervisor. Upon hearing the description, the IR representative gave his opinion that the job sounded like a grade five. He then called Wage and Salary at Elm City and found that a similar sounding job in the Elm City office was already rated at six. Although the Elm City job seemed more complicated, the IR man went into detail to describe the complexities of the local job, *although he knew nothing about the actual requirements of the job.* The representative in Elm City replied that grade six sounded "OK" to him. IR called the plant and told them that "six" looked all right and then told the manager, "I have been building up the job to Elm City and making it sound like it was the Plant Manager." He took credit for getting the job rated at six instead of five, making it clear that he was interceding as a service for the plant manager.

23. IR's role could also be called marginal, since IR was identified with both of the groups involved. This was different from ordinary boundary roles such as the one IR occupies vis-à-vis the union, where IR represents one organization to another. It was also different from the situation where one party's role is marginal because of a lack of identification with either of the other parties. For an analysis of this last situation see Kahn, *et al.* (1964).

On the other hand, IR was called upon to defend Wage and Salary as part of its own organization. On a call from a plant manager to IR requesting some overdue information, an IR man replied by reporting: "They are really swamped. They have had a tough row to hoe ever since they were cut back in the recession."

IR's identification with both the plant manager and the parent unit of Wage and Salary—while the actual people involved were separated from one another—permitted the appearance of intercession on behalf of each group by IR.

The Control of Measurements

Units of organizations have a crucial stake in the way their "output" is evaluated or measured (Blau, 1963). It would be expected that a unit would try to gain as much control as possible over the definition of this measurement. For example, one of the plants of Regional Metal complained because it was evaluated on the basis of cost "standards" rather than profit and loss computations. It claimed that it could sell its products in the geographical area of another plant of the company at a greater profit than the other plant. But, because of the centralization of the controller unit, the plant manager was unable to secure the necessary data to compute profit-and-loss figures. Nevertheless, whether by profit and loss or by cost data, the plant was evaluated by clearly defined standards of measurement. In contrast, much of IR's posture in its relations with the rest of the organization was influenced by the lack of any such clear standards by which to be evaluated or measured. As one non-IR manager said, "IR in general can't be measured. They have the best of the deal."

The lack of measurement was a mixed blessing, however, for it put IR in the vulnerable position of not being able to indicate its accomplishments readily. Consequently, IR tried to retain its nonmeasurable quality in issues dealing with long-range perspectives—such as management-development—but also looked around for areas of success that would submit to precise standards of measurement. The half-year summary of IR "Objectives" made this lack of precise standards an explicit issue and made the point that, in their area, "no news is good news":

Since many Industrial Relations activities concern functions which are not readily measurable in accountable standards, we are forced to use many generalities such as "substantial progress has been made." . . . Also, particularly in the case of labor relations when there is nothing to report because peace and quiet prevails or has been maintained, this "nothing to report" is the equivalent of "progress" or success.

There was a good deal of resentment and frustration on the part of general management over IR's ability to remain relatively aloof from "having to account for itself": "IR turns out paper work of all kinds about what they have done and are going to do, all counted and compiled by themselves."

The difficulty of measuring their contributions and the long-range perspective associated with their efforts led to a further desire on the part of the IR personnel to try to prevent the application of some cost-profit standards. Thus, when one of the IR staff suggested that he could show the return for each cost dollar in one part of his area of responsibility, his IR superior retorted: "We don't want to start the business of trying to measure all IR contributions." Some of the IR staff resented the ambiguity: "We're unable to measure results—it's frustrating. It's [negotiations] a team effort, and we don't know and can't measure it."

Torn by conflicting strategies, they tried to pick and choose those that would enhance their position. IR did desire to develop ways to indicate and publicize its successes. And, if to no one else, IR had to justify its existence to itself. Also, IR had to enter its claim in the never-ending problem of apportioning scarce resources throughout the organization. The ground upon which IR chose to make its stand was that of labor relations and comparative labor costs in competing companies. The "Objectives" made this quite clear: To conduct, or counsel in, the renegotiation of all major labor agreements (totaling 46 in number) of all operating companies on the basis of providing for union wage rates and fringe benefits comparable to our competitors. As we previously noted, the use of competitive labor costs as a measurement of IR's success was one of the forces leading IR to take part in joint bargaining with other companies.

Another tactic was to take the offensive. Regional IR thus reported a shift to "hard-line" labor negotiating in its "objectives":

Placed increased emphasis on fair but firm administration of labor agreements by management and worked to develop greater responsibility on the part of union representatives by insisting on strict adherence to both substantive and procedural provisions of such agreements.

Foster positive programs to further the objective of maximizing productivity on a continuing basis.

The present IR personnel felt that they started their administration saddled with competitive labor-cost disadvantages throughout the member companies. Their attempt to put themselves on a standard basis with their competition meant that, for a while, they actually had to take a harder line. In addition to this, the close and constant interaction between IR and union officials frequently prompted general management to accuse IR of "siding" with the union. A hard line warded off this accusation.

IR's goal of reducing competitive wage costs was directly related to its attempt to prove itself to general management. For example, they attempted to limit only *wage* increases. It was acknowledged that the salary schedule for Rock Products lay at the top of the range for competitive salaries in the geographical area and throughout the industry. And yet IR made no effort even to refer to this problem, *despite the fact that salary costs were 36 percent of the combined wage and salary costs* at Rock Products.

Boundary Wars: Mobility and Control

Despite our references to IR as a corporate-wide entity, no organization, as such, had been set up. There was no budget line for a corporate-wide IR unit. The complexity of relationships and accompanying confusion rested on the overlay of a functional division of labor on top of the more prevalent ones based on product and location. Only the functional lines of reporting appeared to hold IR men together.

The crucial factor in the formation of IR as an organization was the career lines of IR personnel. IR men would ordinarily have little in the way of strong professional identifications to challenge their company identifications. The ties to, and the goals of, their function could exist quite compatibly *within* company identifications. The wider corporate view of their function, with its emphasis on co-ordinated union bargaining, could be enforced only if IR men were held responsible to those of whom this wider view was a prime responsibility. IR's so-called functional responsibility to corporate IR was largely defined

by corporate IR's power over the career lines of company IR personnel—the power to appoint, the power to remove, the power to transfer,
and the power to promote. No matter how identified with, and loyal to,
IR perspectives the incumbent might be, the perspectives would cease
to be important referents if corporate IR did not have these powers.

Predominance of Mobility Aspirations

Control over mobility is important because members of management in large-scale organizations are faced with a constant concern
over their present and future mobility. The organization explicitly consists of a hierarchy of positions; any particular position always is
superseded by another above it. Indeed, mobility may become the
single most important factor in the participant's organizational existence.[24] The opportunities for advancement become important, then,
for securing organizational commitment. They serve as "incentives for
participation" (Simon, 1958:116).

The members of the IR units of Regional Industries were characterized by deep interest and concern over personal mobility. They were
constantly preoccupied with present moves and future possibilities on
both general and personal levels. As a matter of fact, movement was
taken for granted, and hence the major factor was whether one was
moving fast enough:

> Movement is of prime concern here. People are not concerned with
> whether they will move but when and where. Every move that is made, they
> figure what all the subsequent moves will be and where they fit. They are
> constantly concerned with this to the detriment of work. Not that they
> don't do good jobs—but could do so much better.

Mobility among the IR staff was a constant topic of conversation,
though usually under informal circumstances: "When at the bar with
a bunch of guys you get into a discussion about this kind of thing—
various merits and prospects of different people." Some of the IR
personnel had even gone to the extent of figuring the odds for succeeding to higher posts: "To get [the top salary bracket] is a reality now in
IR. Say two chances in IR and seven in operating. In the [next
bracket] two in IR and maybe fifteen in operating."

24. For a general discussion of mobility within industrial organizations, see
Martin and Strauss (1959).

Intercompany Mobility

The greatest opportunity for mobility is provided by the ability of the multicompany organization to transfer people from one company to another.[25] The very fact of movement from one unit to another was important at Rock Products, aside from the idea of promotion. Moving about heightens a person's visibility to those who are in a position to recommend advancement.[26] Staying in the same spot places a greater reliance on the immediate opportunities nearby and on satisfying a specific boss. No one else is likely to be aware of an incumbent's presence. As one disgruntled employee remarked: "Those guys who had moved around and out of the plant had moved up faster." He had been trying to get a transfer from operations management into IR. He thought the movement afforded to the IR employees would present him with greater opportunity for mobility and advancement.

For IR members who had made the move from one company to another, the future possibility of a similar move was a real one. They not only saw the possibility but saw the reason for it lying in their connection to corporate IR and to the position of the corporate IR vice-president:

Just as easy to be in [Alloy] or [Metal] next month as here. With G——as top guy, he naturally knows about people in all areas. I'd take either side of the bet of whether I would be back in [Metal]. These are not arbitrary shiftings. G——takes all conditions into account.

The image of intercompany mobility differed according to level and size of the company. There were those who maintained that fifty percent of the top IR staff had been with more than one company. As a matter of fact, seven of the eight highest members of the IR organization at Rock Products started their careers with another of the Regional companies. In the smaller companies, even the lower-level employee was

25. March and Simon (1958) make the point that "the larger the organization, the greater the *perceived possibility of intra-organizational transfer,* and therefore, the less the perceived desirability of leaving the organization." (Italics theirs.)

26. Those who had moved around, even on a horizontal level, became known much faster around the company and were more "visible" when people had to consider whom to take to fill jobs. Visibility is further discussed in Dalton (1959:176). But Dalton refers more to hierarchical visibility and the visibility of personality, while here we refer to the visibility of roles and visibility due to transfers and movements.

relatively dependent on corporate IR for future mobility. The larger companies hired people at the bottom and generally had enough room for them to move around so that the majority remained with that company. There were even joking references to the "iron curtain" around the employees of one of the larger companies.

The Management of Mobility

Corporate IR made a conscious and continuous effort to maintain the intercompany mobility of IR personnel: if mobility opportunities served as "incentives for participation" within the larger organization, they did likewise for participation in—and identification with—*units* of the larger organizations. Whenever there is any question of an overlap in identifications, the unit able to control mobility gains a proportional edge.

IR was quite explicit about its intentions in its published "objectives":

Completed objectives of using management inventory and development program data, on an integrated basis, for the most effective utilization of Industrial Relations personnel in all companies through intercompany transfers by assembling such data on Industrial Relations personnel and using same in evaluating all opportunities for promotion and/or transfers. Approximately twenty individuals have been transferred between companies since the inception of this program.

And as one informant said, "Considerations about filling posts are in terms of a gigantic chess game."

Mobility and Autonomy

The movement of management manpower was seen as a threat to the autonomy of the separate companies. Established company identifications were broken down in favor of the wider corporate identities when employees saw their mobility opportunities in terms of moving from company to company. The company which lost trained manpower resented the loss incurred in the expense of training: the receiving company suspected the newcomer of having deviant loyalties.

A central unit's ability to take men out of the subunit, as opposed to transferring them in, differentially affects unit leadership and autonomy. Taking a man out means a loss of trained personel and a judgment that another unit's need might be greater than that of the subject unit. When a man is transferred *in,* it may be suspected that he is there as some kind of spy from the central unit. Furthermore, the manager is made aware that he does not have control over choosing his own subordinates:

> F——resisted my putting someone in there because he said it was a threat to his autonomy. He asked if he could fire the guy in six months if he didn't like him. I said he couldn't fire him, but we would move him.

Having men transferred into one's unit seems to offer more of a threat to autonomy than does the removal of a man. Nevertheless, the idea held by a manager's subordinates that they can look forward to mobility beyond their immediate unit—perhaps despite the opinions of their manager—means an increase in identification with the wider organization and a consequent loss of autonomy by the immediate unit.

The actual choice and placement of IR personnel at the Woodside plant were largely in the hands of the IR organization. The company IR Manager placed IR staff, although he usually checked with corporate IR first. Plant management had some veto power over IR personnel, but the power remained unclear because of the virtual absence of any attempt to utilize it. If an appointment was made by corporate IR, there was little question of any kind of challenge by plant management. In the one instance in Rock Products in which plant management wanted an IR man discharged, the IR unit blocked the action. As one official of IR commented, "I felt there might be some justice but thought discharge too severe so I kept the man and he was transferred about six months later." Another instance, the obverse of this, made clear that IR had the power to remove an IR man over objections of plant management. In addition, plant management had no power to promote anyone from one IR position to another.

In any case all the IR personnel in this company were considered to have been put there by the IR manager. In fact the group was identified as a "fraternity" of his men. One otherwise informed respondent reported that "they all played football together in the Army." This was quite false, but it did indicate the identification of the group with the IR manager and his appointive powers.

IR still could not be too obvious about its organizational strength because of the norm of operational decentralization. For example, the following was a report by a member of the corporate IR staff about a placement that IR made in one of the companies:

When we put C——into the [other] company we briefed him ahead of time and told him the first question would be whether in case of conflict between "them" and [corporate IR] who would he back. Of course he said "them," but of course he looks for his next job as an IR job.

IR also used those occasions where it was easy to "give in" in order to "bank" good will with different levels of general management. One respondent offered:

An example is where a man was going from one [Regional Metal] plant to another. He was all packed, and they said we'd like to keep him and look upon him as next superintendent here. He stayed. [It's a question of] keeping in line management's jocks—keeping him happy. I've seen a lot of placements for that reason.

Plant management did explicitly object to one aspect of IR mobility, the "too rapid" turnover of IR personnel. "They [IR personnel] move around so much they have little chance to get oriented. This hurts the company." Plant management found itself faced with some serious problems because of rapid IR movement. The subsequent resentment was best described in the words of one of the plant management officials:

We had to cut down on their moving around so much. They changed so often I got to be the IR superintendent. With most of the contract being unwritten, someone had to be around here for a while. We had to stop some of the latest moves. I told H—— that if he expects to move, he will have to have someone prepared to take his place.

The IR personnel felt that they got more co-operation at higher levels of the company whenever there was a problem about rapid movement. "The trouble usually comes on the plant level where the people are more narrow in their views." The narrower the responsibility, the more serious was the effect of any movement.

A number of contradictory pressures were set up by such rapid IR mobility. Constant mobility within IR built up IR identity but destroyed some of its uniqueness. Constant movement pushed IR men into greater formalization and record-keeping, or bureaucratization, even at the expense of the esoteric aspect of their qualifications, in order to keep themselves free for promotions.[27] On the other hand, without records

27. The notion that increased bureaucratization is needed accordingly as an organization gets bigger, similarly applies if the organization gets "bigger" in the special sense that more rapid mobility inevitably involves larger numbers of people in any single job classification.

of past events and incidents the IR personnel were at a disadvantage even in their own field of specialization. Plant managers who outstayed them became the historical experts. And although this gave the plant manager considerable power over IR, he evidently thought that the necessity of spending so much time was too great a price to pay. Thus, again, the division of labor produced inevitable conflicts.

We have concentrated in this study on the relations between units of the management organization rather than on individual roles. Our attention to these units has been devoted primarily to their functions, their goals, their boundaries, their overlap with other units, and their struggles for autonomy.

We have not ignored the concept of role, particularly when we dealt with the resolution of interunit conflict through the "personality" of labor relations men. But an exclusive concentration on the role misses some of the dynamics of organizational identification.

Were we to focus initially on the role of the Industrial Relations representative, we would have a more difficult time in observing the place of this function in the organization. The role can be utilized profitably only when it is placed in the context of its position within an organizational unit. *Struggles for autonomy in Regional Industries took place between units—not between roles.*

The struggles over the inevitable overlap that existed between IR and Operations were resolved by the very reasons for the division of labor which created the overlap—the need to deal with an outside organization and the desire for standardization. These same pressures played a similar, though more indirect, part at successively higher levels of general management. From the plant-manager level on up, the pressures were responsible for the creation of dual lines of authority.

In contrast to relations with lower levels of supervision, IR personnel did "report to" plant management as well as to higher levels of IR. There were strong pressures for IR to identify with the goals and perspectives of the corporate IR unit because opportunities for advancement generally lay within the IR organization. Plant management's control over the mobility of IR personnel was limited to a veto power. Consequently, perspectives of IR personnel were formed, not only by the present pressures on them, but also from their image of the future within the company and corporation. There were mobility opportunities throughout the entire organization because IR was horizontally organized across different companies.

There was a good deal of ambiguity in IR because the two paths of authority overlapped in their interests and responsibilities. The relations and actions of the IR men were relatively undefined. There were no unambiguous alternatives they could bring to bear on any problem or decision. For this reason, they had to encompass within themselves the ability to handle ambiguity. The lines of authority were not and could not be rigidly defined for the incumbents of such a "boundary" role that permits and even requires a degree of entrepreneurship. The characterization of salesman helped them live with this ambiguity because it helped those with whom they dealt to retain a feeling of authority.

No matter how static a picture of an organization we try to get, we cannot ignore the fact that we catch it in the midst of change. Plant-level IR personnel spent most of their time dealing with a unit that had been steadily losing power to yet other units of the company. Without a historical perspective we would miss the definitions brought to power fights by the participants. Being rooted in positions defined by the past, many participants failed to see some of the transitions. For example, a short while back, Woodside was the only plant in the Rock Products Company. The plant manager for all intents and purposes was in total charge of all company activities except marketing. The addition of more plants necessitated a vice-presidential position to assume that role. Such functions as engineering, which had reported to a plant manager, now reported to a vice-president. It was not that the position of plant manager had lost power but that it was really a new position with a different definition. In fact, the vice-presidential position had been filled upon creation by a plant manager. Retention of position names after the position had shifted led to much confusion over expectations about power.

Bendix (1956:336) has already made the related point that the discretionary exercise of authority increases at intermediary levels of an organization because of the lengthening of the chain of command.

140   FRED H. GOLDNER

Additionally, as functions become specialized into separate units, there is a horizontal spread of decision-making.[28] And the continual pursuit of rationalization assures this. While some positions might be losing decision-making power, a greater number of new positions will be assuming this function. Thus the plant manager may not be making decisions about labor relations, but the new unit of Industrial Relations (with more people) will be making these decisions. The increasing scope and complexity of decision-making are both caused by, and help cause, organizational growth.

The effects of vertical and horizontal spread counter the movements toward centralization and standardization. While decision-making in organizations has moved upwards in terms of centralization, it has also moved outwards: a greater number of persons are involved in decision-making and a greater number of decisions are made. The organization encompasses both centralization and decentralization just as it is in an almost constant state of simultaneous bureaucratization and debureaucratization. As one part of an organization is rationalized, other parts or relations among parts become more ambiguous.

REFERENCES

Argyris, Chris.
   1957 "The Individual and Organization: Some Problems of Mutual Adjustment." Administrative Science Quarterly 2(June):1–24.
Baker, Helen, and Robert R. France.
   1954 Centralization and Decentralization in Industrial Relations. Princeton: Princeton University Department of Economics and Sociology, Research Report Series, No. 87.
Barnard, Chester I.
   1956 The Functions of the Executive: Chapter XVII. Cambridge: Harvard University Press.
Bendix, Reinard.
   1956 Work and Authority in Industry. New York: John Wiley and Sons, Inc.
Blau, Peter M.
   1957 "Formal Organization: Dimension of Analysis." American Journal of Sociology 63:58–69.

28. For accounts of the different kinds of relations this creates, see Sayles (1964), and Strauss (1962).

1963 The Dynamics of Bureaucracy. Chicago: University of Chicago Press.

1964 Exchange and Power in Social Life. New York: John Wiley & Sons.

Chandler, Alfred D.

1962 Strategy and Structure. Cambridge, Mass.: M.I.T. Press.

Colean, Miles L., and Robinson Newcomb.

1952 Stabilizing Construction: The Record and the Potential. New York: McGraw-Hill Book Co.

Colvard, Richard M.

1959 "The Foundations and the Colleges: A Study of Organizations, Professions, and Power in the Arkansas Experiment in Teacher Education." Unpublished Ph.D. dissertation, University of California, Berkeley.

Crozier, Michel.

1964 The Bureaucratic Phenomenon. Chicago: University of Chicago Press.

Dalton, Melville.

1950 "Conflicts Between Staff and Line Managerial Officers." American Sociological Review 15(June):342–352.

1959 Men Who Manage. New York: John Wiley & Sons.

Faunce, William A.

1958 "Automation in the Automobile Industry: Some Consequences for In-Plant Social Structure." American Sociological Review 23:4 (August) 401–407.

Goffman, Erving.

1952 "On Cooling the Mark Out: Some Adaptations to Failure." Psychiatry 15:451–463.

Goldner, Fred H.

1961 "Industrial Relations and the Organization of Management." Unpublished Ph.D. dissertation, University of California, Berkeley.

1967 "Role Emergence and the Ethics of Ambiguity." In Gideon Sjoberg (ed.), Ethics, Politics and Social Research. Cambridge, Mass.: Schenkman Publishing Co.

Guetzkow, Harold.

1966 "Relations Among Organizations." In Raymond V. Bowers (ed.), Studies on Behavior in Organizations. Athens: University of Georgia Press.

Harbison, Frederick H., and Robert Dubin.

1947 Patterns of Union Management Relations. Chicago: Science Research Associates.

Kahn, Robert L., *et al.*

1964 Organizational Stress: Studies in Role Conflict and Ambiguity. New York: John Wiley & Sons, Inc.

Lugard, F. D.
1926 The Dual Mandate in British Tropical Africa. London: William Blackwood & Sons.
March, James G., and Herbert A. Simon.
1958 Organizations. New York: John Wiley & Sons.
Martin, Norman H., and Anselm L. Strauss.
1959 "Patterns of Mobility within Industrial Organizations." In David Keith, and William G. Scott (eds.), Readings in Human Relations. New York: McGraw-Hill Book Co.
Mead, George H.
1934 Mind, Self and Society. Chicago: University of Chicago Press.
Merton, Robert K.
1957 Social Theory and Social Structure. Glencoe, Illinois: The Free Press.
Moore, Wilbert E.
1951 Industrial Relations and the Social Order. New York: The Macmillan Co.
Ritti, Richard R., and Fred H. Goldner.
1969 Professional Pluralism in Industrial Organizations. Management Science (December).
Sayles, Leonard.
1964 Managerial Behavior. New York: McGraw-Hill Book Co.
Simon, Herbert A.
1918 Administrative Behavior. New York: The Macmillan Co.
Simon, Herbert A., Harold Guetzkow, George Kozmersky, and Gordon Tyndall.
1954 Centralization vs. Decentralization in Organizing the Controller's Department. New York: Controllership Foundation.
Simpson, Richard L.
1959 "Vertical and Horizontal Communication in Formal Organization." Administrative Science Quarterly 4:2 (September) 188–196.
Starbuck, William H.
1965 "Organizational Growth and Development." In James G. March (ed.), Handbok of Organizations. Chicago: Rand McNally & Co.
Steiber, Jack.
1959 The Steel Industry Wage Structure. Cambridge: Cambridge University Press.
Strauss, George.
1962 "Tactics of Lateral Relationship: The Purchasing Agent." Administrative Science Quarterly 7 (September) 161–186.
Stryker, Perrin.
1955 "The Subtleties of Delegation." Fortune (March):95.

Thompson, James D.
1967 Organizations in Action. New York: McGraw-Hill Book Co.
Walton, Richard E., and Robert B. McKersie.
1965 A Behavioral Theory of Labor Negotiations. New York: McGraw-Hill Book Co.
Weber, Max.
1946 From Max Weber: Essays in Sociology. H. Gerth and C. Wright Mills (trans.). New York: Oxford University Press.
1947 The Theory of Social and Economic Organization. A. M. Henderson and Talcott Parsons (trans.). New York: Oxford University Press.
White, Harrison.
1961 "Management Conflict and Sociometric Structure." American Journal of Sociology 67:2 (September) 185–199.
Whyte, William H. Jr.
1956 The Organization Man. Garden City, N.Y.: Doubleday Anchor Books.

Some Consequences of Differentiation

RICHARD A. PETERSON

Please let serious consideration rather than sweet words be the mark of my appreciation of Professor Goldner's paper.

Over the past few years the concept of structural differentiation has attained a wide currency in theoretical essays. Professor Goldner's paper—rich in ethnographic detail about the division of labor in a complex corporate organization—affords the opportunity to examine a key assumption about the process made by "differentiationists" and also to use this perspective to order and push forward the analysis of "process and power" in organizations. We will begin by looking at a piece of the differentiation argument as it has developed.

Differentiation in Parsons and in Nature

Goldner's line of reasoning can be summarized briefly as follows: Under market conditions of competition, there is a great deal of uncertainty in the environment of each firm. Firms differentiate various managerial activities in order to bring to bear special expertise and thus reduce uncertainty with the environment.

This picture is in accord with the standard differentiation view presented by Talcott Parsons and others, but Goldner goes on to note that in the instance under consideration, the differentiation of Industrial Relations (IR) out of Production, which has devised to regularize relations with the market for labor, created a new set of tensions and uncertainties *within* the organization.

According to the conventional differentiation view, differentiation creates problems of co-ordination which are managed by the administrative units of the system. But, the tensions described by Goldner are not subject to routine co-ordination because they involve overlapping and crosscutting lines of authority and subunit mission. Thus, the tension caused by differentiation cannot be handled within the bureaucratic hierarchy. Hierarchic ordering is itself one of the points in dispute. The differentiation which Goldner described produces manifold restructuring in the organizations with no clear point of structural stability. In his words, "What starts out as a search for ways to reduce problems and uncertainties in organizations leads, then, to the increase of other uncertainties. Rationalization sows the seeds of increasing complexity and hence of pressures for yet new forms of rationalization." Such a condition of continuing instability is quite beyond the ken of Parsons, for in his view structural differentiation takes place *within* functional spheres so that the emergent structure simply replicates the undifferentiated structure at a higher level of division of labor and technical proficiency. This assumption of functional equivalence is stated most explicitly by Neil Smelser, who asserts that after differentiation, "The new social units are structurally distinct from each other, but when taken together are functionally equivalent to the original unit."

I submit that Goldner's example is typical, and the Parsons-Smelser formulation is a limiting case—that is to say, never found in nature and thus of little interest to the research scholar. Rather than the assumption of functional equivalence, it might be more useful to begin with two expectations, one that differentiation makes possible the crystallization of partisan identifications and actions which could not be clearly developed in the more homogeneous pre-differentiation structure; second, that the new *intra*organizational tensions caused by differentiation lead units to seek alliances with elements outside the corporation in order to consolidate their position within the organization.

Reduction of Environmental Uncertainty

It is instructive to view the ways in which differentiation of IR and all others out of general management reduced environmental uncertainty. IR pressed for and managed a policy of company-wide bargaining with labor unions to prevent the unions from using generous agreements gained in one plant to argue for similar agreements elsewhere. IR's "professional association" with IR men in other firms pressed for industry and labor-markets' area-wide consistency in union contracts. In this way, technical structures were able to dampen the competition-based uncertainty in the cost of labor. Thus, wages increasingly can be treated as a fixed cost subject to administrative calculation. In addition, Goldner shows how an industry-wide union helps to constrain corporations to employ IR specialists and to co-operate with rival firms.

It would be instructive to examine, as Goldner does not, the role of the federal government apparatus—particularly the National Labor Relations Board—in mediating this "consolidation" of competing firms. As I see it, the story goes briefly as follows, the federal labor laws enacted in the 1930s and their "pro-labor" administration made possible the development of nationwide militant industrial labor unions. These eliminated competition between workers for the price of their labor. The growing complexity of the labor laws constrained the employment of legal and IR specialists whose "professional" as opposed to "firm" allegiances facilitated the "arrangement" of labor costs between firms and with the increasingly "professional" union leaders. Over the past three decades, the NLRB has provided the good offices in which the arrangements could be worked out.

Now, all this sounds very much like the emerging *New Industrial State* described by John Kenneth Galbraith. In his terms, the techno-structure regularized the competitive mass left by the enterpreneur-dilettantes who had created, but could not manage, the modern corporation. However, Galbraith leaves us with very much the same expectation as Parsons and Smelser. Just as for the latter structural differentiation makes for no internal tension, just so, for Galbraith, competition based on entrepreneurship is replaced by the smooth *administration* of the technostructure. Galbraith, like Veblen before him, sees the technostructure as an undifferentiated stratum and thus he is not able to see the endemic conflict of interests between elements of the technostructure. Such *internal* conflict is, of course, the *meat* of Goldner's paper.

Escalation of Uncertainty in the Organization

Goldner suggests that the conflict between elements of management engendered by the differentiation of IR out of general managements may be temporary. In any given firm this may be the case, but I think he has presented enough data to show that internal conflict will be endemic in the firm under study as in most other modern corporations.

Let us step back, for a moment, from the study at hand for a somewhat more general consideration. As long as a firm has one plant or major facility and is organized more or less according to the classic bureaucratic model, men will define their careers in terms of the firm. As multiple production units are added and as specialized management units are differentiated, men are more likely to orient their action to the best interest of these units at the expense, in many instances, of other units.

Goldner notes, for example, that IR men have come to see their careers within IR and thus to orient to the expectations of company-wide IR officials rather than to the expectations of their immediate production bosses. This tendency is facilitated by the rapid rotation of IR personnel so they do not develop local plant allegiances to production superiors but depend for their advancement on the evaluation of IR executives.

In addition, to the degree that special management occupations take on the self-conscious trappings of "professionalization," the unit gains outside organization leverage vis-à-vis management and individual practitioners gain the protection of being able to merchandise their occupational skill outside the firm.

Professor Goldner discusses the internal conflict between IR and Production, Production and Maintenance, as well as between Operations and Process Engineers. These conflicts derive from differing definitions of organizational priorities, differing parochial loyalties, and from crosscutting definitions of unit mission. It is logically possible that one contending party might eliminate or absorb the other. This seems unlikely as each party seeks to have its own way in areas relevant to its interest but does not seek to assume sole responsibility. This point is best illustrated in the conflict between IR and Production. IR has taken over much of the management of wage-workers. It has done this in the guise of "selling" its point of view to Production rather than by assuming direct authority. Thus, it avoids the responsibility for administrative decisions while obtaining operational control. Even in an extreme case of power imbalance greater than anything Goldner has found, the more powerful contending segment may maintain the guise of shared authority in order to avoid accountability. Thus, internal conflicts engendered by structural indifferentiation are endemic.

The "Staging" of Conflict with the Environment

Professor Goldner quite properly points to the paradox inherent in IR's quest for organizational power. Its contribution to the firm consists of regularizing and systematizing the relationships with worker and union. To do this takes power out of the hands of Production. Yet, to the degree IR is successful in establishing routine procedures—to that extent its experts are no longer needed. Thus, in theory, the more successful IR is, the more it loses influence.

Goldner points to several specific tactics IR uses to maintain power; for example, it propagates the lawyers' mystique that the labor contract does not mean what it says—that it gains meaning only in terms of the history of arrangements that can be systematically interpreted only by experts in the field, that is, IR men. IR even goes to the extreme of hiding the contract from other management personnel.

These sorts of tactics are redolent of information-hoarding practices of widely different sorts of professionals in organizations; but there is another sort of defense against routinization which Goldner only hints at. He suggests that IR's source of power in specific plant-level issues is "the use of the union as an outside threat. . . . IR [uses] the same source of power, at all organizational levels, to justify the structure of the entire IR organization."

As long as there is real conflict with the union, IR labor relations experts are essential to the life of the corporation. As differences are mediated and accommodated, IR is less vital. It seems quite plausible to me that IR should consort with the union to "stage" conflict. This would have attractions for union leaders as well. It gives them the opportunity to show rank-and-file members that the union leadership is worth the dues being paid.

At the conference Goldner stated that the conflict is indeed real and not staged. Certainly, if IR were not able to maintain this definition they would be accused of conspiracy by other management elements. The conflict may be viewed as real by all the participants, but those familiar with the scenario of union-management negotiations over the past 15 years may be led to ask whether much conflict serves other ends than those usually focal to labor-management relations researchers. To my knowledge, this possibility has not been explored systematically. The complexity of the links between elements of management and various union interests is suggested by Chandler's insightful study *Management Rights and Union Interests*. When developed, such a line of study could tell us much about the patterning of affiliations which cross normatively defined allegiances such as the union and the corporation. Such a study will help lay to rest the assumption of "functional equivalence" of units in the differentiation process and suggest clues as to the general patterns of cleavage and alliance across organizational boundaries.

4

Decentralization in Bureaucracies

PETER M. BLAU

To speak of decentralization in bureaucracies may appear to be a contradiction in terms. For bureaucracies are often defined as organizations in which authority is centralized in the hands of top executives by means of a hierarchical structure. Bureaucratization in labor unions, for example, refers to the development of centralized control by the leadership, which robs the union rank and file of most of its influence over policies and decisions. Thus, the thesis underlying Michels' (1949) "iron law of oligarchy" is that administrative and political exigencies lead to bureaucratization in the form of centralization of authority even in organizations whose very purpose it is to promote equality, such as socialist parties and unions. Weber (1946:197), too, emphasizes that a basic feature of bureaucracies is a hierarchy of authority, that is, "a firmly ordered system of super- and subordination in which there is a supervision of the lower offices by the higher ones."

This research has been supported by grants GS-553 and 1528 from the National Science Foundation, which are gratefully acknowledged. I am also indebted to Sheila R. Klatzky and Richard A. Schoenherr, who have worked with me on this research, and to the generous co-operation extended to me by officials in the federal Bureau of Employment Security as well as in the state agencies. A full report on the study of these agencies is in preparation.

If centralization of authority is considered to be the defining criterion of bureaucracy, it makes, of course, no sense to speak of decentralized bureaucracies. But the centralization of authority in organizations may be conceptualized as a variable—as a matter of degree—in which case the question arises which conditions in organizations are associated with more centralized or more decentralized authority structures.

FORMALIZATION AND STANDARDIZATION

Bureaucratization entails not only centralization of authority and responsibility but also other features of organizations, notably formalization of procedures and standardization of practices. When we accuse an organization of being overbureaucratic, we are as likely to think of red tape, which implies excessive formalization, as of buck-passing, which implies excessive centralization. The performance of the various individuals in complex organizations tends to be standardized to foster uniformity of operations, impartiality of decisions, and co-ordination of diverse tasks. This standardization is typically achieved through the formalization of procedures by means of an explicit, often elaborate, body of rules and regulations. "The reduction of modern office management to rules is deeply embedded in its very nature." "Bureaucratization . . . primarily means a discharge of business according to *calculable rules* and 'without regard for persons (Weber, 1949:198, 215, italics in original).' "

Since Weber notes that two basic characteristics of the typical bureaucracy are operations governed by explicit rules and a centralized hierarchy of authority, he seems to imply that a high degree of formalization of procedures and a high degree of centralization of authority will occur together. However, he (1947:330) also indicates that the impersonal rules restrict the arbitrary exercise of authority by the superior, because the superior is no less bound to adhere to the formally established norms than his subordinates are. These considerations imply that formalization restricts the scope and discretion of centralized authority, which contradicts the inference drawn from Weber's ideal type that formalization and highly centralized authority go together. Hence, no unequivocal hypothesis can be derived from Weber's analysis concerning the relationship between formalization and centralization.

Merton's (1968:255) discussion of the unintended consequences of formalization and standardization has some bearing on this relationship. Strong pressures to conform with formalized procedures in bureaucracies, designed to assure reliable and disciplined performance engender rigidities that impede effective performance in varying and changing situations. "Adherence to the rules, originally conceived as a means, becomes transformed into an end-in-itself; there occurs the familiar process of *displacement of goals* whereby . . . conformance with regulations, whatever the situation, is seen not as a measure designed for specific purposes but becomes an immediate value in the life-organization of the bureaucrat. This emphasis, resulting from the displacement of the original goals, develops into rigidities and an inability to adjust readily." Although Merton makes no explicit reference to centralized authority, his analysis has implications for it. Centralized authority, which means that all subordinates must comply with the directives of top management, implies a rigid decision-making structure, whereas decentralization of responsibilities, which gives officials on lower levels more discretion, implies greater flexibility in decision-making. If strict adherence to formal standards gives rise to rigidity in general, it should also be reflected in a more centralized structure of authority and responsibility.

Here again, however, an alternative line of reasoning leads to the opposite conclusion. Formalized procedures and centralized authority may not be two expressions of the same underlying emphasis on strict discipline, but they may rather be two *alternative* mechanisms for limiting the arbitrary exercise of discretion. The more effectively formal rules and standard operating procedures guide decisions and actions, the less need there is for directives from a central authority to effect such guidance. Accordingly, formalization and standardization would promote decentralization, not centralization, as was inferred from Merton's discussion. The assumption that rigidity and ritualistic overconformity are rooted in excessive assimilation of social norms can also be questioned on other grounds. Psychoanalytic theory (see, e.g., Fromm, 1941) indicates that rigid behavior and compulsive conformity tend to be the result of anxiety and insecurity, and Durkheim's (1951: 241–276) theory suggests that anomie, which is the opposite of widely assimilated social norms, gives rise to anxieties and insecurities. Thus, insufficient rather than excessive identification with social norms would produce rigidity. To be sure, the *psychological* process of anxiety-reduction is undoubtedly not directly relevant for understanding the *social* processes that lead to the development of a rigid authority structure rather than decentralized responsibilities in formal organizations. However, to assume that the social processes set in motion by the thorough acceptance of formalized procedures in organizations have the opposite effect of intensifying rigidity seems questionable.

This brief review of theoretical discussions indicates that they do not imply an unequivocal hypothesis about the influence of formalization and standardization on the centralization of authority in formal organizations. The objective of this paper is to ascertain what conditions in government bureaus affect the decentralization of authority and the delegation of responsibilities by top management, with special emphasis on the influences exerted by the formalization of procedures and strict adherence to explicit standards.

RESEARCH METHOD

To investigate what conditions in formal organizations govern their authority structure requires comparable data on a fairly large number of organizations. A case study could ascertain what characteristics of individual managers or their subordinates induce them to delegate responsibilities, but this is not the question posed here. To answer the question of how the degree of centralization of authority in the hands of top management is influenced by such organizational conditions as size or the extent of formalized procedures, it is necessary to compare a number of organizations differing in size, formalization, and other conditions. Moreover, the number of cases must be sufficiently large to permit multivariate analysis in order to determine which ones of several antecedents of decentralization exert a direct influence on it, or an indirect influence mediated by a third factor, or no influence even though there is a (spurious) zero-order correlation.

A sample of organizations of various types may be used, or the study may encompass all organizations of a single type. The disadvantage of using only organizations of one type is that the generalizations deduced from the findings may not apply to different types. The disadvantage of using organizations of various types is that it is difficult to devise measures comparable across types. The mechanization of a manufacturing concern and a university cannot readily be compared; personnel decisions in a business firm have significance different from those in a government agency operating under civil service; and even size has ambiguous meaning, since 500 employees, for instance, indicate a large school, but a small corporation, and a tiny army. The procedure adopted in the present research is to study all government agencies of a single type.

The data reported pertain to 53 employment security agencies, those in all 50 states and the District of Columbia, Puerto Rico, and the Virgin Islands. (The only agency omitted is the very small one in Guam). The three functions of every employment security (ES) agency are to pay unemployment insurance benefits to those eligible for them, to collect taxes from employers for this purpose, and to provide public employment service to all job applicants and employers who request it. Although ES agencies operate under federal laws with which they must comply and a federal bureau co-ordinates activities and allocates administrative funds, every state agency is autonomous and not part of the federal system. These agencies are not, strictly speaking, independent, just as the communities in a nation are not, but the large variations among them in virtually all respects justify treating them as independent cases in the statistical analysis. The agencies vary in size from 50 to more than 9000, with a mean of 1195 and a very skewed distribution (3.3).

The data-collection was carried out by three research assistants who visited all agencies, spending between one to two days in each interviewing several senior managers, asking additional managers to complete a brief questionnaire, and obtaining information from records. This information was complemented by some available in published sources. Most of the data are objective, such as the distribution of the personnel along a number of different dimensions (by job title, by functional division, by hierarchical level, etc.), the extent of the computer installation, if any, or the form used for the supervisory rating of the performance of subordinates. Some information is based on subjective estimates. For example, the measures of decentralization discussed below are based on answers to questions as to who makes a variety of specified decisions, for instance, hiring a supervisor at the headquarters.

Regression analysis is employed to determine which attributes of these agencies are related to the measures of decentralization. This procedure has the advantage of making it possible to examine the simultaneous influence of various factors on a dependent variable even with only 53 cases, which would not be possible with contingency tables. (Those variables that are not continuous are coded in ranked categories. Eight of the twelve variables used are continuous.) The assumption made is that the decentralization measures are the dependent variables and all other conditions examined are the independent variables that influence them. Since the independent variables comprise such relatively stable factors as personnel regulations, size,[1] and various aspects of administrative structure, it seems plausible to assume that they influence the delegation of responsibilities rather than that they are influenced by it. Inasmuch as the distributions of many variables are far from normal, the requirements of statistical inference are not met. The criterion used for deciding whether or not a certain association exists is, therefore, not that it meets a certain level of significance, but that the regression co-efficient in standard form (b*), indicating the slope of the regression line under controls, is at least 1½ times its standard error, which corresponds to a correlation of about 21.[2]

To measure decentralization we asked several senior managers on which level decisions on numerous different matters are made. Since senior managers at the state headquarters could not be expected to provide reliable information about decision-making on the lowest levels in an average of forty local offices throughout the state, we made no

1. Although size changes from season to season and year to year, these fluctuations have little effect on the basic variations among agencies, since the size of an agency is largely determined by the size of its potential and actual clientele. The correlation of agency size (number of employees) with the state's population is .95; its correlation with number of job applicants is .96; and its correlation with number of unemployment benefit recipients is .98.

2. This is admittedly a weak criterion for rejecting the null hypothesis. But all the associations discussed persist under controls (with the exception of one reversal under controls, which reveals a considerably larger standardized re-gression coefficient), and the conclusions primarily emphasized are based on two independent associations at least one of which is indicated by a standardized regression coefficient more than twice the size of its standard error.

attempt to elicit information about decentralization of decisions to the lowest levels in the organization. Decentralization, then, refers to delegation of responsibilities from top management (including both the director and his deputy) either to middle managers at the state headquarters or to managers of local offices.

Decentralization in these government agencies does not appear to be a unidimensional factor. Numerous correlations between different measures of delegation of responsibilities were low, and some were negative. Whereas these results may be partly due to the lack of reliability of some of the measures, which are based on subjective estimates rather than direct observation, it seems unlikely that they are entirely due to that. Decentralization may indeed consist of several unrelated components. Thus, delegation of responsibilities to the managers of local offices is apparently not related to delegation of responsibilities within the state headquarters. A score was constructed based on five items of delegation to local managers. A factor analysis of seven items pertaining to delegation of responsibilities within the headquarters was performed, yielding four orthogonal factors. Three items representing three of these factors, as indicated by their high factor-loadings, were selected.[3] These are (1) delegation of hiring responsibilities to division heads or lower officials at the headquarters; (2) delegation of some responsibilities for preparing the budget to the same managers at the headquarters; and (3) the influence division heads exercise over major changes in their own divisions, that is, the proportion of division heads who themselves state that they influence major changes.

Thus, measures are available of four nearly orthogonal components of decentralization, none of which has as high a correlation as .17 with any other. Three of them refer to decentralization within the agency headquarters, and one to delegation of decisions to local branches. The first three differ not only in terms of subject matter but also on the basis

3. The fourth orthogonal dimension in the factor analysis seems to refer to decisions of subordinate managers that are indicative of the fact that minor duties have been relegated to them rather than that significant responsibilities have been delegated to them, as indicated by the inverse correlation between the education of middle managers and the "delegation" of these decisions to them. Assigning responsibilities to a subordinate manager entails investing authority in him or requiring him to perform a chore, and one of the four orthogonal dimensions yielded by the factor analysis apparently refers to the latter.

of whether official authority is delegated or actual influence is decentralized. In short, the four components of decentralization are delegation of official personnel authority, delegation of budget responsibilities, decentralization of (reported) actual influence to senior middle managers at the headquarters, and delegation of responsibilities to local office managers.

Indications of two aspects of personnel procedures and one aspect of rating procedures were obtained. Standardization refers to the adherence to explicit criteria in making decisions, whereas formalization refers to the elaboration of explicit criteria for making decisions, usually in the form of written regulations. In respect to personnel procedures, these two factors can be empirically distinguished. The measure of standardization of personnel procedures is the proportion of new appointments based on competitive merit examinations. Although employment security agencies operate under civil service systems, an average of 40 percent of the new appointments are classified as temporary and not based on merit standards of civil service, with wide variations among the 53 agencies, as indicated by the standard deviation of 19 percent. The measure of formalization of personnel procedures is the number of words in the official civil service regulations (estimated by counting the words in a sample of pages and multiplying by the number of pages). Hence, formalization means the elaboration of written personnel regulations. Finally, the index of standardization of the rating procedure is based on whether the form supplied to supervisors for the periodic evaluation of the performance of every subordinate asks them to do so in a descriptive statement or by checking a list of items resulting in a numerical score, with two intermediate categories.

Five other conditions could be identified that influence decentralization. (The reader may want to guess what influence each of them exerts.) The size of the agency is operationally defined by the number of its employees at the time of the survey. Automation is indicated by whether the agency has a computer and the size of its computer installation. The criterion for specifying the number of hierarchical levels at the headquarters is that subordinates report to a superior in charge of them, not salary grades or skill classification. The index of the qualifications of interviewers, who compose the basic service personnel of an ES agency, is the percent of college graduates among recently appointed interviewers. And the proportionate size of the administrative and technical staff, excluding line management, is measured by the percent of the total manhours devoted to staff functions.

RIGIDITY AND FLEXIBILITY

Let us start by examining those organizational conditions that affect decentralization generally, not only specific aspects of it, as indicated by the finding that a condition reveals parallel persisting associations with more than one of the relatively orthogonal measures of decentralization in ES agencies. Three such factors were discovered, and two of the three pertain to the bureaucratization of procedures, specifically, of personnel procedures. First, the standardization of employment practice manifest in the proportion of appointments conforming to merit standards of civil service is associated with decentralization of influence to division heads and delegation of responsibilities to managers of local offices. Second, the formalization of personnel procedures indicated by the extent of written regulations is associated with budget delegation at the agency headquarters and delegation of responsibilities to local managers. Third, the automation of operations is associated with delegation of both authority over personnel and responsibility for the budget to middle managers within the headquarters. (See Tables 1–4; whereas every table represents one dependent variable [decentralization measure], the present discussion is organized by independent variable, requiring reference to two tables in each case.) A fourth variable, agency

TABLE 1
Effects on Delegation of Budget Responsibilities at the Headquarters

Independent Variable	Standardized Regression Coefficient (b*)	Standard Error	Zero-order Correlation
Automation*	0.29	0.14	0.31
Formalization of Personnel Regulations	0.33	0.16	0.34
Size	—0.04	0.16	0.24

Multiple Correlation: 0.44
*Dummy variable: whether or not a computer is used.

TABLE 2
Effects on Delegation of Personnel Authority at the Headquarters

Independent Variable	Standardized Regression Coefficient (b*)	Standard Error	Zero-order Correlation
Automation*	0.48	0.22	0.34
Size	—0.45	0.24	0.22
Levels	0.29	0.16	0.36
Staff Ratio	—0.23	0.14	—0.28
Qualifications of Interviewers	0.20	0.13	0.16

Multiple Correlation: 0.51
*Extent of computer installation, coded in 13 categories.

TABLE 3
Effects on Decentralization of Influence at the Headquarters

Independent Variable	Standardized Regression Coefficient (b*)	Standard Error	Zero-order Correlation
Size	0.30	0.14	0.33
Standardization of Appointments	0.19	0.13	0.18
Salary of Interviewers	0.13	0.14	0.24

Multiple Correlation: 0.41

TABLE 4
Effects on Delegation to Local Office Managers

Independent Variable	Standardized Regression Coefficient (b*)	Standard Error	Zero-order Correlation
Standardization of Appointments	0.32	0.13	0.33
Standardization of Ratings	0.23	0.13	0.28
Formalization of Personnel Regulations	0.21	0.13	0.19

Multiple Correlation: 0.46

size, also is associated with more than one decentralization measure, but since it has contradictory implications for decentralization, its influences will be discussed separately later.

Strict adherence to civil service standards in making appointments as well as the elaboration of formalized personnel regulations would seem to epitomize the bureaucratization of procedures which, according to Merton, engenders rigidities. Yet both of these factors promote decentralization, which implies a less rigid structure of decision-making. The regression analyses show that either aspect of bureaucratization of personnel procedures—though the two are unrelated in our data ($r = -.09$)—is positively associated with two independent measures of decentralization. (For standardization, see Tables 3 and 4; for formalization, Tables 1 and 4.) The hypothesis derived from Merton's analysis that the standardization and the formalization of procedures, inasmuch as they increase rigidity, will find expression in a more rigid authority structure with less decentralized decision-making is clearly negated in these government agencies. On the contrary, both of these aspects of bureaucratized personnel practice tend to promote decentralization and thus a more flexible structure of decision-making.

Rigidity in some respects may breed flexibility in others. Not all aspects of bureaucratization are concomitant. The bureaucratic elaboration of formalized personnel procedures and rigid conformity with these personnel standards do not necessarily occur together, and neither aspect of bureaucratization of procedures gives rise to a more rigid authority structure, at least not in employment security agencies. Indeed, both strict conformity with civil service standards and the elaboration of these formalized standards have the opposite effect of fostering decentralization, which permits greater flexibility. But why do more rigid procedures make the structure of decision-making more flexible.

Strict compliance with civil service standards restricts, of course, the exercise of discretion in making appointments. Some officials mentioned, for example, that the need to conform to civil service regulations makes it impossible to hire as many Negroes or members of other underprivileged groups as would be desirable in accordance with recent presidential directives, because many members of these groups do not meet civil service requirements. This is a clear illustration of rigid procedures that prevent desired adjustments. But the best solution for this problem may be, not arbitrary disregard of merit standards, but the adoption of additional regulations that specify under which conditions merit criteria are to be relaxed. In any case, effective pressures to conform to a given bureaucratic procedure preclude discretion and thus increase rigidity in this specific respect by definition. The interesting question is how such conformity affects discretion in *other* respects.

The very fact that widely enforced merit standards restrict discretion in making appointments assures that all employees have appropriate minimum qualifications. If government agencies were unhampered by civil service requirements in making appointments, the selection process would undoubtedly be improved in some cases, but inferior appointments would occur in others, because political considerations are given weight or simply because the appointing official is not very skilled in personnel matters. The management of a large organization has little control over the qualifications of its personnel, since many were employed under a previous management and many others are in effect hired by junior managers, often distributed in widely dispersed branches. The best guarantee management has that employees meet at least minimum qualifications, therefore, is provided by consistently applied merit standards of employment. Management's responsibility for operations makes it reluctant to delegate decisions if doing so involves much risk. The greater reliability of operations resulting from strict adherence to merit standards in making appointments reduces the risks entailed in decentralization of decision-making and consequently encourages such decentralization.

The interpretation advanced—that strict conformity with merit standards of appointment promotes decentralization because it improves the reliability of performance—implies that other conditions that make performance more reliable also encourage decentralization. The better qualified the employees, the greater reliance management can place in their performance of duties. In fact, superior qualifications do promote decentralization, although only one aspect of it, namely, delegation of personnel authority (Table 2). Another condition that makes operations more reliable is their automation through the installation of computers. Indeed, automation also fosters decentralization, as the interpretation implies.

Students of industrial concerns (see e.g., Whisler and Leavitt, 1948:

41–48) have concluded that automation leads to centralization of authority in the hands of top management, but in these government agencies the use of computers furthers decentralization of decision-making, being positively associated with delegation of both personnel and budget matters (Tables 1 and 2). Automation standardizes operations, not only directly by mechanizing some tasks, but also indirectly by imposing restraints on other tasks performed by employees, inasmuch as their performances must conform to the computer setup. The design of the automated equipment serves as an impersonal mechanism of control, which makes operations partly self-regulating and less dependent on supervisory intervention. The greater reliability of automated operations reduces the risks of delegating decisions, and management's ability to control operations through determining the computer setup and programs diminishes its need to exercise centralized control through issuing directives. These implications of automation encourage delegation of responsibilities.

The rigidity implicit in standardization, whether effected by imposed standards or by mechanization, enhances the flexibility of the decision-making structure in these organizations. Unambiguous standards give rise to an authority structure that permits less rigid task performance in organizations, just as they give rise to personality traits that permit less rigid behavior on the part of individuals. Standards effect flexibility in the case of organizations, however, not through psychological processes, as they do in the case of individuals by relieving anxieties, but through *social* processes. The interpretation does not assume that extensive reliance on merit criteria or automation makes top executives feel less anxious and for this reason less rigid and more inclined to delegate decisions. Instead, it assumes that standardization, by making performance more reliable, provides objective grounds for delegating decisions, because it reduces the risks entailed by possibly poor managerial decisions, and these lesser risks furnish a rational basis for top management's delegation of decisions to subordinate managers. The reduction of objective risks resulting from reliable operations rather than the reduction of subjective anxiety is the mechanism through which standardization promotes decentralization in organizations. Structural conditions influence delegation by changing the objective situation in which top executives find themselves, not merely their subjective experience of this situation.

A question not yet answered is why the elaboration of formalized personnel procedures into an extensive body of written regulations also furthers decentralization. Surely the answer cannot be that many rules produce more standardization than few do. It is far more plausible that one or a few personnel regulations standardize personnel practice to a higher degree than do many different regulations. As a matter of fact, this may be the very reason why the elaboration of formalized personnel procedures encourages decentralization. The requirement to conform to a simple set of personnel regulations has the disadvantage that these standards become a strait jacket into which must be forced all kinds of different cases in a large variety of situations. The same personnel regulations are often not appropriate for the recruitment of highly skilled professionals and that of unskilled clerks; for personnel selection in metropolitan centers and that in rural places or small towns; for finding the most qualified personnel in periods of labor surplus and in periods of labor shortage; for taking into account the government's responsibility to underprivileged groups and its needs for qualified employees. One way to deal with the many exceptional cases not adequately covered by a simple set of rules is to permit officials to depart from these rules at their own discretion, but doing so undermines the important advantages that following personnel standards provides to the organization. An alternative method for coping with a large variety of cases and situations is to devise appropriate personnel standards for each type, supplemented by additional rules specifying under what conditions which standards are to be applied. This elaboration of the system of personnel regulations preserves the advantage resulting from compliance with merit standards of appointments and simultaneously avoids the disadvantages for personnel-selection resulting from either rigid application of inappropriate standards or idiosyncratic departures from standards.

In sum, an extensive body of civil service regulations as well as strict compliance with these regulations fosters decentralization, because an elaborate system of merit standards that takes variations in conditions into account is more efficient than a few standards as an instrument for recruiting qualified personnel and thus improving the reliability of operations in the organization. But civil service is a distinctive system, not found in private organizations. The interpretation suggested is couched in general terms and implies that the formalization and standardization of procedures other than those pertinent to personnel matters would also lead to decentralization, and that this would be the case in other organizations as well as government bureaus. A bit of supportive evidence for this generalization is provided by a study of Pugh and his colleagues (1968:65–105). The sample consists of 46 British organizations in the Birmingham area, the large majority of which are private firms of various kinds. Their operational measures of standardization, formalization, and centralization are based on complex scales and are quite different from those used here, though the underlying concepts are similar, except that most of the items in the standardization and the formalization scale refer to operating rather than personnel procedures. (They report no measure of automation.) Despite these differences, this study also found that standardization reduces centralization ($r = -.27$), and so does formalization (-.27).[4] The paradoxical proposition that more rigid procedures give rise to less rigid authority structures seems to apply not only to American government agencies but also to other organizations.

ADDITIONAL INFLUENCES ON DECENTRALIZATION

We turn now to the analysis of the conditions that influence each of the four different aspects of decentralization, with primary emphasis on those influences not already examined. There is little more to say about delegation of budget responsibilities, since the two factors that affect it—automation and extent of personnel regulations—have been discussed above (Table 1). The zero-order correlation between size and budget-delegation disappears under controls, largely owing to the influence of extensive personnel regulations. Large employment security agencies tend to be part of state governments with extensive civil service regulations, and only for this reason do they exhibit a greater tendency for decentralized budget-decisions than small agencies.

4. The zero-order correlation coefficients are in the table on p. 83 (Pugh, *et al.*, 1968).

Delegation of personnel authority within the agency headquarters is influenced by five conditions, which account for more than a quarter of the variance in it (Table 2). The strongest influence is exerted by automation, which has been previously discussed, as has the influence of the educational qualifications of interviewers. The pronounced influence of automation on personnel-delegation ($b^* = .48$) is partly concealed in the zero-order correlation (.34) and appears only when size is controlled. Both automation and superior qualifications of the personnel make operations more reliable and thus encourage top executives to delegate decisions to their subordinates.

A large number of levels in the hierarchy of authority also increases the likelihood that personnel responsibilities are delegated by top executives to middle managers. The further removed a manager is from the lowest levels of operating employees and first-line supervisors, the more difficult it undoubtedly is for him to acquire sufficient knowledge about these positions to make intelligent personnel decisions on how to fill them. A multilevel hierarchy that removes the top executive far from the lowest levels of employees, therefore, creates pressures on him to delegate personnel responsibilities to middle managers in closer contact with the requirements of the positions to be filled. (Pugh and his colleagues [1968] also found many levels to be inversely correlated with centralization, the zero-order correlation being -.28.)

The larger the proportionate size of the administrative and technical staff in the agency, the less inclined is top management to delegate personnel responsibilities to middle managers. This finding suggests that a large staff component helps the top executive to exercise managerial control and concentrate authority in his own hands without delegating formal responsibilities. It should be noted that cases in which the personnel director, a staff officer, makes personnel decisions are coded as delegated personnel responsibilities. Hence, the finding does not merely indicate that the larger the staff is, the more likely are personnel decisions to be delegated to staff than to line officials; but it indicates that these decisions are less likely to be delegated to either if the staff is large. A relatively small staff to assist top management in discharging its responsibilities puts pressure on management to lighten its administrative burdens by delegating some official authority, such as that over personnel decisions, to subordinate managers.

Large size as such discourages the delegation of personnel responsibilities, but it gives rise to other conditions in these agencies that encourage personnel-delegation, and its consequent positive indirect effect on personnel-delegation outweighs its negative direct effect. This conclusion is based on a dissection of the data in Table 2. The partial regression coefficient in standard form indicates the direct effect of size on personnel-delegation, which is strongly negative (-.45). The zero-order correlation is positive (.22), however, which shows that size exerts even stronger positive indirect effects on personnel-delegation, provided we assume that the other variables in the regression problem are intervening variables rather than antecedents of size, which seems to be the most plausible assumption. (For example, it is less plausible to assume that automation increases the size of agencies than that large agencies tend to install big computers, and similar considerations apply to the other variables.) To ascertain how much of the indirect influence of size on personnel-delegation is mediated by automation, for instance, the zero-order correlation between size and automation (.82) is multiplied by the partial b* in standard form of personnel-delegation on automation shown in the table (.48), yielding a value of .39. Applying the same procedure to the three other intervening variables yields values of .17 for multiple levels, .10 for staff component, and .00 for qualifications of interviewers. The sum of these values must equal, except for rounding errors, the difference between the zero-order correlation and the partial b* in standard form of personnel-delegation on size (.39 + .17 + .10 + .00 = .66; 22- -.45 = .67). Thus, the indirect positive influence of size on personnel-delegation is primarily mediated by automation and to a lesser extent by multiple levels and the staff component.

A large scope of operations increases the significance of managerial decisions and consequently the risks involved in making erroneous decisions. Other things being equal, therefore, large size discourages delegation of responsibilities. But other things are not equal. Large size leads to the introduction of computers and the expansion of automated facilities to cope with the many routine tasks, and automation encourages delegation of responsibilities. Moreover, large size also gives rise to vertical differentiation into multilevel hierarchies and reduces the proportionate size of the administrative staff. These two conditions further increase the indirect positive effect of size on personnel-delegation. These indirect positive influences of large size outweigh its direct negative effect. Feedback processes may well be operative here. Large size not only enhances the implications of managerial decisions and the risks they entail, inclining management to refrain from delegating decisions, but it also increases the volume of management's responsibilities, building up pressures to relieve some of these burdens, by delegating responsibilities or otherwise. The prevailing tendency in large agencies to install extensive automated facilities may be a response to this problem of how to lessen top management's excessive responsibilities, for automation obviates the need for some managerial decisions and facilitates the delegation of others.

In short, large size creates conflicting pressures on top management's decision-making: it heightens the import of its decisions, which discourages delegation, and simultaneously expands the volume of its decisions, which exerts constraints to decentralize. The impact of these conflicting forces can be clarified by considering the decentralization of actual influence as well as the delegation of official authority. The proportion of division heads who report they can institute major reorganizations in their own divisions themselves is primarily affected by the large size of the agency. (It is also somewhat influenced by the strict application of civil service standards, whereas its zero-order correlation with salaries tends to disappear under controls; see Table 3.) The zero-order correlation is .33, and the standardized regression coefficient under controls remains .30. The cross-pressures on top executives in large organizations have the result, first, that they are disinclined to delegate official authority over personnel (the direct influence of size on personnel-delegation is negative); second, that influence over decisions in other areas becomes decentralized despite this reluctance formally to delegate responsibilities (the influence of size on decentralization of influence is positive); and, third, that mechanisms, such as automation, tend to be adopted in large organizations that lessen the disadvantages of delegation and thereby promote the explicit delegation of responsibilities (the indirect influence of size on personnel-delegation, largely mediated by automation, is positive). The pressures of a large bulk of managerial responsibilities lead to the decentralization of some decisions, even without their being formally delegated, and to the development of conditions that facilitate the formal delegation of others.

The final measure of decentralization refers to the official delegation of responsibilities to the managers of local offices dispersed throughout the state, whereas the three other measures referred to decentralization within the agency headquarters. The three factors identified that influence this aspect of delegation all pertain to the bureaucratization of procedures (Table 4). In addition to the standardization of personnel practice and the elaboration of formal personnel regulations, the standardization of rating procedures fosters delegation of responsibilities to local managers. The more objective the criteria are in terms of which supervisors are required to evaluate the performance of their subordinates, the greater is the number of responsibilities delegated to local offices. It appears that the delegation of decision-making to lower managers in physically dispersed branches of the organization depends particularly on the standardization and formalization of procedures. To the extent to which formalized standards restrict the scope of discretion and assure the reliable performance of duties, decentralized decisions become less precarious for effective management and coordination, which diminishes the reluctance to delegate responsibilities way down the line to local managers far removed in space as well as social distance from the top executives at the headquarters. Inasmuch as delegating decisions to many local managers in geographically dispersed branches implies more flexibility than delegating them within the headquarters, the finding that local delegation is most strongly associated with bureaucratization of procedures strengthens confidence in the conclusion that rigid procedures generate a more flexible authority structure.

Risks of and Constraints on Decentralization

In conclusion, two principles of decentralization in organizations under which the various findings can be subsumed will be explicated. Doing so also provides an opportunity for reviewing the results of the analysis presented.

Top management in large organizations is charged with the responsibility for effective operations. The greater the risk of failure entailed by making decisions, the more reluctant will management be, given its responsibilities, to delegate decisions. To be sure, some top executives may be power-hungry, compulsive, or ignorant, and such personality traits undoubtedly affect the reluctance to delegate responsibilities to subordinates, as does the fact that some directors of government agencies are politically ambitious and probably not immune to political pressures. But the present study has no information on these personality characteristics, and their influence on decentralization could therefore not be ascertained. The assumption is that within the limits imposed by personality differences executives seek to discharge their responsibities by finding rational solutions to administrative problems, which makes the delegation of decision-making by them subject to the influences of the organizational conditions here under consideration. One rational criterion is to refrain from delegating risky decisions. All judgments that cannot be made by a simple formula involve some risk, however. Hence, top executives should prefer not to delegate any strictly managerial decisions—only questions that require technical expertness—were there not strong constraints on them to delegate some.

Certain organizational conditions create structural constraints that constitute pressures to decentralize responsibilities. These pressures will usually be resisted, although not always successfully, unless other organizational conditions facilitate decentralization by reducing the risks it involves. The nature of the decision affects both of these factors. Some managerial decisions require technical knowledge, since managerial and technical considerations cannot always be clearly separated, which creates pressure to delegate these decisions to professional experts. An illustration is the preparation of the budget for operating automated facilities, which necessitates expert knowledge of computers, and this may be one of the reasons why automation is associated with budget-delegation in these agencies (Table 1). Very simple decisions, on the other hand, entail little risk and thus facilitate delegation. Aside from the nature of the decision and the personal attributes of top executives, however, conditions in the organization also influence decentralization, some by creating pressures to decentralize, and others by reducing the risk of decentralization.

The large size of an organization expands the volume of managerial decisions beyond the capacity of the top executive and his deputy, and it thus exerts structural constraints that promote decentralization. A large number of clients to be served by an agency, a large number of employees to serve them, and a large number of branches in different locations—each of which is correlated with either of the others more than .90—increase the responsibilities of top management beyond endurance, generating pressures that lead decision-making to spill over downward. A large staff can aid top management in withstanding these pressures and maintaining authority concentrated in its own hands. But the larger an agency, the smaller is the proportionate size of its staff,[5] which implies that larger organizations do not require as large a staff ratio as small ones and that it would be uneconomical for a large organization to devote a large proportion of man-hours to staff activities. A proportionately small staff intensifies the pressure on top management to delegate responsibilities. Large organizations also have more hierarchical levels than small ones, and a multilevel hierarchy further constrains top management to delegate some authority to middle managers less far removed from the bulk of employees. Thus, a multilevel hierarchy and a small staff ratio generate pressures to decentralize, and large size does so most of all, in part directly and in part indirectly, by increasing hierarchical levels and reducing the staff ratio.

Conditions in organizations that make operations more reliable facilitate the delegation of responsibilities by making it less risky. The use of computers automates the more routine tasks, and superior qualifications of interviewers make the less routine tasks relatively self-regulating and independent of supervisory guidance. These conditions make operations less liable to serious disruption by poor managerial decisions, which are occasionally inevitable if responsibilities are delegated to a number of middle managers the quality of whose judgment is necessarily variable. The standardization of rating procedures limits the discretion that can be exercised on lower levels and thereby lessens the risk entailed by delegating decisions to local managers. The standardization of personnel procedures diminishes the risk of decentralization for a different reason. Strict adherence to civil service standards makes the

---

5. The zero-order correlation, with size logarithmically transformed, is $-.60$. Studies of industrial concerns and of hospitals have also found that the ratio of administrative staff declines with increasing size, though their measure of the staff ratio is not the same as the one used here. (See Bendix, 1956:221–222, and Anderson and Warkov, 1961:23–28).

performance of tasks more reliable by assuring that employees meet minimum merit requirements. The formalization of personnel procedures into an extensive body of regulations, which enables these standards to take into account variations in positions and situations, further raises the quality of the personnel and the reliability of their performance by averting the dangers of either applying an inappropriate standard or disregarding any standard in personnel-selection. All of these factors that make operations more reliable—automation, qualification of personnel, standardization of rating, standardization of personnel practice, and formalization of personnel procedures—foster decentralization.

The two forces affecting decentralization—the constraint of burdens and the reduction of risks—exert conflicting pressures in large organizations. For the heavy load of managerial decisions in large organizations engenders constraints to decentralize, but the wide implications of managerial decisions in large organizations enhance the risk of delegation. One result of these cross-pressures is that large size seems to give rise to inadvertent decentralization not intended by top management, as indicated by the findings that the direct effects of large size are to reduce the official delegation of authority (over personnel) to middle managers but increase the actual influence (over instituting change) that accrues to them. Another manifestation of the same conflicting forces is that large size directly discourages delegation of personnel responsibilities but simultaneously promotes conditions, such as automation, which encourage delegation of personnel matters. The pressures to decentralize are resisted until they give rise to conditions that limit the risk of delegation.

Characteristics of government agencies that are generally considered to be expressions of bureaucratic rigidity, such as an elaborate body of strictly enforced civil service regulations, paradoxically lead to the development of a less rigid authority structure, in which decentralization permits more flexible decision-making. The principle that delegation is a function of risk-reduction can explain this paradox. Both the standardization effected by merit standards and the formalization manifest in an extensive body of personnel regulations improve personnel-selection, and the resulting greater reliability of operations fosters delegation by reducing its risks. The indirect nature of these social processes should be noted. The findings do not simply show that the reliable execution of duties by officials on a given level encourages delegation of responsibilities to these officials, which would hardly be surprising. Civil service standards affect primarily the qualifications of the personnel on the lowest level of the organization. What the findings imply, therefore, is that the reliable performance of the operating personnel promotes delegation of responsibilities to managers several levels above them, because their effective performance makes operations less dependent on variable managerial judgments. Lest it be thought that these conclusions are confined to civil service, which is subject to special political pressures, it should be mentioned again that a study of 46 British organizations, most of them private firms, also found standardization as well as formalization, in this case referring largely to operating rather than personnel procedures, to be inversely associated with centralization. The limits on the exercise of discretion imposed by formalized procedures and standardized operations seem to permit the development of a less centralized authority structure, in which directives from top management place fewer restrictions on the exercise of discretion.

Another paradox is implicit here; it should be made explicit. With slight exaggeration, one could say that managerial decisions in organizations are either significant, in which case they are not delegated, or delegated, in which case they are not significant. There is an element of truth in this caricature. Since the top executive is accountable for effective operations in the organization, he will tend to reserve the most important managerial decisions for himself. To be sure, his decisions will be much influenced by the counsel of subordinates in whose managerial ability he has much confidence as well as by the advice of those whose professional expertise he lacks, but his obligations as top executive require him to assume official responsibility for the most crucial administrative decisions himself. However, this means neither that there are no variations in decentralization nor that only trivial responsibilities are delegated. The pressures to decentralize differ among organizations, and so do conditions that have developed, partly in response to these pressures, to reduce the risk of delegation. As a result, senior middle managers in large employment security agencies, for example, not only exercise more important responsibilities than their counterparts in small agencies but probably also make decisions of greater consequence than the top executives in the smallest agencies. Besides, the delegation of responsibilities in a given sphere that may appear to be relatively unimportant at the time has unanticipated consequences by establishing precedents that cannot easily be set aside when decisions in this sphere assume greater significance, further enlarging the scope of responsibilities of middle managers.

Middle managers in organizations undoubtedly often exercise major responsibilities, but this is most likely to be the case if impersonal mechanisms of control lessen the risk of delegation and give top executives some ultimate controlling power. The nature of management's controlling power, however, is fundamentally altered when impersonal mechanisms are substituted for orders issued through a chain of command. Thus, automation empowers the top executive to control operations by determining the design of the computer installation and the type of programs to be used, and it requires employees to adapt their activities to the computer setup, but conforming to these impersonal constraints is a very different experience from submitting to the orders of superiors. Personnel regulations that govern the selection of applicants exert control over operations, and so do top executives who determine selection criteria (directly in private firms and indirectly in government bureaus) and who decide which positions should be expanded. Such control through personnel-selection, however, does not involve obedience to commands from superiors by subordinates. The existence of impersonal mechanisms of control does not imply, of course, that managers in formal organizations never issue directives with which subordinates are expected to comply. But I do think that the prototype of the bureaucratic hierarchy in which control is essentially exercised by giving commands to subordinates is increasingly being replaced by a different authority structure in formal organizations in which control is primarily exercised through impersonal mechanisms.

REFERENCES

Anderson, Theodore R., and Seymour Warkov.
1961 "Organizational Size and Functional Complexity." American Sociological Review 26:23–28.
Bendix, Reinhard.
1956 Work and Authority in Industry. New York: Wiley.

Durkheim, Emile.
  1951 Suicide. Glencoe: Free Press.
Fromm, Erich.
  1941 Escape from Freedom. New York: Farrar & Rinehart.
Merton, Robert K.
  1968 Social Theory and Social Structure. New York: Free Press.
Michels, Robert.
  1949 Political Parties. Glencoe: Free Press.
Pugh, D. S., et al.
  1968 "Dimensions of Organization Structure." Administrative Science Quarterly 13:65–105.
Weber, Max.
  1946 Essays in Sociology. New York: Oxford University Press.
  1947 The Theory of Social and Economic Organization. New York: Oxford University Press.
Whisler, Thomas L., and Harold J. Leavitt.
  1958 "Management in the 1980's." Harvard Business Review 36:41–48.

Power Behavior and Decentralization

F. L. BATES

Peter Blau's paper presents an interesting and important theory of decentralization of power in bureaucracy. His central thesis is that decentralization of decision-making will occur in an organization as the risk of subordinates' making incorrect decisions is reduced. In other words, when top level management feels that the risks of allowing lower level managers to make decisions are reduced, they will tend to allow more decisions from the lower level.

Blau points out that such risks will be reduced if the rules and procedures of the organization are clearly and definitely specified. Therefore, as "routinization" in the Weberian sense occurs, decentralization of authority and power will tend to follow. This, Blau points out, is contrary to what would be expected on the basis of Weber's discussion of bureaucracy. Weber would have tended to see centralization and routinization as two positively correlated aspects of bureaucratization.

Professor Blau's thesis and the data that he has used to test it show that an increase in routinizations and the use of automation (a kind of computer routinization) are accompanied by a decentralization in power.

There can be little quarrel with this thesis and these findings, except one that is based on challenging Blau's definitions of decentralization and power.

It seems to me that Dr. Blau has tended to define power too narrowly, and because of his restricted definition there appears to be a disagreement with Weber's notions. Power behavior in an organization includes a variety of actions only a few of which Blau has used to measure decentralization. It can be argued that the following six types of actions all amount to power behavior: (1) Directing the activities of others; (2) Making rules which apply to the behavior of others; (3) Enforcing the rules with respect to others; (4) Setting goals and objectives for others; (5) Selecting personnel to occupy offices, hiring, promoting, firing; (6) Making decisions that lead to one of the above for others.

Blau measures power, and consequently decentralization, using items which fall under 5 and 6 above. There is a hint that he also includes 1, directing the activities of others, as power behavior although he has no direct measure of it. In contrast he uses items which fall under 2 and 3 and possibly 4, as measures of routinization.

It is my belief that the items used as measures of routinization really measure one type of power, while those used to measure power decentralization measure a second type of power. If this were true his thesis could be restated as follows: As power over behavior through the statement and enforcement of rules becomes centralized at the top of an organization, power over behavior in the form of directing activities, selecting personnel, and making operational decisions will tend to be decentralized. As in Blau's original argument, it can still be stated that centralization of power types 2, 3, and 4 will reduce the risk to top management of delegating power types 1, 5, and 6 to lower levels of the organization.

If this argument is correct, then Blau's data tend to confirm Weber's notions partially and to qualify them in an important way. Routinization of power can result in decentralization of certain kinds of power activity. Such routinization, however, in and of itself, represents a form of centralization. Thus centralization and decentralization occur simultaneously with respect to different types of power behavior.

Some Additional Questions

RICHARD H. HALL

My over-all reaction to this paper is extremely positive. This reaction is to this particular piece of research and also to the broader studies of which it is a part. An obvious but intriguing impression that this paper gives is of the great complexity of organizations. Cross-pressures and conflicting forces in complex organizations are vividly portrayed. The paper exemplifies careful research design and data-collection. The interpretation is clearly grounded in the data. At the same time it provides food for thought for additional research.

The section on methodology is clear and explicit, providing the reader with the rationale for the research decisions that were made. At the same time, it would be beneficial to have some examples of the kinds of questions asked and the nature of responses received. Examples of questions and responses would provide the reader with a basis for deciding if he too would place organizations in the kinds of categories used by the author. The measure of the formalization of personnel procedures (number of words in the manual) is a good "hard" measure; I wonder, however, how good an indication of formalization this actually is. I can envision situations in which unwritten expectations are highly formalized. A subjective question regarding the extent of "informal" formalization would have been very useful here. The next point is not strictly methodological but is part of the over-all research strategy. This particular paper is obviously part of a larger package (Blau-Meyer). One wishes that the author would provide some comparative data from the other kinds of organizations under investigation, even if these were speculative because of the incompleteness of the total project. Although the author tends to believe that it is difficult to combine dissimilar organizations (the fact and basis of dissimilarity must be identified), it would be extremely useful to know if the centralization-formalization

177

relationships hold up outside employment security divisions. I hope that this kind of data is forthcoming.

A basic problem I found with this paper was that there was no information regarding variations among these employment security agencies. While they are charged with administering the same basic program, there are undoubtedly variations in terms of emphasis given particular programs, rate of innovation of new programs, and the kinds of technologies employed. Examples of these variations can be found in the extent and rate with which programs for helping minority groups or the culturally disadvantaged are designed and implemented. There is a fair amount of research which suggests that these kinds of variations can have important structural implications. Without this information, therefore, the findings must be taken as tentative. (Examples—a highly innovative organization might be less formalized and more centralized. The source of this might be the innovativeness, rather than some of the other structural characteristics considered).

In somewhat the same vein is some lack of clarity regarding the content of the things that are delegated to the local offices. It would be extremely useful to know the kinds of decisions that are passed down, since the particular tasks performed at different levels and in different areas can have widely variant knowledge bases. What I am suggesting here is that some indication of the intellectual complexity of the kinds of decisions allowed at decentralized points would be useful in determining whether there was actual decentralization of important decisions or simply a distribution of routine and largely programmed decision-making power.

Some unanswered questions are raised in the section dealing with standardization and decentralization. The findings indicate that standardization, better qualified employees, and automation are all related to decentralization. The high levels of standardization and automation give rise to the question of what the people do. We have these highly qualified personnel in a situation of delegated something, but with highly standardized and routinized procedures. What may be happening here is that there is in fact *less* decentralization. We need more information on the kinds of things that the personnel in the decentralized locations actually do. Certainly the procedures do not cover all contingencies. At the same time, the reader cannot be sure if decentralization actually has occurred in fact, rather than simply apparently.

Related to this last point is another questionable interpretation. The paper states that the presence of extensive and intensive rules allows the decentralization of authority. Mightn't this actually be a form of centralization, since the *power* still resides in the central authority? The presence of extensive rules is not unlike the presence of an assembly line—impersonal control mechanisms exist which limit personal discretion and at the same time allow less direct supervision. This gives an aura of decentralization, but it may not exist in practice. Here again, more information might clear up these inconsistencies. The British data certainly lend support to Blau's interpretations, but I wish we had more information to allow us to accept them without these reservations.

The first implication from this research is that, as in factory work, impersonal control mechanisms can be introduced to regulate the behavior of members of administrative agencies. While Blau attributes this to the growth in size of the organizations, to me it is more fruitful to look beyond size. Blau notes that decisions to expand areas of service contribute to the growth process and thus to formalization. Size thus is not the primary cause. Rather, it lies in the decision process itself. Key factors here would appear to be environmental pressures for more services and the development of new technologies. These would seem to tell us more about organizational development than the size variable.

A second implication of this research is that organizations do in fact try to cope. Cross pressures indicate the difficulties in processes of coping and the likelihood that any change will lead to further needs to cope.

An additional question raised by these findings regards the future of these organizations. If the lower level managers do in fact operate with little discretion (power) due to the formalized and standardized system discussed, what will happen when they advance to higher positions? In a sense, this seems to be a verification of some of the ideas and implications of Whyte's *Organization Man*. The amount and kind of discretion of the lower level managers thus remains a key and open question.

A variable which has been largely omitted from the discussion here is the level of professionalization of the employees. Since some of Blau's earlier work on this project focused on this variable, it would be interesting to learn the way in which this variable interacts with the formalization-decentralization variables. It certainly would be an additional cross pressure, but, more important, it would also be a major source of conflict if the literature on professionals in organizations is at all correct. The high levels of formalization and standardization would appear to be diametrically opposed to most professional values.

Finally, the question raised in the section on methodology must be raised again. To what extent can these findings be generalized beyond Employment Security divisions (or English industrial firms)? I hope that the data to answer this question are soon forthcoming.

5

Patterns of Organizational Adaptation: A Political Perspective

EDWARD HARVEY
RUSSELL MILLS

Particularly in a period of rapid social and technological change, a most theoretically fruitful process for study in organizations is adaptation. The adaptive process is that in which an organization's resource-deployment and operating strategies are adjusted to cope with internally generated stress or perceived changes in the external environment. The aim is to structure optimally the organization to achieve its goal and to cope with threats to its continued existence.

The focus on adaptive processes pursued in this paper is considered an analytically useful strategy for two reasons. First, adaptive processes are common to all organizations and as such offer a frame of reference for comparative analysis. Second, the process is a dynamic one and thereby revealing of the relationship between organizational structure and action over time.

In order to limit the number of variables under consideration, however, the following discussion will be restricted to profit-making organizations. Profit-making organizations share a common type of boundary relationship in which internally generated resources (e.g., a product or a service) are exchanged for external resources which the organization needs (e.g., raw materials, capital) on a supply and demand basis in a competitive or at least potentially competitive market situation.

181

In nonprofit organizations that obtain resources from third parties (e.g., governments) and are thus less dependent upon competitive market situations, adaptive processes are likely to take quite different forms.

Variations in Organization Adaptability

A number of authors have concerned themselves with the specification of factors influencing the degree of adaptability in organizations. A. K. Rice (1963:17), for example, has argued that maximum flexibility, consistent with over-all integration, obtains in organizations when: (a) Control of parts is by results rather than by detailed inspection; (b) Parts have both whole tasks and maximum autonomy; (c) Communications are selective, rapid, and undistorted.

In practice, these conditions suggest that: (a) Control should be through people rather than through procedures; (b) Those in charge of part-enterprises should have both the responsibility for, and the authority required to carry out, their tasks; (c) Differentiation within the organization should ensure that each level in the hierarchy has genuinely discrete and distinctive primary tasks; (d) So far as is possible, lines of command should be short, with the minimum number of levels consistent with adequate over-all control.

W. M. Evan (1966:51–53) approaches the question of variations in organizational adaptability via the concept of organizational lag; that is, administrative decisions in organizations tend to lag behind technical innovations. In Evan's view, administrative innovations filter through the organization from the top down, while new technical patterns filter up from the lower levels. Evan argues that as organizational lag diminishes, organizational adaptability increases. Clearly, one condition for optimal adaptability, in terms of this scheme, would be for this filtering or trickle effect to be operative in both directions at the same time.

A number of authors have also viewed the process of formalization in organizations in adaptive terms. W. H. Starbuck (1965:480) argues that

As an organization gets older, it learns more and more about coping with its environment and with its internal problems of communication and coordination. At least this is the normal pattern, and the normal organization tries to perpetuate the fruits of its learning by formalizing them. It sets up standard operating procedures; it routinizes reports on organizational performance; it appoints specialists in areas of consistent need; it discovers the effective factorings of the organizational tasks and delegates the factored components to sub-units. The organization's need for and capacity for formalization increases as it grows.

Other authors, including Jerald Hage (1965–66) and Warren Bennis (1966), have taken the apparently opposing position that increases in formalization in organizations actually serve to diminish adaptability. As we shall undertake to point out, however, the interpretation of the role of formalization vis-à-vis adaptation in organizations is contingent upon the kind of adaptive process under consideration.

While suggestive of a number of sources of variations in organizational adaptability, then, the views outlined above are not sufficiently convergent to provide a general theory of variations in organizational adaptibility. In fact, certain divergencies, such as differential interpretations of the role of formalization, suggest the need for theoretical strategies to add clarification. In this regard, it would seem of considerable importance to differentiate types of adaptive process. For example, adaptive processes of a predominantly routine character might well be facilitated by formalization. Conversely, in situations of an innovative character, organizational adaptability might well be facilitated by lesser degrees of formalization. One aim of this paper will be to develop this contention further by identifying and discussing a number of different basic paths along which the adaptive process can proceed.

It is also suggested here that any adaptive process in organizations can be discriminated along a number of dimensions for the purposes of analysis. Three such major analytic properties of the adaptive process are time, conflict, and effectiveness. In empirical terms, of course, the referents of these dimensions are interrelated in a number of evident ways. For example, one might hypothesize that the greater the conflict during adaptation, the longer the process will take, and, consequently, the lesser the effectiveness of the adaptive process. Instead of examining such empirical interdependencies, however, it is our intention to focus in some detail on one particular variable dimension of the adaptive process—that of conflict.

In this connection, a basic assumption behind the argument of the paper is that adaptive changes are always to some extent disruptive of the status quo and that such changes will always be resisted by parts of the organization which feel threatened by the proposed modifications. Any adaptive change will thus result in at least some degree of conflict within the organization between those subunits where the proposed change is perceived as beneficial to subunit interests and those subunits where it is believed that the proposed change will weaken the subunit's position within the organization. A subunit is defined as a group of individuals within the organization charged with a formally defined set of responsibilities directed toward the attainment of a basic but circumscribed goal of the organization, such as research and development, or the maintenance of fiscal records.

If we define conflict as expressed differences of position between individuals or subunits in organizations as to what form adaptive processes should take, we can then find considerable support in the literature for the above-stated assumption that adaptive processes generate at least some measure of conflict in organizations. In this connection, the reader is referred to cases reported by Cyert, Dill, and March (1958–59), Jacques (1951), Brown (1960)[1], Chamberlain (1960), Archibald and Villoria (1967)[2], and Morison (1962).

Our concern, however, goes beyond offering support for the contention that adaptive processes generate conflict in organizations. Rather, a second major aim of the paper will take the form of an attempt to identify variables which are related to variation in the amount of conflict associated with adaptive process in organizations. The analysis will be somewhat extended by relating the same set of variables to variations in the kinds of power relations obtaining between individuals, subunits, and levels in organizations during adaptive process.

Very generally, the basic approach to organizations taken here is an attempt to synthesize elements from the equilibrium and conflict models of social systems (see van den Berghe, 1963). The adaptive process itself is seen as an essentially equilibrating or homeostatic

1. The material reported here is a good example of the gradual way in which the recommendations put forward by Jacques (1951) were implemented with respect to the accommodation of conflicts between different interests within the organization.

2. Refer to the conflicts generated by the introduction of a network-based management system in a large aerospace corporation.

mechanism for returning an organization to a type of balance or for improving its stability. This is not to say that adaptive changes always accomplish this aim. In fact, in some cases, adaptive changes may be actually maladaptive or may generate so much internal conflict that the organization is forced into a position less stable than before the change was contemplated.

Although the adaptive process is the organizational mechanism for coping with internally generated and externally imposed changes, it is not seen as being intrinsically eufunctional or dysfunctional for the system. Judgments of this type must be made on the empirical basis of the results of specific adaptive processes. This raises questions concerning what constitutes comparable indexes of organizational effectiveness.

Following from this conception of the adaptive process, the basic structure of relationships between the organization's subunits is characterized as being "political." This does not mean, on the one hand, that subunits are purely competitive with irreconcilably opposed interests as are social classes in Marxian analysis. Nor does it mean, on the other hand, that the subunits and their interaction merely bear a eufunctional relationship to the persistence of the larger organizational system.

"Political" does mean that the subunits can be characterized as either primarily competitive or primarily co-operative, depending on the exigencies of the situation in which they are involved. A conceptualization of organizations as "political systems" is now spelled out in greater detail.

THE ORGANIZATION AS A POLITICAL SYSTEM

One finds in complex organizations a division of the work involved in the realization of the organization's general goals. For our purposes we shall conceive of this division of the organization's work in terms of the organization's subunits. Although such subunits have specialized tasks in the organization, they are often interdependent. That is, they form the parts of the organization's general work process. Another characteristic of organizational subunits is that they are usually claimants in common on the scarce resources of the organization (March and Simon, 1958:122). It follows from this that subunits are likely to develop their own subset of goals within the organization. That these subunit goals may be incongruent with the general goals of the organization has already been demonstrated in the literature (see Kaplan, Dirlam, and Lanzillotti, 1958; Selznick, 1949). Given the possibility of specific subunit interests on the one hand and the likelihood of the interdependence of subunits relative to general organizational goals on the other, we may raise the question of what organizational mechanisms there are for the accommodation of differentiated subunit interests and the realization of general goals. In this connection, March (1962:672) has suggested that

a business firm is a political coalition and the executive in the firm is a political broker. The composition of the firm is not given; it is negotiated. The goals of the firm are not given; they are bargained.

By this definition, then, one may see the organization as a coming together of different interests, a "political" coalition of subunits in the sense that a particular interest (theoretically at least) remains in the organization only as long as there is "something in it for them." Such differential interests are of course amplified as well as instigated by technical specialization and functional differentiation within the organization.

Given this situation of implicit or explicit conflict, there arises the question of what mechanisms enable organizations to endure. First, there is the process of bargaining, which may be seen in operation at two levels. There is, to begin, the basic "bargain" that certain members of the organization will be production workers, certain others executives, and so on, which serves to mark out the general dimensions of the coalition and to give a measure of stability to the enterprise. This may be seen as kin to the notion of a general policy or charter in an organization; many members of the organization may have widely different interpretations of the policy or may not even know what it is. Its mere presence, however, acts as a binding force. This primary bargaining, then, serves to establish a measure of organizational stability and also provides a base for secondary bargaining, the "jockeying to improve one's position" within the organization.

We have mentioned that the subunits of an organization make differential claims to scarce organizational resources. The extensiveness of the claims is a reflection of the subunit's importance to the organization. Thus, for example, the engineering division of an organization is likely to have a greater claim on the organization's resources than, say, the typing pool. To maintain itself, the organization's coalition must balance claims against resources through the processes of bargaining. The bargaining process defines the dimension of a "side payment" (an allocation of organizational resources by one subunit of the organization to another subunit), which the coalition can bear and which the subunit will accept. The "side payments" assume various forms, such as money, services, the allocation of authority, equipment, and so on (see Cyert and March, 1963:29).

The coalition is precisely feasible because not all of its members are simultaneously engaged in making demands on the coalition's scarce resources. This is further guaranteed, however, through formal arrangements which specify sequential attention to the claims of the different subunits. The basis of such a sequence would most probably be the functional significance of the subunit to the organization as a whole or perhaps the degree of authority that the subunit possesses within the organization. Arrangements of this type mean that the total claims of the subunits, at any given time, are not likely to be sufficient to exhaust totally organizational resources at the same point in time. The difference between the two is the organization's "slack" or resource pool (Cyert and March, 1963:36–38, 155–157). Its presence may be viewed as a critical condition for the continuation of the organization.

One of the most common organizational phenomena during the adaptive process is the formulation of special-interest coalitions composed of only a limited number of the organization's subunits. At certain points during the adaptive process, horizontally or vertically differentiated subunits may perceive that they have certain interests in common which they can pursue more effectively by consolidating the pressure they can exert on other subunits and the decision-making center.

If the special-interest coalition is to be successful, the interests of the subunits composing it must be close enough so that they can act as a single unit and thereby exert more effective pressure than could any of the subunits alone. The subunits composing the special-interest coalition must also be convinced that the benefits they will receive from the action of the coalition will be greater than they would receive outside the coalition. In some cases a subunit which will be vitally affected by an adaptive decision may attempt to attract less-involved subunits into a coalition by making side payments to them. The value of these side payments must clearly be commensurate with the contribution which the less-involved subunits make to the coalition.

It is the contention of this paper that in the modal processual development, special-interest coalitions are strongest when the organization is still temporally remote from finding a solution to the problem and tend to break down as the organization approaches a final decision. Divergent interests will increasingly tend to emerge from the matrix of common interests that bind the coalition together as the organization comes closer to taking a decisive step on the adaptive process. For example, several subunits of an organization may coalesce to force the organization to construct a new building, but the closer the organization comes to agreeing to this demand, the weaker the coalition will become, as each subunit then attempts to maximize the amount of floor space it will have.

These distinctions, then, form the major components of our conception of organizations as political systems. This general focus on organizations has been succinctly put by Tom Burns(1961–62:257):

While the corporation is hardly a microcosm of the state, study of the internal politics of universities and business concerns may develop insights contributing to the understanding of political action in general.

Corporations are co-operative systems assembled out of the usable attributes of people. They are also social systems within which people compete for advancement; in so doing they may make use of others. Behavior is identified as political when others are made use of as resources in competitive situations. Material, or extra-human, resources are also socially organized. Additional resources, resulting from innovation or new types of personal commitment, alter the prevailing equilibrium and either instigate or release political actions. Such action is a mechanism of social change.

By way of summary, then, political behavior is defined as behavior by individuals or, in collective terms, subunits within an organization which makes a claim against the resource-sharing system of the organization. Such claims are frequently, although not invariably, rationalized as being necessary or desirable in order that the individual or subunit can continue to carry out organizational duties effectively.[3] Finally, in addition to taking up the question of political behavior in organizations, we have discussed organizations as political systems, in this latter connection following Cyert and March's conception of organizations as coalitions.[4]

With this conception of organizations as political systems in mind, we shall now go on to identify in more detail basic modes of adaptive process in organizations and some of the possibilities for political behavior obtaining in the course of such adaptive sequences.

MODES AND SEQUENCES OF ADAPTIVE PROCESS

The adaptive process has two basic constituents: a problematic situation confronting the organization, and a solution arrived at by the decision-making centers of the organization to cope with the situation. Both of these constituents can be differentiated along a continuum referred to here as the routine-innovative dimension. A routine situation is defined as a situation that the organization has faced before, while an innovative situation is a situation that is completely new to the organization. A routine solution is a solution that the organization has used to cope with the problematic situations in the past, while an

3. The major assumption resting behind this definition is that as long as the organization continues as a resource-sharing system, political behavior will obtain. It is further contended, however, that adaptive processes are likely to threaten existing patterns of resource-sharing and that, in consequence, organizational politics become particularly activated in the course of such decisions. It should further be stated that we assume that the different interests held by different individuals and subunits within organizations are the major source of organizational politics. In this connection, however, we, as observers, can only say whether individuals or subunits within an organization are in positions such that a given decision process can objectively affect them differently. This is quite different from stating what are the objective interests of such individuals or subunits. The latter procedure is of course permissible if one has statements of what interests are from such individuals or collectivities. However, to look at structural position and then proceed to impute interests is, in our view, an untenable procedure.

4. There are, of course, other ways of defining a political system such as Dahl's (1963:6). In our view, however, Dahl's definition has less built-in receptivity to change than March's coalition-formulation in that the form the organizational coalition takes over time can be highly variable, and it is for this reason that we have chosen to follow the latter formulation.

innovative solution is defined as a solution that has not been used before and for which there are no precedents in the organization. Although in many empirical cases problematic situations and solutions may contain both routine and innovative elements, the two constituents of adaptive process will be dichotomized here for the purposes of analysis.

A cross-tabulation of these two basic constituents produces the following table:

SOLUTION

		ROUTINE	INNOVATIVE
Problem	ROUTINE	A	B
Situation	INNOVATION	C	D

In the case of a routine problem situation, two basic courses of action obtain within the organization. A routine solution may be imposed, to deal with the situation in the same way it has always been dealt with in the past, or a totally new way of solving the problem may be developed, thus leading to an innovative solution. In the case of an innovative problem situation, the same set of possibilities is faced within the organization. An attempt can be made to impose a routine solution on the new problem, or an attempt can be made to find an unprecedented solution to suit the unprecedented nature of the problem situation. We shall now outline some of the factors associated with the selection in organizations of different adaptive paths or strategies.

Basic Path-Selection

Although there is a tendency for routine problem situations to be met with routine solutions and for innovative problem situations to call forth innovative solutions, it is suggested here that the propensity to impose routine solutions in both types of problem situations is related to various contextual and organizational variables. As conceived of here, contextual variables are properties of organizations in relation to factors in the organization's environment. Organizational variables, as treated here, are conceived of primarily as internal properties of organizations. The four contextual variables considered are: (1) The size of an organization relative to its competitors; (2) The age of the organization relative to its competitors; (3) The degree of competitiveness an organization faces in its market situation; (4) The degree to which the technological sector of which the organization is a part is changing rapidly or slowly. The two organizational variables considered in this connection are: (1) The degree of diffuseness or specificity of the organization's technology. A technologically diffuse organization is defined as one producing a wide range of different products. As the range of products narrows, technical specificity is said to increase. (2) The degree of formalization of the communication system of the organization.

This list of variables does not, of course, purport to be exhaustive of all factors possibly influencing basic path-selection. Making use of the variables listed, it can now be hypothesized that the tendency to impose routine solutions on all types of problems is most likely to occur in organizations: (1) that are relatively large compared to their competitors; (2) that have been in existence for a relatively long time compared with their competitors; (3) that face a relatively uncompetitive market situation; (4) that are part of a technological sector that is changing relatively slowly; (5) that have a relatively technically specific production process; (6) that have relatively formalized communication channels.

Organizations of this type will be considered to be in "low-threat" contexts.

The general theoretical perspective informing the first four hypotheses is an assumption that, in general, the less the environmental pressure on an organization, the greater the propensity to rely upon routine procedures in situations calling for adaptation. The last two hypotheses are better understood in the light of the foregoing discussion of organizations as political systems. From that perspective, it would appear plausible to argue that structural arrangements which emphasize predictability and stasis are more likely to reinforce continuation of routine patterns around which interests have come to form rather than to promote innovative activity.

Carry the argument a step further, it is hypothesized that the tendency to impose innovative solutions on all types of problems is found in organizations: (1) that are relatively small compared to their competitors; (2) that have been in existence for a relatively short time compared to their competitors; (3) that face a relatively competitive market situation; (4) that are part of a technological sector that is changing relatively rapidly; (5) that have a relatively technically diffuse production process; (6) that have relatively unformalized communication channels.

Organizations of this type will be considered to be in "high-threat" contexts.

The extent to which these different environmental and organizational characteristics can be collapsed into an index of "threat" will obviously have to be demonstrated empirically. Although we intend to take a theoretical liberty and build our discussion on the assumption that these characteristics can be collapsed and treated unidimensionally, it is clearly possible that they may have distinguishably different effects on the adaptive process.

A further differentiation should be made relative to the two cells of the table in which the nature of the solution imposed appears to be less appropriate to the nature of the problematic situation. These are cell B, in which a routine problem is met with an innovative solution, and cell C, in which a routine solution is imposed on an innovative problem. In some organizations these solutions may be perceived as being effective, and the adaptive process may be brought to a conclusion; while in other organizations a gap between the nature of the problem and the nature of the solution may be perceived, and the organization may go on to impose another solution more appropriate to the nature of the problem it is facing. It is hypothesized here that the tendency in both cells B and C to perceive the first solution as being ineffective and to impose a more appropriate solution is related to the organization's being in a "moderate-threat" context; that is, in an intermediate position on the six previously listed dimensions.

There are several quite different organizational contexts subsumed under the general concept "moderate-threat" context. Some organizations in this category might be high on some of the preceding dimensions and low on others, while others might occupy an intermediate position on each one of the dimensions. The effect which these variations have on the adaptive process should be investigated, although we believe it to be premature to differentiate theoretically the concept "moderate threat" at this point. For the purposes of our argument, "moderate threat" is not meant to refer to any precisely defined situation or to any absolute position on a scale of "threat," but merely to characterize the broad range of situations between contexts which are clearly "high threat" and those which are clearly "low threat".

Thus, in a *routine problem situation,* we hypothesize that the tendency to impose a routine solution and stay with it is related to the organization's being in a "low-threat" context; that the tendency to impose an innovative solution and stay with it is related to the organization's being a "high-threat" context; and that the tendency first to impose an innovative solution, to perceive it as being ineffective, and then to impose a routine solution is related to the organization's being in a "moderate-threat" context.

In an *innovative problem situation,* we hypothesize that the tendency to impose a routine solution and stay with it is related to the organization's being in a "low-threat" context; that the tendency to impose an innovative solution and stay with it is related to the organization's being in a "high-threat" context; and that the tendency first to impose a routine solution, to perceive it as being ineffective, and then to impose an innovative solution is related to the organization's being in a "moderate-threat" context.

We do not mean to imply that organizations in "moderate-threat" contexts always follow this two-stage sequence of finding a solution to a problem; in fact, this may be a relatively rare occurrence. We do maintain, however, that among a given set of organizations, those in "moderate-threat" contexts will have the greatest probability of following this course.

Sequence Within Path

The argument up to this point has been concerned with identifying basic modes of adaptive process and with a consideration of some factors which appear to lead to the emergence of one kind of adaptive pattern rather than another. In addition to this differentiation between paths, however, *within each path* it is possible to differentiate a sequence of stages. The central aim in developing such sequential models is to provide a framework in terms of which one may interpret the implications of a number of organizational variables vis-à-vis the political process within given paths of adaptation.[5]

5. For other models of adaptation in organizations, see Gore (1956) and Lundberg (1964).

In this connection we shall first develop a sequential model of the innovative problem–innovative solution process. As it would be somewhat redundant to develop completely separate models for the other three types of adaptation identified, we shall instead simply note the basic ways in which they differ from the innovative problem–innovative solution model. This will be accomplished through a discussion of processual differences following from routine problem situations and processual differences following routine solutions. At the conclusion of this process we will have in effect enumerated what we take to be the major stages associated with each of the four adaptive processes identified.

A further important distinction which must be introduced at this point is the matter of the scale of the adaptive process. Clearly, innovative and routine problem situation–solution sequences may have either far-ranging or quite limited effects within the organization. It is assumed here that while all adaptive processes tend to activate political behavior within organizations, large-scale adaptive processes will be more productive of political behavior than small-scale adaptive processes.

The balance of the argument in this section, then, will be developed as follows. First a sequential model of innovative problem–innovative solution processes will be outlined with particular reference to the potential for political behavior at various points in the process. Other types of problem-solution processes will then be discussed in contrast with the innovative-solution process. The various stages of the adaptive processes discussed here are ordered along the temporal dimension of their anticipated empirical sequence. It should be emphasized in this connection that although the following sequence of steps is what we would expect, it is by no means presented as a necessary or invariant order of events. In their present form, the models we advance are best viewed as heuristic frames of reference designed to facilitate the analysis of the politics of adaptive processes.

A Sequential Model of Innovative Problem–Innovative Solution Processes

Issue-perception and formation of goals. "Issue-perception" refers to the identification in terms of some kind of cognitive structure of an event or pattern of events that in some way demands an organizational response. "Goal-formation" is simply the process of delimiting and giving direction to the response.

If we are correct in viewing an organization as a coalition of different interests, it obviously becomes unlikely that the emergence of a problematic issue will be met by a consensual definition of what the problem is. One would also expect this divergence to carry over to the goals in terms of which solutions are sought. Yet the adaptive processes which emerge along the lines discussed above are certainly directed toward some sort of goal, however unclear or loosely formulated it may be. In this connection, Cyert and March (1959) have criticized the notion that organizations have a well-defined set of a priori goals in terms of which they solve all their problems. Instead, these authors have argued that "the goals of a business firm are a series of more or less independent constraints imposed on the organization through a process of bargaining among potential coalition members and elaborated over time in response to short-run pressures" (Cyert and March, 1963:43).

Thus when a problem comes to impinge upon an organization, whether its direction of causation is from the external environment or from within the organization, the formulation of some sort of goal vis-à-vis the problem is, after perception of the problem, the next step in the adaptation process. This process of perceiving the problem and formulating relevant goals has two implications for the earlier discussion of the political system of organizations. First, the actual problem may be differentially perceived by different members of subunits of the organization. Second, the goals ultimately formulated may well represent particular interests within the organization.

This line of argument is not designed to suggest that organizations are without any a priori goals. On the contrary, organizations have at a very high level of diffuseness certain very general goals relating to such factors as what constitutes, broadly speaking, an acceptable market share or adequate volume of sales.[6] It is our contention, however, that these very general goals provide only a context in which specific goals are developed and bargained over. As we have tried to suggest, it is these specific goals that are of crucial importance in adaptive processes.

Search and the use of expectations. The delimitation of goals relative to an issue leads to two closely interrelated processes. The first of these

6. The conception of an organization's general goals is used here in the sense that Cyert and March (1963:40–43) have specified five general goal areas.

is organizational search and is defined as the investigation of different action possibilities relative to a given issue and in terms of certain goals. The second process involves the development of expectations in terms of information gathered in the course of search processes. Thus, for example, officers of an organization might evaluate from a cost perspective three possible solutions to a given problem. Should they select one on the basis that it appeared it would yield the cheapest and most effective outcome, they would then have engaged in the process of developing expectations.

In view of what has been said concerning the organization as a political system and the bargained nature of organizational goals, certain difficulties emerge in those theoretical approaches to organizations and adaptive process that appear to assume, implicitly or explicitly, that search processes and the use of expectations are governed by a model of rational action.[7] We would prefer to treat rationality as a variable, and in this connection we shall specify some factors which serve to limit its operation in the organization generally and during these processes in particular.

We would point, for example, to the cognitive limitations on complete rationality reflected in the descriptions of four adaptive processes by Cyert *et al.* (1958–59). This evidence strongly indicates that the decision-makers in question obtained little or no information on alternative choices during the search procedure. In all cases the amount of information resulting from search procedures was quite limited compared to what might "ideally" have been obtained.[8] The same cases and Chamberlain's (1960) account of a policy decision in a telephone company also indicate that the amount of calculation of the costs involved in these adaptive processes, especially with regard to minimizing expenditures and maximizing outcomes, was also very limited. In the cases cited, much of the comparison of advantages was directed toward satisfying conflicting subunit interests, a process in which bargaining power and

7. A number of theorists in the field have stressed organizational rationality in such terms as the maximization of efficiency and operation in terms of highly specific goals. See, for example, Etzioni (1961:11); Parsons (1956:64); Weber (1956:586); Moore (1962:30 and 1963:86–7).

8. Obviously a truly omniscient search is virtually impossible; however the search procedures described in these cases do not even begin to represent a fairly complete investigation of readily available information.

authority are likely to give direction to adaptive outcomes before calculated costs do.

We would also suggest that the earlier comments regarding subunit interests and bargaining over goals have implications for the question of rationality in organizations, especially insofar as the latter has been linked up with the notion that processes of organizational adaptation represent efforts to maximize rationality in terms of clearly formulated, a priori goals. In this connection, findings reported by Cyert *et al.* (1958–59), and Jacques (1951) indicate that goals become defined *after* an issue has been perceived. It is also apparent from these findings that such goals reflect a process of conflict and interest accommodation between organizational subunits with differential bargaining power rather than in any sense being representative of what is "rationally best" for the organization as a whole. A closely associated case would be the operation of career strategies within the organization as factors bearing on the operation of rationality. Buren (1962), for example, has pointed out how personal career interests within the organization can influence the discovery and development of issues for adaptation processes regardless of the "rational" significance of such issues to the organization as a whole.

Choice of solution. The perception of an organizational problem, the goal-formation process, the gathering of information, and the use of expectations have been discussed here as elements of a sequential model of the politics of organizational adaptation processes. Ultimately, however, the individual or group of individuals within the organization who possess the legitimate authority to do so proceed to decide whether or not a particular course of action can be formalized. It is this process that defines our conception of choice of solution. It should be noted that even the process of choice involves the possibility of political behavior. For in the context of a given choice, the deciding officer or officers have the opportunity to express a preference between the remaining alternatives or, in rejecting all alternatives, they may undo a sequence of political processes in favor of an entirely different course of action.

Redefinition. The fact that a choice is made by an individual or group invested with authority does not guarantee that the course of action implied will be immediately or enthusiastically carried out by all remaining incumbents of the organization. We define this possibility that other members of the organization may seek to evade or modify such outcomes as "redefinition."

Melman (1958), for example, in his study of Standard Motors, speaks of a double decision system in which one system is constituted by management's prerogatives to set production figures while the other system is constituted by the workers' capacity to decide within certain tolerances how much will *actually* be produced. In this connection, Melman (1958:19) has observed:

> The decision systems of the management and of the workers have been found to be operative as separate, distinct, unilateral systems, each performing the function of decision making on production. To be sure, the decision system of the employer has been by far the more important one in the scope of its effect on production. In the operation of the industrial enterprise, however, the worker decision system has already had clear and traceable effects on the decision system of the employer.

Thus even when an adaptive choice has been made, the way in which it is put into effect may depend on the way it is received by those who possess the power of this counter-decision system. Clearly, the politics of adaptive processes do not come to an end with choice of solution.

Processual Distinctions in Routine Problem Situations

In the case of routine problem situations, "issue-perception and goal-formation" do not form a separate stage of the adaptive process. A routine situation, by definition, has been faced before, and thus some types of organizational precedents for handling it are available. Routine situations are invariably anticipated, and thus perception of the problematic issue is continuous and does not enter the decision-making process at a definable point to cause problems which can be clearly differentiated from those of the "search and expectations" stage. In routine problem situations, search procedures are more likely to be regulated normatively and limited to an institutionalized scope, whereas in innovative situations, for which there are no precedents, search procedures would likely involve exploration of a much broader range of possibilities.

Processual Distinctions Following Routine Solutions

The redefinition stage, so crucial when an innovative solution has been decided upon, is minimized or even eliminated in the case of routine solutions. If a solution is routine, very similar decisions have been made in the organization before, and the consequences of such decisions have been incorporated into the operating structure of the organization. These organizational precedents for the way in which the results of such decisions are defined and absorbed by the organization set limits on the ways in which the results of similar decisions can be incorporated. Since the range of possible choices is narrowed, post-decision conflict is minimized. Thus, for example, in an annual departmental budget-allocation decision, not all parties to the process may be satisfied with the outcome. Possibilities for redefining the outcome are very limited, however, in view of the typically well-established routine mechanisms for putting the decision outcome into effect. Efforts of dissatisfied parties are more likely to be directed toward improving strategies for the next budget year, rather than concentrated on redefinition efforts which are not likely to produce significant results.

Summary and Flow Charts

The different paths which adaptive processes may take in organizations and the sequence of processual stages within each path will now be summarized in flow charts. As was previously discussed, in the case of both routine and innovative problem situations, the tendency to follow Path 1 is related to the organization's being in what has been referred to as a "low-threat" context. This means that it is large and well established compared to its competitors, faces an uncompetitive market situation, and has a specific and stable technology. The tendency to follow Path 3 in both charts is related to the organization's being in a "high-threat" context. This means that it is small and less well established compared to its competitors, faces a highly competitive market situation, and has a diffuse and rapidly changing technology. The tendency to follow the process in Path 2 will tend to be followed in organizations that are at intermediate points on the dimensions of threat.

VARIATIONS IN CONFLICT AND POWER RELATIONS DURING ADAPTIVE PROCESS

We have now reached a point where, in terms of the sequential models outlined, the potential for political behavior during in-path se-

ROUTINE PROBLEM SITUATION

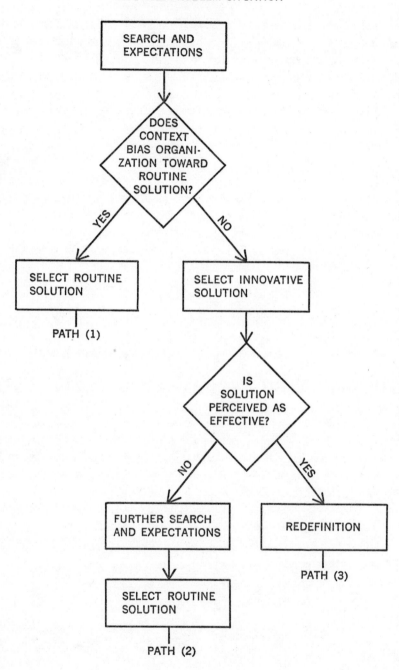

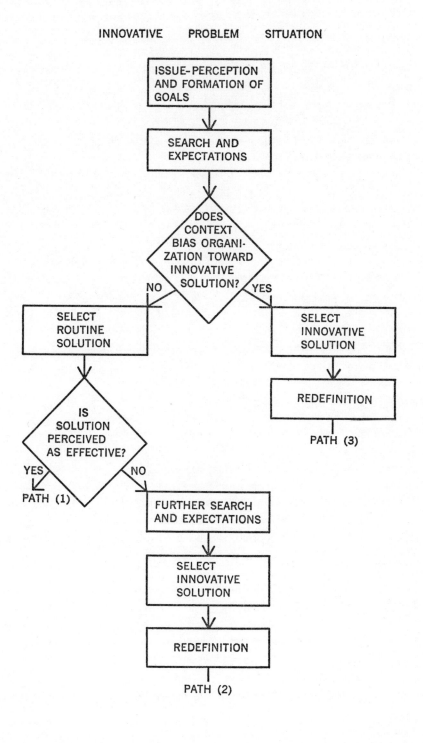

INNOVATIVE   PROBLEM   SITUATION

ISSUE-PERCEPTION
AND FORMATION OF
GOALS

SEARCH AND
EXPECTATIONS

DOES
CONTEXT
BIAS ORGANI-
ZATION TOWARD
INNOVATIVE
SOLUTION?

NO   YES

SELECT
ROUTINE
SOLUTION

SELECT
INNOVATIVE
SOLUTION

REDEFINITION

PATH (3)

IS
SOLUTION
PERCEIVED
AS EFFECTIVE?

YES   NO

PATH (1)

FURTHER SEARCH
AND EXPECTATIONS

SELECT
INNOVATIVE
SOLUTION

REDEFINITION

PATH (2)

quence has been illustrated. It remains, however, to suggest sources and types of variations in such political behavior.

It is argued here that there are two particularly significant dimensions of political behavior in organizations. One is the *amount of conflict* which the adaptive process generates. This could obviously be further differentiated into various components of conflict such as intensity and extensiveness, although these theoretical refinements will not be attempted at this time.

The other dimension of political behavior to be considered relates to the model *types of power relations* which will obtain under specific types of organizational conditions during adaptive processes.

Power is defined here as the ability of an individual group to act out successfully its character or to impose extrapolations or projections of its inner structure upon its environment (Deutsch, 1963). Power relations in organizations are therefore defined as relations between individuals or subunits in which each is attempting to impose its own inner structure on the organization's internal environment—aims which are to some extent incompatible.

As used here, "power" is a generic variable from which we derive a number of subtypes of power relations. Our derivation of subtypes proceeds from the postulation of two major dimensions of power relations in organizations. One dimension is the degree of legitimacy of the exerted power as defined in terms of the norms and formal structure of the organization. The other dimension is the extent to which the wielder of power can impose sanctions (either normative or nonnormative) for failure to comply. For effective use of power at the low end of this continuum, in which fear of sanctions is not a major factor, it is maintained that effective power must be based on other attributes of the wielder of power such as special knowledge, abilities, or contacts he may have.

Dichotomizing and cross-tabulating these dimensions, for the purposes of analysis, produces the table on page 203.

Weber (1947:152) defines power as "the probability that one actor within a social relationship will be in a position to carry out his own will despite resistance." The definition of power with which we operate here is clearly much broader than this and is motivated by a felt need to conceptualize the general force resting behind all attempts to affect

LEGITIMACY OF POWER

		HIGH	LOW
Ability to Impose Sanctions	HIGH	Legal Authority	Coercion
(Based on abilities, contacts etc.)	LOW	Rational Authority (Expertise)	Persuasion-manipulation

outcomes in social relationships, whether these attempts take the form of outright coercion, influence, or the exercise of legitimate authority. In our view, of all the terms considered, "power" appears to lend itself most effectively to this generic use.

In terms of our distinctions, the cell labeled "coercion" would most closely approximate what we take Weber to mean by "power." One of Weber's major types of authority, "rational-legal," has been differentiated in terms of our scheme in the light of Parsons's cogent criticism that

Weber . . . confused two distinct types of authority:
(a) authority which rests on "incumbency of legally defined office,"
(b) that which is based on "technical competence."

Finally, persuasion and/or influence has been identified as a separate variant.

Sources of variation in the amount of conflict and types of power relations obtaining during adaptive process will now be analyzed in terms of five organizational variables and certain aspects of the adaptive problem situation itself. The five organizational variables with which we are concerned are organizational differentiation by subunit; levels of authority; the ratio of managers and supervisors to nonsupervisory personnel; program-specification; organizational technology. These variables will be defined and discussed in detail below. The aspects of the adaptive problem situation which concern us are whether it is routine or innovative and whether it is large scale or small scale.

A major difficulty with the approach we take here is that the implications of these factors for political behavior in organizations during adaptive process will be taken up one variable at a time. Clearly, however, actual organizations represent empirical clusterings of all the variables we have identified in addition to other possibly relevant variables. Thus, for example, let us anticipate our argument that the potential for political behavior during adaptive process increases with the number of subunits and number of levels of authority in an organization. How, in fact, would one deal with the empirical case where an organization contains many subunits but few levels of authority? Even though there is some reason to believe that the variables we identify vary together in the same direction (see Woodward, 1965), it remains clear that ideally some measures should be devised for weighting each variable dimension with regard to its implications for political behavior during adaptive processes. For the present, however, we shall restrict our argument to a consideration of the implications of each variable for political behavior.

The Problem Situation

The nature of the problem situation facing an organization is one of the main sources of variation in the amount of conflict and the nature of the power relations which arise during an adaptive process. It is hypothesized that because of their implied threat to established resource-showing patterns, innovative problems will produce more conflict in organizations than will routine problem situations. It is also hypothesized that the unprecedented nature of the problem and consequent absence of guidelines will increase the probability that political behavior associated with innovative problem situations will be characterized by power relations low in organizational legitimacy. In both instances, the tendencies referred to would increase as the scale of the adaptive process increased. The reciprocal hypothesis, of course, is that political behavior in routine problem situations is more likely to be characterized by the use of legitimate types of power.

Taking legitimate power alone, it is hypothesized that innovative problems are more likely to call forth rational authority while routine problems are more likely to be solved through the use of legal authority. Expertise is only the best base of power the first time a problem is faced. In subsequent similar situations, nonexperts can reimpose the solution used the first time, and, as a result, the value of expertise is deflected.

Subunit Specialization in Organizations

It is difficult to think of an organization that does not entail some kind of division of work directed toward the attainment of its outputs. The degree or extensiveness of this division of work is, however, a variable matter, and if one considers any given empirical range of organizations, one will find that some organizations have more specialized subunits than others. It is our contention that subunits in an organization can become for their incumbents a more important focus than the organization as a whole. That is to say, commitment to an involvement in a subunit lends to the development of a particular way of looking at organizational events. In addition to providing this kind of cognitive focus, we have also held that subunits are involved with other subunits in the process of sharing the scarce resources of the organization. The mechanisms in terms of which the members of a given subunit seek their "fair share" have been identified as organizational politics. The processes through which balancing and integration of these claims take place have been referred to as the political system of organizations. Insofar as resources are always scarce in an organization, organizational politics always exist to some extent and, in our view, are particularly activated by adaptive processes which threaten the existing system of resource-allocation. Working from this basis, we would hypothesize that as the number of subunits in an organization increases, so will the potential for political conflict during adaptive processes.

No plausible hypothetical relationships may be advanced concerning relationships between the number of subunits per se and specific types of power relations. However, it would appear plausible to argue that the types of subunits which enjoy primacy within the organization may well be a factor influencing the character of power relations. In organizations, for example, where the research and development function is of prime importance, it would seem reasonable to argue that power relations during adaptive process would be characterized by considerable emphasis on rational-expertise forms of authority. Conversely, organizations characterized by primacy of subunits dealing with routine production functions would be more likely to be characterized by the exercise of legal authority as the predominant mode of power relations during adaptive processes.

It is also possible that the nature of the subunits present within an organization might cause the adaptive process to unfold differently in different types of problem situations. For example, there are some subunits of industrial organizations such as research and development departments which are keyed to the solving of innovative problems and to the imposition of innovative solutions. Other subunits such as financial or accounting departments are more keyed to the solving of routine problems (budget-allocations, investment decisions, etc.) and to the imposition of routine solutions. The presence of such subunits in an organization and the nature of the distribution of power and resources among routinely oriented subunits and innovatively oriented subunits might affect the amount of conflict during adaptive processes and bias the organization towards a certain type of solution.

Levels of Authority

A "level of authority" is defined as a formally delimited zone of responsibility along the organizational hierarchy, bounded at the lower limits by delegation of authority to a lower level and at the upper limits by the necessity of "reporting to" a higher level in the organization. Because of the kind of specialization that inevitably takes place in formal organizations, it clearly becomes increasingly difficult for any single person to co-ordinate and supervise organizational activities. The delegation and multiplication of the loci of authority is the result. While this process is clearly necessary for the continued functioning of the organization, it is not without dysfunctional implications as, for example, the literature on informal organization would suggest.[9] A frequent point made in such literature is that formal channels quite often do not represent the best way of getting things done. It is further argued here that levels of authority, like subunit specialization, serve to differentiate and that this differentiation provides structural bases for political differences and conflicts within the organization.

On these grounds, we hypothesize that the greater the number of levels of authority in an organization, the greater will be the amount of conflict during adaptive processes. We also hypothesize that the greater the number of levels of authority in an organization, the greater will be the tendency for power relations in the organization to be based on the wielding of low-legitimacy types of power, since the finer the distinctions between levels of authority, the less legitimate power each level will have to control the level immediately beneath it and the more freedom it will have to evade decisions made by the next-highest level.

9. See, for example, Gouldner (1954); for a general review of the literature, see Blau and Scott (1962).

When legitimate power is thus deflated, it is hypothesized that non-legitimate power will be used as an alternative.

Ratio of Managers and Supervisors to Total Personnel

A manager or supervisor is defined as an incumbent of the organization charged with the responsibility of overseeing and co-ordinating the work of others in the organization. Increases in the proportion of managerial or supervisory staff to total personnel are generally closely related to the degree of differentiation in terms of subunits and levels of authority. As in the case of the two preceding measures of differentiation, it is also argued here that as the percentage of managers and supervisors increases, the number of persons within the organization having a potential or actual interest in the adaptive process increases and, in this sense, increases the possibility of political disagreement or conflict.

Managers and supervisors can also increase the number of adaptive processes which an organization must go through by generating new problem situations and exacerbating relatively minor ones for the purposes of advancing their own careers within the organization.

Program-Specification in Organizations

Programs are defined as the mechanisms or rules in terms of which an attempt is made to give direction to organizational activity (see March and Simon, 1958:142). Specification refers to the variable extent to which such programs are detailed or spelled out. The following constitute three major areas of organizational programming: (a) Role-programming, or the formalization of duties and responsibilities as in sets of job specifications; (b) Output-programming, or the formal delineation of steps through which raw materials pass in the course of becoming the organization's outputs. The automobile assembly line is a particularly good example of how such programming can be built into organizational technology. Such programming of outputs can also be observed in very different kinds of organizations. In a university, for example, the earning of a Bachelor's degree precedes the Master's degree which in turn may precede the Doctor of Philosophy degree. (c) Communication-programming, or the formal specification of the structure, content, and timing of communication within the organization.

For example, certain organizations specify these processes very closely through the establishment of standard letters or memoranda, the use and timing of which is specified by code numbers.

It would seem plausible to assert that all but the simplest organizations attempt some programming of their activities. To suggest, however, that the areas of organizational activity are subject to programming is not to suggest that the *degree* of specification in such programs is in any way necessarily the same for all organizations. Rather, it is contended that the degree of specification in organizational programming is highly variable from organization to organization and that this variability has certain implications for political conflict in organizations. In this connection, it is suggested that highly specified programs tend to provide yet another structural support for the entrenchment of intraorganizational differences. For example, the presence of a highly specified output program can generate change-resistant arguments such as "let's do it by the book." Close programming of role specifications may be viewed as somewhat analogous to subunit specialization insofar as the structural maintenance of political diversity is concerned. Finally, the close programming of communication networks may lead to omitting from communications considerable content, the relevance of which is not immediately definable in formal terms.

Thus, the hypothesis offered is that the greater the degree of program-specification in an organization, the greater will be the amount of conflict during adaptive processes. We would also hypothesize that the greater the degree of program-specification, the greater the tendency for power relations to be based on legitimate types of authority, since a high degree of programming implies that legitimate methods of regulating the organization are well entrenched in its structure.

Technology

Although the conceptualization of technology as an aspect of organizational structure may present some problems, it is nonetheless clear that it is an element of organizations which can be politicized during adaptive processes.

There would appear to be two relevant dimensions for conceptualizing organizational technology. The first, referred to as the technical specificity–technical diffuseness dimension, deals with the range of products which the technical processes of the organization yield. The other dimension is the speed at which the technology which the organization uses in its production process is changing.

It is not contended that the relative specificity or diffuseness of an organization's technology directly affects the amount of conflict which will be generated in the organization during adaptive processes. It is contended, however, that this aspect of technology will have an indirect effect on conflict during adaptive processes through its effect on the structure of the organization. In this connection, there is some evidence to suggest that organizations which have more specific technologies also tend to have more subunits, levels of authority, etc.[10]

Since hypotheses have already been presented relating each of these structural variables to amounts of conflict during adaptive processes, we now hypothesize that the more specific the organization's technology, the greater will be the amount of conflict during adaptive processes, since the organization is more likely to have structural arrangements which predispose it to conflict.

We maintain, however, that the relationship between the rate of technological change and the amount of conflict during adaptive processes is much more direct. Since a stable technology implies that technological adaptations are made infrequently, we hypothesize that when a problem situation does arise, a greater amount of conflict will obtain in organizations with slowly changing technological processes than in organizations in rapidly developing technological fields. The underlying assumption is that the more frequently change is coped with, the more is learned about controlling conflict-generation.

Thus, it is hypothesized that the greatest amount of conflict will be found in technically specific organizations with stable technological processes, while the least amount of conflict will be found in technically diffuse organizations with rapidly changing technological processes.

It also seems likely that the specific types of power relations which obtain in organizations during adaptive processes may be related to their technologies. Because a rapidly changing technology presumably requires a greater reliance on technical expertise than does a stable

10. For another discussion of performance programs in organizations see March and Simon (1958).

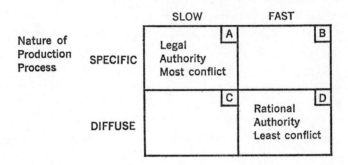

technological process, it is hypothesized that during adaptive processes power relations in organizations operating in rapidly changing technological fields will be characterized by the use of rational authority, while power relations in organizations in stable technological fields will be characterized by the use of legal authority.

It is hypothesized that Cell A will be characterized by the greatest amount of conflict during adaptive process and by the use and predominance of legal, as opposed to rational, authority. Cell D will be characterized by the least conflict during adaptive processes and by the use and predominance of rational, as opposed to legal, authority. Cells B and C represent technological states which, we are hypothesizing, will lead to intermediate amounts of conflict and to the use of both types of legitimate authority.

Throughout the paper, organizations have been described as political systems with special reference to decision-making during adaptive processes. For the purposes of analysis an arbitrary "beginning" and "end" have been assigned to the adaptive process in the form of the arising of a problem situation and the finding of a solution. In reality, the adaptive process is most probably constant and circular in that each solution "feeds back" into the organization in the form of new problems which require attention.

The nature of the problem situation was looked on as the first major input into the adaptive process. If the problem has been faced and dealt with by the organization before, we have postulated that it will generate amounts of conflict and types of power relations quite different from a problem situation that is completely new to the organization.

The second major set of variables that was considered to affect the unfolding of the adaptive process involves four aspects of an organization's environmental relations and two aspects of its internal structure. These variables were hypothesized to determine "path-selection," that is, the nature of the solution or solutions which an organization will attempt to impose on a problematic situation. It was postulated that organizations in "low-threat," "moderate-threat," and "high-threat" contexts will each follow different decision paths in dealing with problem situations.

The third major set of variables which affect the adaptive process is concerned with aspects of organizational structure that can become "politicized" during adaptive processes. It was hypothesized that these variables do not determine path-selection but do determine the nature of behavior within each path; that is, the amount of conflict and the modes of power relations which obtain during the processual development towards a solution. A set of hypotheses was developed relating various structural characteristics of organizations to these dependent variables.

For heuristic reasons, a set of stages of the adaptive process has been included in the theoretical argument. No attempt has been made, however, to develop propositions relating structural variables to "stage-specific" amounts of conflict or to "stage-specific" modes of power relations.

REFERENCES

Archibald, R. D., and R. L. Villoria.
    1967   Network Based Management Systems. John Wiley and Sons.
Bennis, Warren.
    1966   Changing Organizations. Boston: McGraw-Hill.
Bennis, Warren, *et al.* (eds.).
    1962   The Planning of Change. New York: Holt, Rinehart and Winston.
Berghe, Pierre L. van den.
    1963   "Dialetic and Functionalism." American Sociological Review 28:695–705.

Blau, Peter M., and W. Richard Scott.
 1962   Formal Organizations: A Comparative Approach. San Francisco: Chandler Publishing Co.
Brown, W.
 1960   Explorations in Management. New York: John Wiley and Sons.
Burns, Tom.
 1961–62 "Micropolitics: Mechanisms of Institutional Change." Administration Science Quarterly 6:257–281.
 1962   "Des Fins et des Moyens dans la Direction des Entreprises." Sociologie du Travail 4:209–229.
Chamberlain, N.
 1960   Management in Motion. New Haven: Labor and Management Center, Yale University.
Cyert, R. M., W. R. Dill, and J. G. March.
 1958–59 "The Role of Expectations in Business Decision Making." Administrative Science Quarterly 3:307–340.
Cyert, R. M., and J. G. March.
 1959   "A Behavioral Theory of Organizational Objectives." In Mason Haire (ed.), Modern Organization Theory. New York: John Wiley.
 1963   A Behavioral Theory of the Firm. Englewood Cliffs, N.J.: Prentice-Hall.
Dahl, Robert A.
 1963   Modern Political Analysis. Englewood Cliffs, N.J.: Prentice-Hall.
Deutsch, Karl.
 1963   The Nerves of Government. Glencoe: The Free Press.
Etzioni, A.
 1961   A Comparative Analysis of Complex Organizations. New York: The Free Press.
Evan, William M.
 1966   "Organizational Lag." Human Organizations 25:1(Spring): 51–53.
Gore, W. J.
 1956   "Decision Making in Federal Field Offices." Public Administration Review 16:281–290.
Gouldner, Alvin.
 1954   Patterns of Industrial Bureaucracy. Glencoe: The Free Press.
Hage, Jerald.
 1965–66 "An Axiomatic Theory of Organizations." Administrative Science Quarterly 10:284–320.
Jacques, E.
 1951   The Changing Culture of the Factory. London: Tavistock Publications.

Kaplan, A. D. H., J. B. Dirlam, and R. F. Lanzillotti.
 1958   Pricing in Big Business. Washington: Brookings Institution.
Lundberg, C.
 1964   "Administrative Decisions: A Scheme for Analysis." In W. J.
         Gore and J. W. Dyson (eds.), The Making of Decisions. Glen-
         coe: The Free Press.
March, James G.
 1962   "The Business Firm as a Political Coalition." Journal of Politics
         24:672.
March, James G., and Herbert A. Simon.
 1958   Organizations. New York: John Wiley and Sons.
Melman, Seymour.
 1958   Decision Making and Productivity. Oxford: Blackwell.
Moore, W. E.
 1962   The Conduct of the Corporation. New York: Random House.
 1963   Man, Time and Society. New York: Wiley.
Morison, Elting E.
 1962   "A Case Study of Innovation." Pp. 592–605 in Warren G.
         Bennis *et al.* (eds.), *The Planning of Change*. New York: Holt,
         Rinehart and Winston.
Parsons, Talcott.
 1956   "Suggestions for a Sociological Approach to the Theory of
         Organizations." Administrative Science Quarterly 1:64.
Rice, A. K.
 1963   The Enterprise and its Environment. London: Tavistock Pub-
         lications.
Selznick, Phillip.
 1949   T.V.A. and the Grass Roots. Berkeley, University of California
         Press.
Starbuck, W. H.
 1965   "Organizational Growth and Development." In J. G. March
         (ed.), Handbook of Organizations. Chicago: Rand McNally.
Weber, Max.
 1947   The Theory of Social and Economic Organization. In A. M.
         Henderson and Talcott Parsons (trans.) and Talcott Parsons
         (ed.). Glencoe: The Free Press and Falcon's Wing Press.
 1956   Wirtshaft and Geselleschaft. 4th ed. Tuebingen.
Woodward, Joan.
 1958   Management and Technology. London: H.M.S.O.
 1965   Industrial Organization: Theory and Practice. London, Oxford
         University Press.

Three Problems for Future Consideration

DAVID W. BRITT
WILLIAM P. SMITH

We would like to address ourselves initially to Harvey and Mills's discussion of adaptive process modes. The author suggests that the adaptive process has two basic constituents: a variably problematic situation and a solution arrived at by the decision-making centers of the organization to adapt to the situation. Both situation and solution were dichotomized on a routineness-innovativeness dimension and cross-tabulated to form a fourfold table. The initial statement concerning the relationship between variations in situations and solutions is that there is a tendency or strain toward innovative situations being countered by innovative solutions and routine situations being countered by routine solutions. In other words, we should find most of the cases within the table falling on the diagonal. Following this, it is suggested that other variables might be introduced to explain the occurrence of cases which do not fall on the diagonal, that is, whether some organizations are more likely to choose a routine solution no matter what the nature of the problem situation (within limits). Contextual variables (representing environmental pressures) and the organizational variables (representing degree of formality of the structure) are collapsed into the degree of contextual threat variable in order to provide a tool for analyzing the deviant, off-diagonal cases. There are three problems with this analysis that may deserve further consideration.

Initially, the four contextual variables (relative size, relative age, market-situation competitiveness, and rate of change in the technological sector) are perhaps deducible from a statement concerning environmental pressure (as the authors suggest), but each of the variables suggests a relationship of sufficient complexity to warrant further individual investigation. The problem which must be avoided in the collapsing of a number of variables into a more abstract one is the inclusion of variables whose relationship to the dependent variable of interest—in this case, solution choice—changes for different values to a degree that makes the placement of particular cases questionable. For example, relative ages of the combatants in a market situation where they are fighting for control of the available resources would seem to have varying effects, depending on the total ages involved. If age does bear a positive relationship to the degree of the organization's knowledge of the environment, then with a low rate of fairly constant change in the environment, there might not be too much more to learn past a certain age. Hence a diminishing effect would be observed as the organizations approach senility. But who is to say that environments change at a relatively low and constant rate? With a higher or somewhat fluctuating rate of change, the backlog of available solutions built up by an older organization might even prove to be a hindrance to adapting to the environment—thus making the relationship, given certain conditions, curvilinear. A similar argument could possibly be made for relative organizational size, if size gives some indication of the degree to which organizations are able to mobilize resources to help in an interorganizational contest, and if the larger organization found itself increasingly hindered (relative to the smaller organizations) by governmental constraints on the mobilization of resources.

A somewhat different problem is confronted if the distinction between the variables in the original cross-tabulation and the variables used to explain off-diagonal cases (contextual threat) breaks down. We are thinking here particularly of the rate of technological change variable, (although the same argument appears to apply for some of the other contextual and environmental variables included under threat). Rate of technological change has been used as a correlate of environmental uncertainty or complexity, and what seems to be the intent of situational innovativeness. Incidentally, we do not believe that it makes any difference whether the relationship between rate of change and the other variables is spurious or not: the main problem is having the variables related strongly to the cross-tabulated dimensions. In this particular case, to suggest that the contemporaneous rate of technological change is inversely related to the probability of opting for a routine solution is like trying to argue that a case falls off the diagonal because it should fall on the diagonal. Actually, the resolution may be quite simple—if the crucial variable is experience. The temporal separation of contemporary and past rates of technological change (or changes in market competitiveness), although presenting some other problems, would seem partially to resolve the present one. This strategy, coupled perhaps with the ommission or further specification of the age and size variables, enables such reformulations as the greater the rate of technological change which has been successfully dealt with in the past, the greater the probability of finding adequate existing routines. As an aside, the notion of success or effectiveness might be problematic; one possibility might be to use as a criterion or base line the proportion of resources controlled by that particular organization (after Yuchtman and Seashore).

A third problem comes to the fore when discussing moderate threatening contexts—a problem analogous to that of status inconsistency. The question which should be asked is, what are the consequences of having organizations which have all moderate scores classified with those that have some extreme scores which average out? Using the present framework, would an organization, for example, that was relatively old and large, yet in a competitive market situation, resolve situational problems in the same way as a moderately old, large organization in a moderately competitive market situation? One might predict that in the former case the amount of pressure on the organization is greater than in the latter consistently moderate case, since the competitiveness is probably forcing the organization toward increasingly large-scale changes.

The other section to which we would like to address ourselves is Harvey and Mills's discussion of variations in conflict and power relations during the adaptive process. This section we found interesting but somewhat confusing. Because of limited space however, we shall have to confine ourselves to presenting in brief one of the cases with which he deals and then asking some questions which seem to overlap the other areas of variables which he considers in this session.

Discussing the relationship between innovativeness of the problem environment and variations in conflict between subunits, the authors suggest that a variable of considerable importance is the degree of implied threat to the established resource-sharing patterns of the organization. Innovative problem situations are postulated as being positively related to the degree of resource-sharing threat; the latter variable is then said to be positively related to the amount of conflict between subunits. The authors then deduced from this relationship a positive relationship between degree of innovativeness of the problem situation and the probability of conflict between subunits. They suggest, further, that the degree of conflict experienced between subunits, given an innovative problem situation, will increase under large-scale changes, that is, those which have far-ranging effects within the organization. At this point we would ask two questions: first, how does the scale of the change affect the probability of inter-subunit conflict; does it affect the probability of conflict through the resource-sharing threat variable that supposedly mediates the innovativeness of the environment effect or does it have some other processual relationship to the probability of conflict? Second, is it possible to conceive of other ways in which the degree of innovativeness of the problem situation might affect the probability of subunit conflict, aside from its relationship through the threat to established resource-sharing patterns? The second question leads to consideration of the hypothesized relationship between innovativeness of the problem situation and the probability of use of some form of legitimate power as a control device within the organization. Here the link suggested by the authors is one involving the probability of presence within the organization of some relevant guidelines for handling the problems presented by the innovativeness of this situation; if relevant guidelines are present, then presumably legitimate power would predominate as the main control device. Also, the degree of innovativeness of the problem situation is supposedly inversely related to the probability of obtaining relevant guidelines; the simple deduction here then is that there is an inverse relationship between the degree of innovativeness of the problem situation and the use of legitimate power as a control device. This relationship too is supposedly increased by the presence of large-scale changes: again we would ask in what ways scale affects the probability of the use of legitimate power; does it have an effect only through the former variable of presence of relevant guidelines within the organization? In other words is scale inversely related to the probability of finding relevant guidelines? Second, could innovativeness be related to the probability of use of legitimate power as a control device

FIGURE 1

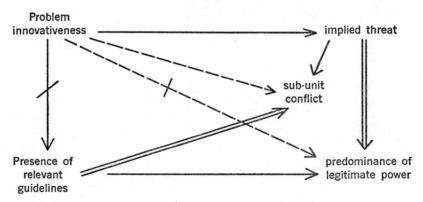

Postulates from the original model are indicated by single solid lines.
Deductions from the original model are indicated by single broken lines.
Possible elaborations are indicated by double solid lines.
Slashed lines denote inverse relationships; unslashed lines denote
   positive relationships.

in some way other than that suggested by the authors? These questions
dovetail somewhat into a consideration of perhaps more of the paths
than the authors have considered. For instance, could innovativeness
and degree of scale affect both the established resource-sharing patterns within the organization and the probability of presence of relevant
guidelines within the organization, and both of these latter variables
affect both conflict and the use of legitimate power as a control device?
(See Figure 1).

Another problem with respect to conflict as a dependent variable
arises when we consider the likely relationship between choice of an
innovative solution and amount of conflict. In discussing specific hypotheses relating conflict to organizational variables, Harvey and Mills
suggest that innovative problem situations are more likely than routine
problem situations to create conflict, but do not clearly state the same
relationship for innovative *vs.* routine solution choices. However, the
same relationship is strongly implied when the authors state that redefinition is not a step in routine solution—thus an opportunity for
conflict which exists for innovative solutions does not appear for routine
solutions. And in fact, the very concept of routine implies that much of

the potential for conflict, present in the unfamiliar innovative process, is absent.

However, some of the conditions said to create conflict would seem to predispose the organization to selection of routine solutions—and therefore lessen conflict. Thus an organization with many subunits, many levels of authority, a high ratio of supervisors, and a high degree of program-specification seems likely not only to have entrenched interests among subunits (which creates conflict), but also to have established routines. Indeed, it seems reasonable to assume that some of the characteristics listed for "low threat" organizations, such as high relative size and age, and formal communication networks, should be directly correlated with the conflict-generating characteristics such as number of subunits, etc.

This contradiction might be resolved by consideration of the relationship between organizational variables and conflict for innovative *vs.* routine solutions separately. For example, an organization with a large number of subunits might ordinarily choose routine solutions (because they are available), but when it does choose an innovative solution, it may experience greater conflict than an organization with fewer subunits. The same or the opposite relationship might be obtained for routine solutions; the important point is that the solution choice itself is related to amount of conflict, and that the conflict-related organizational variables may operate clearly only if the variance in conflict due to solution choice is somehow removed from consideration.

Finally, the authors make a (to us) startling suggestion about the capacity of an organization to learn how to control the generation of conflict. They address themselves specifically to change in technological processes, suggesting that the more frequently change is coped with, the more is learned about controlling conflict-generation. There are two observations we would like to make about this statement. First, there seems no reason to limit such a statement to technological change, at least in the context of this paper. It takes very little imagination to modify this statement to read, "The more frequently any given aspect of the organization or its environment produces conflict, the more is learned about controlling conflict-generation." Such a statement has profound implications for the entire theoretical edifice of Harvey and Mills.

Second, the notion of controlling conflict-generation, though intriguing, is not sufficiently spelled out for any serious examination of its consequences to be undertaken. Surely the concept of routine solution may be taken as a form of conflict-management or prevention; indeed, one point of view, from the social psychological literature, is that norms and roles represent attempts to reduce open interpersonal conflict. Perhaps the best approach to this problem would be to examine co-ordinating or executive structures within the organization when dealing with questions of control of conflict, while looking at more insular, specialized sub-units for conflict-generation. But the question as to what conflict-controlling devices might be needs attention prior to any such analysis.

6

Political Economy:
A Framework for Comparative Analysis

MAYER N. ZALD

The publication of the *Handbook of Organizations* (March 1965) confirmed what many students of complex organizations already knew: although a vast number of studies, concepts, and approaches have been developed for the study of organizations, there is little apparent unity among them. The absence of unity is in part a function of the number of "basic" and "applied" disciplines involved—e.g., psychology, sociology, political science, and economics; industrial management, operations and systems analysis, public administration, etc. As Victor Thompson (1966) has emphatically noted, the disunity is also a function of the absence of integrative frameworks guiding and giving focus to the disparate strands of research.

One such integrative framework is provided by the political-economy approach to the study of organizations. Starting from analogies to the nation-state and national economies, the political-economy framework focuses on the intersection of the polity structure and political life of organizations with the economy and economic life within organizations.

The political-economy approach to the study of organizations was originally developed to help explain the direction and processes of organizational change. It proved, I think, very fruitful in explaining the

221

transformation of the Young Men's Christian Association in America over the last one-hundred-twenty years and the more recent transformation of the YMCA of Metropolitan Chicago (Zald, 1970). The advantages, as compared with other theories, of the political-economy approach for the study of major organizational change have been stated elsewhere (Zald, 1968) and need not be detailed here.

In brief, the political-economy approach focuses on proximal internal and external determinates of change; thus it retains focus. It links change to organizational structure *and* goals as opposed to leaping from internal problems to leadership decisions; thus, it spells out a rather complete causal and contingent chain. Because it assumes that organizational character shapes decision premises, it allows room for both "rational" and "irrational" decision premises to enter into organization choices; thus, it avoids the biases of rationalistic and irrationalistic approaches to organizational change.

But this approach also has the advantage of being useful as a *middle-range, integrative,* theoretical framework for the *comparative* study of organizations. The framework is of the "middle range" because it assumes many of the assertions or concepts of social-system analysis and the general theory of action. Instead of dealing with "universals" and completely general propositions, it attempts to develop concepts, propositions, and variables that will order a range of specific organizational forms and processes.

The approach used here provides an *integrative* framework because it specifies the interrelation of a range of organizational dimensions and types of organizations. Some of these dimensions have been central concerns of other students of organizations, but their interrelation with other important dimensions has been left unspecified. It is also an integrative framework, because it brings within one over-all framework and language system a wider range of *types* of organizations than is usual, e.g., it is not restricted to bureaucratic organizations or businesses, etc.

Because the framework states the range of variation between organizations on crucial (in the sense of pervasive and powerful) variables, it is useful for comparative work. It is useful for the comparative study of major types of organization *and* for the comparative study of organizations *within* major types. For example, government departments may all have major bureaucratic components yet differ significantly on dimensions contained within the framework.

This paper emphasizes the usefulness of the framework for integrative and comparative purposes. It is a "working paper," for, as will become apparent, I am still developing the concepts and analytic distinction.

The Basic Concept

In its most generic sense, political economy is the study of the interplay of power, the goals of power-wielders, and productive exchange systems (Cf. Buchanan, 1964). As used here, political economy is neutral to the question of the market's value as a mechanism for registering preferences, producing goods, and distributing income. In its nineteenth-century meaning, of course, political economy referred to that system in which politics or government was so ordered as to encourage the free play of market forces in determining the allocation of resources. In its more general sense, however, political economy refers only to the relations between political and economic structures and processes.

When applied to nations, the term refers to description and analysis of the interplay between the institutions of government and law, fortified by coercive power, and the economy, or the system of producing and exchanging goods. James Willard Hurst's monumental *Law and Economic Growth: The Legal History of the Lumber Industry in Wisconsin, 1836 to 1915* (1964), for example, relates how government's initial desire for rapid economic development brought about legal policies for disposal of public lands in Wisconsin, how the laws of property and contract led to certain patterns of private usage and, finally, how changing goals and conceptions of the public good influenced regulations of property-usage and the use of state money (conservation) in relationship to this property.

As this capsule summary of Hurst indicates, political economy is more than the study of a power structure as it affects economic structure. Also involved is a study of the *ends* desired and enshrined in the economy and polity. In these terms laissez faire economics was a normative system of political economy which, given the advantages of the division of labor, with profit as an incentive, strove to maximize

over-all production of material goods. By allowing market forces to
determine profit and production, society would capitalize on the benefits of the division of labor.

Both in political science and sociology, conceptualization (although
not empirical study) of the polity has focused on this goal-determining
aspect of government and the political process. For instance, Norton
Long (1962) points to the value of analyzing community constitutions
that is, to the study of community rule and the ethos or values of
dominant groups as a way of answering the central questions raised
by Aristotle for the study of politics.

In sociology Talcott Parsons has also focused on the political process
as the major arena of goal-determination and allocation for a society.
His relevant point is that study of an organization's political economy
must be concerned with the goal-shaping aspects of goals as these are
embodied in dominant groups. *Whose* goals are maximized and with
what consequences must be a central concern.

Beyond a study of an organization's goals and powers, what else is
implied in taking a political-economic approach to organizations? There
must be a form of institutional analysis focusing on the interaction of
values and control groups with the supply of resources and demand for
services of clients and funders. The term economy focuses both on the
internal allocation of men, money, and facilities and on the external
supply of resources and clients. Internally, of course, the mechanisms
for allocating men, facilities, and money are carried out by traditional
rules of thumb, intergroup bargaining, and hierarchical assignments.
The internal economy of no organization can be described as functioning precisely according to pure market processes. (This empirical fact
makes it harder to separate the internal political processes of organization from those of the internal economy.)

The term economy should not be conceived narrowly as limited to the
exchange of money for services. Rather what is exchanged is a number
of goods, or incentives, that bind men to each other. Following Barnard
(1938:134–181) and derivatively Wilson and Clark (1961), a wide
range of incentives can be explicated. Men are bound to organizations
by promises of values fulfilled and promises of friendship and prestige,
as well as by monetary contracts for the exchange of goods and services.

That this framework deals with the major political and economic factors in an organization does not rule out attention to many traditional concerns of the sociology of organization; professions and professional socialization, role relations and role conflict, and even the "fit" between personality and role can be included. Basing this analysis on political economy, however, suggests that these more traditional concerns must be subordinated and intermeshed with the dominant concern for the political-economic interactions and structure. For example, the attitudes and values of professional staff in an organization are not important as indicators of satisfaction, or morale, or even as a reflection of organizational ideology: they are only important as they articulate with the polity and economy. In a sense then, the political-economy approach abstracts for analysis two key sectors of a social system. Processes of socialization and pattern-maintenance are not dismissed but are treated only as they affect the political economy.

If the approach is to be more than a guiding metaphor, it is necessary to elaborate its major components. What are the major political and economic processes and structures of organization? How do they relate to each other? What is the variation among organizations on each of the central dimensions? What are some of the propositions about organizations that can be generated from these concepts and dimensions?

ORGANIZATIONAL CONSTITUTIONS

Just as nation-states and primitive societies have constitutions, so do complex organizations. These constitutions guide (constrain) the operation of the ongoing political economy. An organization's constitution is its fundamental normative structure. The constitution of an organization or, for that matter, of any enduring social system, is a set of agreements and understandings which define the limits and goals of the group (collectivity) as well as the responsibilities and rights of participants standing in different relations to it.

The term "constitution" is often used in both a narrower and a broader sense than we use it here. Narrowly, it refers to a specific, usually written, set of agreements as to the structure and rights of actors (collective and individual). Yet constitutions need not be written and written constitutions need not be binding. Broadly, the constitution sometimes refers to a total pattern of organization and the relationship among its parts (cf. Stinchcombe, 1960; Bakke, 1959). In the sense we use it, the constitution of an organization is more limited than the pattern of social organization since it refers to a conceptually defined normative order; the pattern of social organization contains elements which are neither normative nor conceptually defined. By constitution we will refer to a historic and conceptually defined normative order.

Organizational constitutions regulate behavior in at least four normative sectors: incentive exchanges, the range of discretion of positions, organizational "ownership," and collective goals and means. First, constitutional norms vary according to the norms binding individuals into the organization (that is, according to the "contract" or terms of exchange existing between organizations and their individual members). These norms of exchange determine the amount of energy, time, and commitment that the organization can expect from different members. They also determine the extent to which organizations have discretion over wide ranges of members' behavior.

"Incentive theory" and "compliance theory" have their major interest in the variations among organizations in the terms of exchange. Wilson and Clark (1961) distinguished between material, solidary, and purposive organizations in terms of three different kinds of incentives that bring about three different kinds of commitments. Etzioni's (1961) categories (coercive, utilitarian, and normative) overlap Wilson and Clark's and have much the same focus. An organization has a fragile polity if its norms of exchange are fundamentally weak and non-binding.

Second, constitutional norms specify the range of discretion and the decision responsibilities of officers, groups, and units. Rights and responsibilities are deeply embedded in different kinds of functional, territorial, and hierarchical units. The federated-corporate distinction may be the broadest distinction in this regard, but even within corporate structures, questions of functional responsibility, autonomy, and levels of centralization may become basic constitutional parameters having great import for the polity's operation. It is quite clear that many crucial changes in modern society involve these constitutional norms regarding the rights and responsibilities of different groups. To cite only one widely known example, the range and rights of management as contrasted with unions involve the central constitutional norms of business corporations.

Third, constitutional norms are deeply embedded in the relationship of an organization to the society of which it is a part. These norms involve such basic premises as: To whom is the organization responsible? Under what conditions? The norms linking these organizations to society may undergo change during crisis periods. For example, an organization's right to use business property for profit may be modified in wartime. Moreover, the norms linking an organization to the larger society may be relatively unstated or even unknown except during such periods of crisis as wars and disasters (Thompson and Hawkes, 1962).

Finally, constitutional norms specify the focuses of collective action (that is, concerns falling inside or outside the zone of indifference of the organization and its subgroups). These include goals, target groups (clientele), and technologies (means). The clarity, specificity, and breadth of these focuses of collective action become involved in the ongoing political life of the organization as groups contend for their actual definition.

It should be clear that constitutional norms differ from organization to organization, not only substantively, but also in their import and intensity. Some organizations may change clientele groups or even goals with but little consequence if the former have few attachments to the latter.

Constitutional norms set limits for behavior, and it may be rare for participants even to be aware of the norms. One way to illustrate a constitutional norm is to ask what would happen if it were violated. For instance, what would happen if an NAACP leader asked his members to support the Ku Klux Klan? Stunned disbelief and accusations of insanity! (When Reverend Bevel said he would support James Earl Ray, the first response of many was that he was having a nervous breakdown.)

Constitutional norms set zones of expectation (zones of indifference). These indifference sectors may be broad or narrow. However, all zones of indifference need not be constitutional. If, for instance, the zone of indifference is merely habitual, few sanctions will be invoked by its violation; little power will be mobilized for its protection.

Empirically one recognizes constitutional norms by two kinds of indicators. Negatively, violation of basic norms leads to withdrawal of resource-commitment (including members) and/or major conflict, accompanied by *perceptions* of violations of major norms. Positively, basic norms are indicated by their reaffirmation and articulation by spokesmen for the collectivity.

Many comparative typologies of organizations are constructed out of the polar extremes of each of the constitutional dimensions. Numerous typologies are founded on basic differences in the terms of exchange (Wilson and Clark, 1961; Etzioni, 1961; Warriner, 1965; Gordon and Babchuck, 1959), difference in goals (Zald, 1963; Bidwell and Vreeland, 1963), rights and responsibility of groups and units (Sills, 1957). Also, they have been constructed out of conditions of responsibility (Blau and Scott, 1962), and the common sense classification of "public-private."

There is no special merit in showing that these constitutional dimensions have had traditional value in typological exercise. (All that would necessarily demonstrate is the ability to construct a concept of a constitution out of the history of sociological research. In fact, the dimensions were developed over time by pondering inductively-intuitively basic organizational "agreements" needed for an organization to function—they were not "derived" from a more general system framework. It is possible that they could be.) What is important to note is that the four dimensions are addressed to four fundamental problems of social systems:

(1) The motivational bases of individual commitment or participation in collectivities. (And what are the consequences of differences in these bases?) (2) The distribution of decision prerogative with the organization—the internal power-distribution. (3) The distribution of decision prerogative between the organization and the outside world— the external power relation. (4) The collective focus of the organization—what its work shall be.

I will not argue that there might not be other dimensions of constitution. I will argue that analysis of organizational constitutions will always include at least these four dimensions.

Note that organizations exhibiting all combinations of positions on all constitutional dimensions are unlikely to be found. For instance, because federated constitutions allow independent spheres of action, organizations are unlikely both to have federated constitutions (internal-polity dimension) and to be constitutionally responsible to a single major external decision center (external-polity dimension). Or again, organizations based on solidary incentive norms are unlikely to have also highly differentiated task norms, because such differentiation of task destroys or interferes with cohesion required for maintenance of solidary norms.

The congruence of organizational constitutional dimensions deserves further elaboration. Another topic deserving elaboration is the "sources" of basic norms. Some, for instance, will be rooted in the social structures of society. More important for our task is the implication of constitutional norms in the ongoing operation of the political economy.

THE OPERATING POLITICAL ECONOMY

The operating power system and the operating economy of an organization are constrained by and contain constitutional norms. We consider the power system the actual means by which decisions are influenced. There need not be much difference between the constitution and the actual power system, but it is a fundamental postulate of sociology and political science that, in a changing social system, there is likely to be a continuous state of tension and adjustment between them.

The actual power system is the patterned use of social influence in an organization. Use of the term "polity" or "power system" indicates that we wish to include more actors in this pattern than simply those who formally make and execute decisions. In its more inclusive form, a polity refers to the whole web of groups and individuals, internal or external to an organization, that possess resources to sanction decisions.[1]

1. Following the usage current in political science, we use the term polity to refer only to those groups or positions having an active and somewhat organized influence on the process of decision-making. Certainly, upper level staff are included within the boundary of a polity. Also included would be groups holding major sanctions, such as unions or professional associations. In the national polity individual voters (i.e., those who register preferences relatively passively, intermittently, and without direct interaction with decision-makers) are the outer edge of the polity, but interest groups which speak for an articulate mass interest are certainly part of the polity. Similarly, for organizations, individual workers and/or stockholders become important to the political process as their interests aggregate to affect decisions, and so do the aggregations of interests of suppliers of major inputs (e.g., labor, capital, raw materials, facilities).

Polity analyses examine the institutionalized and authoritative patterns of decision control as well as the less regular and even "illegitimate," but systematic, influence processes. Analysis of polity focuses on the ends of decisions that are made, the channels to utilizing influence, the characteristics of influence-holders, and the distribution of power.

Where the polity is the power-and-control system of an organization, the economy is the productive exchange system of an organization. By definition organizations are less inclusive than societies. They have relative specific "products" or services which they offer in exchange for support by members of society. Just as an organizational polity has an internal and external aspect, so too, does an organization's economy. Although it is somewhat unusual to discuss an economy *within* an organization (Parsons would call it the "adaptive system"), our usage is consistent with its usage in the phrase "political economy" and is, we think, easily justified.

It will be convenient to analyze political economies into the structure processes and interaction of four broad sectors: external political environment, economic environment, internal polity structure and process, and internal economic structure and process. Figure 1 illustrates these sectors.

The over-all framework is undergirded by a very general and very weak assumption—that processes originating in any one of the sectors may impinge in some organizational cases on any of the other sectors.

We assume that the internal polity affects and/or is affected by the internal economic structure and process. And we also assume that some organizations to some extent can affect the external political and economic environments in which they are involved. However, for many there are some elements of both economic and political environment that are highly impervious to organizational action. For example, the economist's pure competitive market (homogeneous products, many suppliers, many buyers, low barriers to entry), leaves no room for an organization to affect the market and its position in it. Similarly, governmental constraints (an external political process) on an organization's internal economy through safety laws and regulations are, in the short run, impervious to action. In the long run, of course, organizations may coalesce to attempt to change such regulations.

Although in this last example the external polity effects the internal

FIGURE 1.

MAJOR COMPONENTS OF POLITICAL ECONOMY

	Environment Structure and Process	Internal Structure and Process
POLITY	Associations of similar organizations (trade associations)	Power-distribution and major value constellations
	Relationship with major suppliers and buyers of factor inputs	Demand-aggregation
	Regulatory agents	Succession system
	Indirect parties	
ECONOMY	Characteristics of factor "markets" (labor, capital, etc.)	Allocation rules Accounting-information systems
	"Raw materials" supply	Incentive system
	Characteristics of demand and clientele "Industry structure"	Task- and technology-related unit differentiation

economy, a complete behavioral chain would have external-polity processes affecting internal polity, which transmits rules and allocates resources to the internal economy. That is, power-holders could (and sometimes do), refuse to comply with governmental regulation, thus eliminating a constraint over the internal economy. Interconnections between environmental and internal processes are elaborated below.

Political and Economic Environments

There are both distinctive differences and a degree of overlap in consequences between the environmental political and economic relations. The distinctive difference is that political relations involve attempts to influence the decision premises of the parties to the relationships. Organizations, in attempting to achieve ends, form external alliances, curry favor, and conform to the requirements of agents having greater power. On the other hand, strictly economic relations in the environment involve no attempt to change organizational goals; instead the willingness to buy a product or sell labor represents a registering of preferences. Only as these preferences are aggregated by the decision centers do they influence goals and operating procedures (e.g., the buyer shopping for a Cadillac registers a preference; he does not, by himself, influence design.)

Where individual buyers and suppliers represent minor proportions of organizations' exchange relations, they can be considered economic. But where they become "significant" proportions of an organization's supply sources or product-users, these relations may take on political connotations, and promises and threats (overt and covert bargaining) may be used to influence decision premises. As these relations stabilize, and as structural mechanisms, such as co-ordinating and consultative committees, are developed, formal political structures emerge.

External Polity.

The extent to which external political negotiations and relations develop into stable structures, including sanctions for nonconformity, is important for several reasons. First, *the greater the sanction and resource control of the other party, or the coalitional alliance, the less the autonomy of the focal organization* (the organization that is the object of analysis).

Second, *the more a focal organization is bound into a stable external political structure, the more areas of internal policy-setting are influenced by the coalition.*

Possibly more important than the *extent* of external political involvement are the types of relationships. First, political relations develop "horizontally" among organizations having similar "products." Horizontal relations have two focuses: control of relations *among* the similar units—price-fixing, establishing territories—and control of relations between the organizations as a group and agents in the impinging environment—government, unions, etc.

Second, political relations develop "vertically" among suppliers of resources, distributors, and buyers of products (Palamountain, 1955). These include suppliers of labor, raw materials and facilities, and capital.

Typically, we have thought of the relationship of large suppliers of capital (major stockholders, banks, government) as different in kind from the suppliers of other resources, because capital suppliers have, in capitalistic countries, a different legal status. They sometimes have rights of "ownership," and rights of ownership are associated with rights of appointing executive leaders, formulating goals, etc. But under some conditions user and supplier groups may claim these rights. For instance, student-power advocates emphasize their rights to have a voice in appointing professors or even presidents of universities, and in other countries "ownership" may pass to either the state or the workers—suppliers of labor. Either vertical or horizontal political relations may lend to a de facto transfer of "ownership"—that is, to a change in legitimate usage and discretion.

The external political relations discussed above are between groups having a *direct* stake in organizational interrelationships and exchanges. Even such groups as the National Council of Churches or the Western Railway Men's Association have a stake in the constituent organizations' contributions to them and to their constituent organizations' conformity with the "umbrella" organization's policies.

But sometimes direct stake is muted or diffuse. First, organizations attempt to influence or co-opt people or groups indirectly affecting the flow of resources, whether legitimacy, capital, or sales. Dupont gives professors educational tours, politicians befriend editors, pharmaceutical houses pay for trips of aspiring doctors, heads of correctional institutions befriend judges and editors.

Second, a major component of an organization's external political involvement lies in its relation to the state. Obviously, nation-states vary dramatically in the extent of control exercised over organizations. Within nation-states different organizational sectors are subject to varying degrees of regulation. Both points apply to all types of organizations—utilitarian, solidary, or purposive; churches, businesses, or social clubs. One might expect that the more centralized the state, the greater the range of organizations coming under state supervision. Furthermore, the more "important" are organizational goals and procedures, the more likely is the development of state regulatory provisions.

Description and comparison of external political relations force us to study the tangled web of external supporters, competitors, and enemies of an organization, focusing on the alliances, commitments, and structural mechanisms through which organizations relate to the power nodes

of their environment. Attention is paid not only to the structure of the
political environment, but to the level of politicalization as well. Terryberry (1968) has argued that organizational environments are becoming increasingly populated by other organizations. The important facet
lies in its implications for goal-setting and influence processes.

Economic Environment.

In this framework, the description and comparison of economic environment draws heavily on concepts developed by economists in the
theory of the firm, price theory, and in institutional economics.

Price theory emphasizes the interaction of utility, income level,
supply and demand, and the elasticity of supply and demand in relation
to price. The theory of the firm relates the combination of the factors
of production, fixed and variable, to marginal and average cost curves
and to profit; it focuses on internal allocational and production decisions.
Since the theory of the firm is usually characterized as a "quasi-stationary
equilibrium model," it is limited from the point of view of those interested in institutional growth and change. Institutional economists, especially industry specialists, tend to focus, although with less analytic
precision, on the more dynamic change factors in industrial environments.

The historical changes in the quality and aggregate levels of factor
inputs and in technology for *industries* are related to attempts to change
the external polity of organizations. For instance, the oil industry historically was faced with increasing demand and increasing supply. But
it was also faced with cyclical discoveries of crude oil and stepwise
technological advances that led to surges in capacity and drastically
fluctuating fixed costs and profits. Recourse to government quota-
setting and monopoly practices changed the ability to absorb fluctuations (Chazeau and Kahn, 1959).

Institutional economists also tend to be more descriptive of the
social-system characteristics of the environment—what are the special
characteristics of buyers and sellers that affect organizational decisions?
What are the distribution chains? On the input side, organizations deal
with a variety of specific markets—labor, raw materials, capital—each
with its own internal differentiation and supply-demand characteristics.
On the output side, organizations vary in the number of products they
offer and in the structural characteristics of product markets.

Social scientists other than economists have become increasingly concerned with aspects of economic environments. For instance, Lorsch and Lawrence (1968), building on the work of James D. Thompson, have related the *heterogeneity* and *instability* of environments to the internal structures and co-ordinating mechanisms of organizations. Although sociologists have begun to pay more attention to economic environments, there has been no apparent integration of their work with the theory of the firm and price theory. As a consequence, all of the problems of the economies of scale, and fixed and variable costs as related to demand and supply levels and rates of change have been ignored. Yet, it is here that the impetus to organizational change, the resources for growing salaries and other "minor" features of organizational life are found.

Students of social-movement organizations have long been concerned with problems caused by the changing level of demand. (Messenger, 1955; Zald and Ash, 1966). But economic environments of other kinds of organizations should also be studied. For instance, sociological studies of mental hospitals and prisons, even though dealing with the historical development of internal structures and goals, rarely focus on the supply of patients and prisoners. This literature has focused on internal staff-patient/prisoner relations. Yet, at least for the mental hospitals, there is tremendous flux in the input-output and processing procedures; there have been massive changes in technology, the speed of processing patients, the characteristics of those in the hospital and those outside, and the distributional network of patients.

Although the supply-demand matrix is relevant to almost all organizations, many nonprofit organizations have a fundamental dichotomy between who pays for service and who directly receives the service. Whether the client of the mental hospital is considered to be the state or the patient, the separation of payee from receiver means that pricing preference mechanisms are somewhat irrelevant (Etzioni, 1958). In a "welfare-service" state they are a growing edge of organizations. And the language of political economy is a relevant language for these indirect-service organizations.

Finally, many topics treated as economic ones by economists are political ones for us. Economists emphasize the pricing policies of monopolists or oligopolists, but for us the goal-setting and influence process of monopolists and monopsonists, oligopolists and oligopsonists may be even more important.

The dimensions of any organization's external political economy are in large part determined by its position on the fundamental dimensions of organizational constitutions discussed earlier. For example, except for social movements with well-insulated support bases, most social-movement organizations are subject to radical shifts in demand, depending upon issue-arousal.

Again, the particular constellation of interest groups, attitudes about them, and funding arrangements, which have led to prison's peculiar modes of organizational change, are tied to fundamental expectations about what prisons are supposed to accomplish, who has responsibility for them, and what should be the relations among groups within them. Since these constitutional dimensions are related to the external political economy of an organization, it is our expectation that the comparative approach suggested in our discussion of constitutions will illuminate important differences in external political economies.

The political economic environment directly impinges on, and interacts with, the internal political economy. It imposes constraints and presents opportunities to an organization. Goals and procedural choices tie an organization into a web of users, suppliers, distributors, and to a set of influences, relationships, alliances, and hostile antagonists.

Some aspects of the external political economy exert influence through impinging on decision-makers' perception of opportunity in the environment. Others, such as state laws, impose rigid constraints, and still others exert pressure on role effectiveness, which in turn leads to pressures for changing internal rights and responsibilities.

Internal Political Economy

The internal polity is the system of control and influence. One of the things it controls is the system of transforming "raw material" into finished products. In this conception every organization has a productive task, subject to a greater or lesser division of labor and requiring the combination of the factors of production to satisfy performance criteria. The statement holds whether describing a manufacturing corporation selling auto parts, a prison managing prisoners, an insurance company managing money in relation to claims, or a social-movement organization managing membership sentiment and effecting change in its environment.

The general analytic distinction between polity and economy is clear; but, both conceptually and empirically, specific polity and economy processes may be difficult to disentangle. However, there will be little difficulty in showing how these processes operate and are connected to the rest of the political economy.

Internal Polity.

The internal polity is an organization's internal power system: the systematic manner in which power is distributed, mobilized, utilized, and limited. As in any social system (and to repeat our earlier discussion), power is utilized to achieve or to maintain a set of goals and values. These ends may be personal or collective.

Three aspects of internal polities have proved to be extremely important for both empirical and theoretical work. First, examining the *amount and distribution* of power reveals a central structural aspect of a polity. One aspect of analyzing the distribution of power is to reveal its sources. Second, because of differences in constitutions, economies, and power-distributions, organizations vary widely in their processes of *demand-aggregation* and in *conflict-resolution*. Third, an important aspect of a political system is the manner in which change occurs in central positions. Related to resource control, changing goals, and power structure, *succession systems and processes* are a fundamental political reality.

Amount and Distribution of Power. Any comparative approach to organizational politics must analyze variation in power structures. Whether one is doing comparative research within a subclass of organization—such as among utilitarian organizations (constitutional dimension of incentives) or hospitals (goal dimension), or between different types [2] such as comparing social-movement organizations and

2. Most comparative research studies that collect data on several organizations typically study variation within a major subtype, e.g., Lorsch and Lawrence (1968), businesses; Street, Vinter, and Perrow (1966), correctional institutions; Georgopoulos and Mann (1962), hospitals. However, the more strictly theoretical comparative works—e.g., Etzioni (1961), Clark and Wilson (1961), Babchuck and Gordon (1959)—find it useful to use a broader palette. Their theoretical strategy is to identify major variables, while the empirical work demands comparability of measures and control of many organizational parameters.

utilitarian ones, the question of power *distribution* is raised. Less common, though we think equally important, is the question of the *amount* of power mobilized in a social system (Huntington, 1963; Tannenbaum, 1962).

Power is the ability of a person or group, for whatever reason, to affect another person's or group's ability to achieve its goals (personal or collective). In Emerson's (1962) convenient formulation, if A and B are in fact in a social relation, it is likely that B also can affect A's goals, and the empirical problem becomes that of specifiying relative resource control. The distributional question involves examining the relative ability of one group or position to control resources (including legitimate decisions) vis-à-vis others. The question of the *amount* of power in the system involves the over-all resources utilized to influence other groups.

Distribution of Power. Two main questions concerning the distribution of power have been traditional:

(1) What affects the distribution of power among functional groups or positions?

(2) What are the differences in the *vertical* distribution of power between and within organizations?

Students of manufacturing firms, department stores, governmental bureaucracies, hospitals, correctional institutions, and mental hospitals have described and attempted to explain the sources of power of formally equivalent groups. (The "equivalence" comes only from the fact that no formal or authoritative—that is, explicit, accepted symbolic authorization—legitimation is given to the unequal distribution of power.)

There would seem to be two major *sources* of difference in the horizontal distribution of power; on the one hand, the contribution and functional importance of a particular group in the *work-flow* processing of the organization's raw materials to achieve organizational goals may be a strong economic source of differential power. On the other hand, horizontal differences may be attributable to a group's position in *defining* the internal information flow, rules of the game, and external environment relevant to control and evaluation of the internal economic system. Comptrollers' offices, research and development units, budget offices, and long-range planning units gain their power from controlling information and definitions relevant to functioning. Sapolsky (1966), for instance, attributes to the unprogrammability of "taste," that vital ingredient of department-store buying, the inability of department-store comptrollers to raise their influence level effectively.

Where the source of horizontal power often flows directly from a unit's or position's role in the processing of raw materials, variation in the vertical distribution of power more often relates to polity sources, ownership, and legitimate authority. The internal economic structure may put limits upon and force a shift in the structure of vertical power, but it does so through challenging the effectiveness of the control system.

The literature contains a number of concepts that refer to aspects of the vertical distribution of power—e.g., span and hierarchy of control. Characterization of the over-all distribution of power in organization is found in the concepts of centralization-decentralization and federated-corporate. Similarly, the literature on church polity focuses on "episcopal," "connectional," and "congregational" structures. The polar types refer to the relation of a "center," or executive office, to a periphery, or constituent units.

Although these polar types have in common a concern with the vertical dimension of power-distributions, they are not parallel concepts. For instance, the question of centralization-decentralization largely applies *within* a corporate structure: it refers to the degree of delegation—parceling out—of the "executives' " legitimate powers. On the other hand, the federated-corporate distinction has to do with whether there are fundamental *unit* rights and constraints on the over-all collectivity. In congregational church polities, the powers of the center are even conceived as being illegitimate or, at best, delegated by the constituent units.

Note that the literature on social-movement organizations pays little attention to the vertical dimensions of organizations. Because of the weakness of the incentive bases, most meliorist movements have little control over their members, leaders are in a weak position vis-à-vis members, and formal hierarchies may have few powers attached to them. Only as we examine political parties which combine a variety of incentives does a vertical dimension emerge (Duverger, 1954). Thus, although the vertical distribution of power can be described for all organizations, there is wide variation both within and between types of organizations.

In discussing the sources of the vertical distribution of power, one must account for the amount of vertical differentiation *and* for the distribution of power among the positions. The concept of an effective span of control is one important way of accounting for the amount of vertical differentiation. Effective spans of control combined with over-all "size" of productive work force determine the number of vertical levels. The range of effective spans of control is related at the production level to characteristics of technology and raw material as well as to devices for evaluating performance. But ideological factors and the cultural history of a group enter in as well.

Four main factors appear to affect the relative distribution of power between centers and constituent units: (1) Historical ideology of organizational elites. The founders and developers of organizations carry with them "theories" of proper authority structure. In the case of the founders of protestant denominations many were rebelling against the hierarchy of the Roman Catholic Church. Changing ideologies of management has also affected the level of centralization of business firms. (2) The resources controlled by central-peripheral units. Where the constituent unit controls vital resources—stemming from legal positions or from their relative self-sufficiency and alternatives—constituent units have great autonomy (much as professors with high market values have greater autonomy than those getting raises at the sufferance of their chairmen). Sills (1954), reports that a formally corporate structure was transformed into a perceptually federated one because of dependence on local commitment. (3) Task requirements encourage varying degrees of centralization or decentralization. The hostile environment of conspiratorial parties leads to high centralization. On the other hand, for business organizations, great complexity of product output and market is usually believed to press away from a centralized structure (Chandler, 1962). Vertical and horizontal sources of power-distribution may be closely linked in a particular case. For example, doctors became dominant in hospitals because of their functional skills (horizontal) *and* because they often owned or founded the hospitals, or were perceived as legitimate rulers there. Their position was translated into constitutional prerogative. The transformation of both the capital base of hospitals and the skills needed for administration have eroded both their vertical and horizontal power positions. (4) Amount of power. Two organizations might have similar distributions of power —that is, profiles of power-measurements over similar positions might be exactly parallel—and yet be very different in the overall *amount* of power mobilized in the system. An organization has a "low" power system if there are few resources mobilized to influence others, if units or positions conduct their affairs with few explicit attempts at influence from other units. A high power system (internally directed power) is characterized by a great number of influence-attempts. An example will clarify:

The phrase "the politicization of the University" essentially refers to the transformation of the traditional autonomy of departments and administrative offices into the center of influence-attempts from previously supine groups. (One university president told me that decisions which had always been left solely to his office's discretion had become a center of controversy. Local bar associations began pressing him about the law school deanship appointment, student groups wanted to influence the choice of the manager of the student union, etc.)

What are the sources of amount of power in a system? The over-all level of influence in an organization is a function of the level of non-routinized interdependence and/or the perception by groups or positions of the control of their own reward-deprivation balance by other groups or positions. The perception of a reward-deprivation balance controlled by others is in part a function of goals; the group or person who likes the status quo is unlikely to use his time, energy, and resources for influence unless there is a threat to the status quo.

The extent of nonroutine interdependence is a function of both goals and technology. In a study of correctional institutions for delinquents, for example, we found great differences between two institutions dedicated to treatment goals, because one of them focused on milieu-treatment and the other on individual counseling (Zald, 1962). The emphasis on manipulating the milieu led to a great number of meetings and consultation between clinical staff and cottage parents and, hence, to many more influence-attempts.

Differences between organizations in the amount and distribution of power can be described in static and structural terms. But the topic also bears on fundamental aspects of organizational change and conflict-resolution.

Demand-Aggregation and Mechanisms for Resolving Conflicts. There is a curious hiatus in the literature on organizations. Social conflict is linked to social change in studies of society, but in studies of organizations conflict and change are often treated as relatively unconnected subjects. An exception is industrial sociology where union-management conflict is linked to social change.) Much of the literature on organizations takes a short-time perspective and deals with enduring structural bases of conflict. Furthermore, much of the literature on organizational change starts from the *introduction* of the change and asks about the effect on (a) organizational structure or (b) individual morale (Mann and Hoffman, 1960). Thus, the intersection of large-scale change and conflict is bypassed. "Why do elites or members initiate change?" and "What is the social process of change?" are topics that are lightly treated.

Obviously, the political-economy approach can be used in describing enduring structural conflicts and their resolutions. Staff-line conflict, interprofessional relations, superior-subordinate conflicts, and interdivisional conflict, all smack of the stuff of competition for scarce resources, relative power positions, and the like. One of the distinctive advantages of the political-economy approach, however, is its illumination of the *processes* of change.

One of the central points made by students using the "systems" approach to the study of politics is that institutionalized political systems are the focus of aggregated demands for collective outputs. Through politics, individuals and groups attempt to change both individual and collective rewards. In this approach the distinctive feature of politics is that people who have grievances attempt to redress them not directly (although power may be used in this way) but through demands on authoritative officeholders. Officeholders are more or less responsive depending upon the resources they control, the competitive definitions of collective policy, and their own goals and values.

Organizational change, as distinct from sheer increase or decrease in size, involves changes in policy, products, goals, market, technology, and interunit relations. Whether or not the change is "irrational" or "rational," it involves a process in which (a) the current state of the organization or some aspect of it is in some sense unsatisfactory; (b) some unit or group proposes an alteration in the unsatisfactory state; (c) the proposal is or is not translated into a decision and an organization's program or policy; and (d) the new policy does or does not reduce dissatisfaction with the state of affairs. Variations in political structure—vertical and horizontal power-distributions and "amount" of power mobilized—help account for the patterns of organizational change and conflict.

Several propositions, some truisms, are useful in presenting a political model of demand-aggregation and organizational change: (1) Specific dissatisfaction within an organization and the formulation of an issue occurs in the group or section whose interests are hurt by the status quo, e.g., assembly-line workers, not stockholders, complain about assembly-line speedups; stockholders and upper management gripe about profit levels, growth, and dividend payments; upper executives criticize functional departmentalization and press for radical decentralization. External to organizations, "issue entrepreneurs" (e.g., Ralph Nader) mobilize demand for change.

(2) If an organization is highly centralized and power is concentrated in a small executive core, change depends either upon aggregating fractionated external and internal power sources into a unified opposition, or upon capturing the ear of the "elite." On the other hand, the more there is a dispersal of power in an organization, the more likely are forms of coalitional politics. Federated organizations, like some unions, or bodies of collegial equals, like the New York Stock Exchange, have forms of parliamentary politics. If they require unanimity or near unanimity for adoption of any changes, then the intensity of the motivating issue must indeed be strong. In the most radically dispersed organizations, social-movement organizations, in which the executive cadre control members *only* by dint of persuasion, or in confederations in which collective decisions (assembly votes) are considered only as advisory—e.g., Baptist assemblies, the early phase of the national YMCA movement—the adoption of change-proposals is essentially based on consensus. Among confederated organizations, the greater the homogeneity of elite perspectives and of environmental conditions, the more rapid the adoption of proposals for change.

John Q. Wilson's (1966) model of organizational innovation suggests that the greater the decentralization of an organization the more *proposals* for change will be initiated, for decentralization gives people a greater stake and sense of involvement. But he also suggests that highly decentralized organizations will also have a low rate of proposal-adoptions because each unit must get others to consent and none has more power than others. On the other hand, in highly centralized organizations, fewer proposals for change will be initiated, but those that are can be adopted easily ("by a wave of the King's wand"). Wilson argues essentially that the balance of a large number of proposals and a high rate of adoptions occurs in neither radically centralized nor decentralized organizations; he restricts himself to collectivity-wide proposals. It is likely that decentralized and federated organizations have a much greater rate of *individual unit* changes than centralized organizations; for the power to initiate and adopt internal changes is located in each unit.

How are collective demands generated in organizations? How is a perception of an issue translated into a social process of contending parties? When we are studying organizational conflict among small groups of managers, the social psychology of coalition-formation may be most appropriate, and for tactical lessons we may turn to Machiavelli. But where we are talking about the aggregation of diverse and dispersed individuals into relative coherent pressure groups, social-movement analysis is most appropriate.

Within organizations, several factors would seem to be conducive to social-movement formation. First, the greater the group solidarity and self-esteem, stemming from social status and/or professional homogeneity, the more likely a collective identity is to be found (Sayles, 1958). Since professional and highly skilled groups often have universalistic standards of performance, when the status quo departs from these standards collective action is likely to take place.

Second, if a subordinate group is to make collective demands, it must be insulated from repressive action on the part of the superordinates. The Wagner Act helped industrial unions in this country by controlling the ability of employers to retaliate against employees involved in union-building. In academia, liberal norms of freedom of expression *and* professors' absolute dependence on the good will and commitment of their graduate and undergraduate students have conditioned the response to internal social movements.

Finally the task structure and exigencies that facilitate communication and the development of grievances may be conducive to social-movement phenomena (Burks, 1961).

Some demands for change result in new policies which effectively solve the problem or reduce dissatisfaction. Other internal strains and conflicts are chronic, based on enduring fissures in the body politic, and their solution is based more on ways of channeling and handling conflict than on removing the causes of conflict.

Organizations develop a number of institutional mechanisms for resolving what could be disruptive conflicts. Capital-allocation committees use criteria of equity rather than economic standards; review procedures are institutionalized; appeal boards and collective-bargaining procedures come into existence. A general hypothesis: the more superordinates are dependent on subordinates, and the more vertical power is equally divided among several groups, the better-developed are criteria of equity and quasi-judicial mechanisms (Cf. Scott, 1965; Pondy, 1964).

Succession Systems and Political Behavior. Organizational changes occur not only through the aggregation of demand; they also occur through succession processes, leading to the systematic selection of new perspectives into executive office. Unfortunately, students of organizational leadership have been enamored with the personality styles of leaders or, slightly better, with the expectation pattern of subordinates and the superordinate-subordinate role-interactions (Grusky). The broader systemic implications of succession choices, except in a few studies (Grusky, 1963; Guest, 1962; Levinson, 1964; Carlson, 1962), have been ignored.

Yet it is patent that (1) how key executives are chosen varies with the internal political structure of organizations and (2) the outcome of succession choices may, under specific external and internal conditions, have a large impact on organizational directions and policies.

Organizational succession systems range from crown-prince systems, in which the chief executive chooses and trains his own replacement, to elective *leadership* systems in which executives serve on the short-time sufferance of a politicized, conflict-ridden, and involved electorate. Succession systems range from regularized ones, allowing for a chain of successors to be established, to those that take place through spasmodic and clandestine organizational coups d'état.

Let us specify the structures and processes of political economies that affect succession systems. At least three main factors must be considered in understanding recruitment and succession to higher office: (1) the distribution of power; (2) the degree of consensus about performance adequacy and the location in the power system of perceptions of inadequacy; (3) the career channels of "standard" and "deviant" executive leadership.

Who chooses key officeholders is, in most organizations, a fundamental aspect of constitutions, closely related to constitutional prerogatives attached to specific offices or groups. Constitutional provisions often specify not only who chooses the chief executive, but conditions of tenure in office and the timing and process of selection. In general, the more the constitution vests power in a broad-based "electorate," the more tenure in office is explicitly limited and defined. Examples of short-tenure electoral systems are found in Protestant congregational polities.

The higher the concentration of power, the more likely are "crown-prince" systems. Such is the case in larger corporations with either family ownership, or highly dispersed ownership that effectively concentrates control in the chairman's hand.

Systematic conflict and, indeed, regularized competition are most likely in federated organizations or in organizations that have several powerful but disparate nodes of power. Edelstein (1967) has persuasively argued that competition for office in trade unions is most likely when the constituent units have histories of autonomy. (This analysis of the relation of power-distribution to succession rules is somewhat superficial, for it ignores many interesting mixed cases: e.g., highly centralized systems with democratic succession principles attached to the upper levels—the Roman Catholic Church and that perennial favorite of sociologists, the "democratic system with oligarchic tendencies.")

Although, as noted above, "crown-prince" systems depend upon a high concentration of power, there is one difference between the two cases cited—family-owned corporations and dispersed ownership. The family-owned corporation is, hypothetically, in a position to ignore market and economic considerations, up to and including bankruptcy. On the other hand, where ownership is widely dispersed, inadequate profit-performance depresses stock prices and leads, potentially, to accumulation of blocs of stocks by investors who see recovery possibilities. Similarly, in business corporations with contending blocs of stockowners, minor fluctuations in their economic status may be the occasions for votes of confidence and attempts to win over previous backers of the incumbents. I cite these cases to indicate the interdependence of power systems, succession processes, and performance adequacy.

Performance adequacy is evaluated in most organizations along several dimensions. The causes of inadequacy may be internal or external and may be more or less subject to executive control. Regardless of whether the causes of inadequacy are under executive control, since key offices are charged with responsibility for the collective, replacement is most likely at times of inadequate performance. Latent conflicts are brought to the fore at such times, and competition for office is exacerbated. (Voluntary organizations may differ here: the low rewards of a failing organization may discourage office-seeking.) Also, where a crown prince has been established, we suspect that the discreditation of the regime may discredit the crown prince.

Not only does performance inadequacy lead to dismissal of incumbents, but continuing inadequacies lead to high rates of turnover. High rates of turnover in key positions, of course exacerbate inadequacy.

Performance adequacy or inadequacy is also related to the selection of candidates with "standard" or "deviant" careers. From a political-economy perspective (as contrasted with traditional social-psychological ones) a career is a labor-market mechanism that, over time, combines occupational and social backgrounds to "fit" specific job requirements. Most relatively stable organizations develop standard patterns of recruiting key executives. Career routes leading to high office develop, with options. The standard pattern is determined both by the perceived requirements of competence of top officers and the opportunities to develop those competencies provided in organizations. American Civil Liberties Union executives are recruited from liberal lawyers, railroad executives from operating railroad men, etc. Standard patterns filter out those with marginal skills or deviant career paths.

The standard pattern is affected by the internal political economy of an organization. For example, small organizations may not have sufficient internal divisions of labor to provide training for executive succession. They then have to rely on contact with other, similar organizations for identifying new executives (Carlson, 1962).

When performance has been "inadequate," however, whatever groups control succession may develop perspectives that lead away from standard pattern choices; the choosing of a successor becomes a period of political reassessment and deviant career patterns become relevant to executive choice. Thus, for instance, as the railroads became bankruptcy-prone and later merger-oriented, legal skills became relevant and traditional operating skills were downgraded. Or, in the Young Men's Christian Association, confronting the urban crisis led to an emphasis on program imagination rather than business efficiency (Zald, 1965). The point is that the careers of individuals intersect with an organization's changing political economy.

Internal Economic Structure and Process.

The internal polity articulates with the internal economic system in several ways. First, authoritative power centers make choices among "product" lines, technology, and the system of integrating roles and units. Second, both in inducing factors of production into the organization and in maintaining their usage once committed, political-economic choices are made which reflect the balance of resources in the organization and the relative power of different units. Commitments to a division of labor, to a grouping of roles into higher order units, and to technology become the basis for the development of group identity and solidarity, the development of strategic control of resources, and, therefore, power.

Three aspects of internal economies merit systematic attention: (1) the division of labor, technologies, and interunit exchanges; (2) mechanisms and criteria for allocating resources and recording costs and information about performance adequacy; and (3) incentive economies and their consequences.

It is fairly easy to see the division of labor and product-processing as being an essential part of the internal economy. But the accounting-information and incentive systems might analytically be treated as part of the polity. The accounting-information system is established by authoritative power centers and functions to provide authoritative information. It serves as an internal substitute for a price system. Once the accounting system is established, the variable data, monetary and otherwise, recorded in it signal to participants efficiency and effectiveness vis-à-vis other units and the outside world. I argue below that the *choice* of accounting rules is based on political-economic considerations, and that once in operation the accounting rules operate like a sloppy price system to guide the allocation of resources.

A similar point can be made about incentive economies. Barnard's (1938) original argument was that different organizations have stocks of different kinds of incentives which they exchange for labor-commitment. In this sense, an economy exists; but authoritative power-wielders not only control stocks, they make choices about how they should be allocated, thus rewarding and depriving different groups. An incentive system is both economic and political in actual operation.

Division of Labor, Technologies, and Inter-Unit Relationships. Economies are systems for producing and exchanging goods. Basic to any economy, whether free market or centrally controlled, are considerations of specialization, role differentiation, and division of labor. Specialization and differentiation within an organization are, in turn, largely functions of the state of the arts (technology) for producing a specific "product," the variety of "products" offered by the organization, the scale (size) of the organization "required" both to produce and to distribute production to the "market," and the organization's geographic dispersion.

Each of these factors has consequences for the amount of role and unit differentiation, as well as independent effects on the political structure and difficulties facing organizations. For example, holding other things constant, as differentiation increases, span of control decreases, as does organizational loyalty. Greater complexity (holding size constant) requires more supervision and administrative personnel (Anderson and Warkov, 1961; Rushing, 1967). Further, the more nonroutine the tasks, the more discretion must be left to lower level personnel (Thompson and Bates, 1957). In addition, a unit's weight in organizational counsels varies directly as it controls or is perceived as involved in the organization's functionally most difficult subtasks

(Perrow, 1961; Crozier, 1963). Finally, routinization and stabilization of output processes facilitate increased centralization and reduce co-ordinating problems.

These problems of the relation of the "socio-technical" system to the distribution of intra- and interunit power, to supervisory strains, and to problems of group cohesion have been a central concern of sociologists for the last twenty years. One advantage of the political-economy framework is that it treats the "socio-technical" system itself as a dependent variable.

The socio-technical system in most organizations is not rigidly fixed. It changes as a function of competitive pressures, the profit potential and capital investment requirement of an innovation, and the innovative orientations of the executive elite (Mansfield, 1968). Similarly, as labor costs increase, pressures to mechanize increase. Adopting new technologies may require large capital expenditures, changing both external political and economic commitments (long-term debt) and changing the scale of market required to utilize efficient production. Similarly, adoption of a new technology and related role differentiation changes the social relations internal to the organizations.

Just as, within the political-economy framework, the adoption of technology can be treated as a substantive problem, so, too, can that historic problem of increase of administrative personnel. Sociologists typically treat increases of administrative personnel as a response to internal complexity and co-ordination, a control-of-economy problem. They have ignored the goals-and-choice aspect. As Williamson (1964) and Pondy (1969) indicate, however, managerial elites may have a "taste" for profits or increased staff (and I would add for short-range and long-range profits). Thus, Pondy shows that industries having higher percentages of owner-managers have lower staff ratios compared to industries having lower percentages of owner-managers, controlling for size and technology. This line of argument ties into the debate over managerial capitalism associated with Berle and Means (1934) and recently continued by Galbraith (1967).

The topic of the shape of the internal economy has been most fully developed for utilitarian organizations; for complex, large, and finely tuned internal economies do not exist to any great extent where organizations do not have control over their members regularly and for long periods of time. Although social-movement organizations do have internal divisions of labor and role differentiation, they are of simpler types. Only as social movements change does analysis of skill competence and division of labor become especially interesting. For social-movement organizations, the central economic problem is finding a set of incentives to ensure member participation; so often the stock controlled by the organization is extremely weak (Zald and Ash, 1966).

Incentive Allocations. One component of the internal economy is the distribution of rewards and sanctions to motivate role performance. It was asserted earlier that one central normative principle of organizational constitutions is a set of exchange terms. What is to be gained by joining an organization? Analytically, this is a problem in the relation of an organization to the external environment. Even *within* major types of organizations, organizations differ in the *amount* of incentive *resources* they control. Their ability to retain and motivate members will depend upon their stock or supply.

The incentive necessary to maintain a member's motivation may well differ from that necessary to obtain his initial membership (e.g., a person joining an organization for purposive values may stay because of solidary relations). And it is probably the distinctive contribution of the human relations school to have emphasized the "extra-contractual" and "extra-monetary" incentives that bind men to utilitarian organizations.

This approach goes beyond that of the human relations school. Since I conceive of incentives as part of a comparative political-economy approach, eventually I must be able to treat within this framework monetary and non-monetary incentive systems, including symbolic ones. Incentives vary not only in the "needs" they satisfy but in their tangibility, their divisibility, and their pervasiveness. Futhermore, incentives are defined in a social and political matrix and are associated with particular kinds of social structures.

The effects of differences in incentive bases for organizations with similar goals has been nicely demonstrated by James Q. Wilson (1961). In "The Economy of Patronage" he poses the questions of under what conditions political parties are more likely to be ideologically riven by factions and when they can resemble a bureaucratic of patrimonial machine. The core of his analysis has to do with the number of patronage positions (material incentives), controlled by the "leader." He estimates that Chicago has three to four times as many patronage positions for districts of comparable size as does New York. He then argues that the material base of these positions allows the mayor to be able to mobilize more party workers without persuasion than the mayor of New York. To a greater extent, people in New York have to be attracted by purposive incentives, but in our society these are relatively weak, and in a complex situation each group attaches a different weight to issues. Thus, the party tends to be fractionated and faction-ridden.

Incentive analysis is important not only for comparing different kinds of organizations but for studying organizational change. Major change usually upsets the balance of incentives, affecting participant motivation. It is obvious that rising and declining incentive stocks affect the expectations and comparison-level alternatives of members. Moreover, within an organization, allocation of incentive to one group or unit affects the satisfaction/dissatisfaction levels of members in other units, contributing to patterns of mobility within the organization and affecting, possibly, decisions to remain with an organization.

Within organizations, incentives are allocated to motivate performance. From the point of view of organizational elites, incentives, like other resources (capital expenditures), are allocated in terms of the elites' perceptions of organization tasks and enhancement of their own values and performance. They are aided in their allocational work by various accounting and forecasting mechanisms which summarize both the internal and external state of the organization. Many of these information summary and transmittal mechanisms may be informal and based on direct observation. But others are based on quite extensive, formalized, accounting-information systems.

Information Systems: Budgeting and Accounting Systems. Information systems are created by accountants, quality-control experts, and other specialists in measurement as "readings on the current state of the organization." By comparing past readings and projecting future ones, the relative satisfaction/dissatisfaction level of elites and relevant audiences can be affected. They are created for, and largely used by, influence-wielders.

In this sense they are part of the polity. But for the most part they represent indexes of the state of various aspects of the productive exchange system, and in this respect "stand for" the economy. Furthermore, rules developed by organizational elites and powerful external authorities operate to channel the flow of resources with the organization.

It is not too important whether the budget and accounting and information systems are considered as largely part of the economy (because they represent it) or as part of the polity (because they are used by its agents). Possibly they should be treated as important connecting tissues of political economy. It *is* important to understand the way in which these information-accounting systems are developed, used, and fit into organizational structure.

Unfortunately, until very recently sociologists and political scientists of a behaviorist persuasion largely ignored information systems. Like the sociologist of medicine who never questions the doctor's diagnosis, the sociologist of organization has tended to accept accounting systems as given—as professionally and abstractly dictated. Except for a few political scientists and economists interested in tax policy, these topics have been seen as "boring, dry topics for narrow-minded money-grubbers."

The irony is, of course, that these systems often are major bones of contention within and without organizations. We can modify Lasswell's famous phrase "who gets what, when, how" to "who is charged with what, when, how." Anyone following the debates over the financial statements of conglomerate corporations in 1968 and 1969 knows that the emergence of this form of corporate organization is related to tax and accounting rules, subject to debate and discretion, and that, if conglomerates decline, it will be because external authorities (including the Securities Exchange Commission) impose rules for their regulation.

If our discussion seems to overemphasize the use of information systems in business organizations, one need only turn to universities and churches to find parallel examples. Indeed, the statistical records of established denominations are used by staff to evaluate ministerial performance, production targets are established in relation to various goals (e.g., missionary giving, Sunday school attendance, and the like), and among the cognoscenti a debate goes on over the interpretation of membership statistics.

It may be that social scientists have ignored accounting systems because by the time they personally experience them they have become deans and chairmen, no longer doing research! In any event, who controls what budget, what shared costs are allocated, what a teaching charge is, what a fellowship change is are matters of no small import in universities.

Concern with the budgeting and accounting processes in government, and with the political effect of such innovations as PPBS (Program-Planning-Budgeting System) provides one step in the direction I am proposing (Wildavsky, 1964; Wildavsky, 1967). Furthermore, some accountants and "management-science" experts have become interested in the behavioral effects and sources of these systems (Gynther, 1967).

At this point I can at best propose a paradigm for investigation. Resource-allocation within organizations is a function of traditional rules, intergroup bargaining, mechanics for deciding conflict, and elite perception of new areas for growth, change, or defense. One level of investigation would be an examination of the *structural mechanisms* for reaching decisions. For example, following Pondy's (1964) lead, we might study institutional structures and the organizational rules used to reach decisions on allocating resource capital for investment and major facility change.

A second level of investigation is suggested by the *history and development* of the accounting and allocating rules themselves. For example, what factors encouraged the development of charging units a fixed interest cost on loans or allocating costs in a given ratio to different functions? On what basis do social-movement organizations determine staff salaries or percent of membership income to be shared between national and local units (e.g., in the National Association for the Advancement of Colored People or the American Civil Liberties Union)?

A third level of investigation would be the *consequences* of different allocational and accounting procedures. Who benefits? Which functions are supported and which slighted? Where are different information and account functions located in the organizations? Which departments gain in importance, and which lose because they do or do not control the information system or have special access to information from the system? The introduction of computerized information systems has only made more obvious the existence of a potential relation between the control of information systems and the control of key decisions. An increase in organizational complexity is reflected in the strategic importance of information systems and the offices that manage them.

Accounting systems reflect the ethos of organization as well as the internal power system. Organizations have choices between "conservative" and "radical" accounting rules (e.g., in charging depreciation, setting up reserves, and the like). The accounting system may favor short-run efficiency over long-run risk-taking (rules for capitalizing or treating research and development costs as current expense), or, in the YMCA, efficiency versus program-service.

Finally, organizational change reflects itself in the resources allocated to different functions and in the system used for processing information. For essentially stable organizations, it will become apparent that allocation rules are made up of traditional accounting procedures with a percentage increase or decrease depending upon total income projected for a given year (or whatever period is used). Crecine (1966), studying municipal government, has found that department heads request and receive a budget based on last year's expenditures plus or minus the percentage increase (decrease) in revenue projected by the municipal executives' financial office. Only as new programs are initiated or old programs expanded is this formula changed. For other organizations, (particularly those in rapid flux), resource-allocation and criteria for allocation will constitute central concerns of organizational elites. And the nature of the information system itself will be subject to change as organizational ethos changes.

The political-economy framework was initially developed because organizational analysis seemed inelegant and diffuse when utilized to study the causes and dynamics of organizational changes. Any general social-system approach to organizational change must include a host of variables, some of which will be political and economic, to explain change.

My focus on the political-economic variables is intended to provide a more *efficient* and *illuminating* approach than is possible with a more general framework. This approach postulates that economic and political forces, structures, pressures, and constraints (1) are among the most significant motivators of change and (2) are the key factors shaping directions of change. The political-economy approach is efficient because it concentrates investigation on two key processes and structures and their interrelation; a general social-system approach is too diffuse.

This approach is illuminating, I think, because it allows a greater explication of political and economic processes and structures within organizations than most sociologists and political scientists have heretofore provided. It forces the researcher to a more finely wrought conceptualization of organizational polity and economy than has been the norm. Virtually all students interested in organizations (not decision-making) utilize some concepts of power and exchange, as well as their synonyms and related terms. Without explicit focus on polity and economy as the central objects of analysis, however, a rich set of distinctions and analytic units has not been developed.

Although the political-economy framework was originally developed for the study of organizational change, here I have emphasized its utility as an integrative framework for comparative work. Major independent variables in many comparative studies have been shown to be aspects of a political economy. By systematically tracing out their position in a political economy and by paying attention to other major components, oversimplified explanations can be avoided; yet at the same time a delineated range of interlocking variables can be explored.

As a first step in developing our approach, I have turned, whenever possible, to the fields of economics and political science. The concepts used by these disciplines (at the most general level) are often applied to whole societies or to nation-states. However, since political scientists are centrally concerned with the aggregation, structure, mobilization, utilization, and limitations of power and economists with the consequences of differing exchange systems and terms, it has been useful to scan these disciplines for concepts and ideas applicable to organizations.

No claim is made that this essay presents a "complete" political-economy approach. At this point our concept of an internal polity is more fully developed than other aspects. For some purposes, different concepts or aspects of polity and economy might be elaborated. For example, there has recently been an interest in the judicial and internal legal systems of corporations. What appeals system, if any, do employees or members have? What rights are vested in the individual, and how are individual rights protected? For a battery of concepts relevant to analyzing an organization's legal system, the student might well turn to that part of political science which examines judicial processes and comparative legal structure.

What of the theoretical status of my framework? At least two generations of social scientists have been nurtured in a model of the scientific enterprise that perceives formal theory and experiment as science's exemplar. Some philosophers and historians of science (e.g., the late Norwood Russell Hansen, 1958) would argue, however, that these models are only formalizations of "truths" emerging from a much looser pattern of discovery.

Even if the hypothetical-deductive method constitutes a late stage in the establishment of scientific truth, few would deny its value for clarifying the logical status of concepts and providing economical explanations. The political-economy framework can be used to generate specific predictions and in one case has already demonstrated its predictive values (Wood, 1967). No claim is made, however, that this framework has reached an advanced state of development.

The political-economy framework is not a substitute for decision theory, the human relations approach, or the concept of organizational rationality. It does claim to have organic connections to these approaches when they are used for empirical research. If, for example, organizations are conceived as rational instruments, the political-economy approach suggests that their rationality depends upon specifying rationality for what groups, or elites, with what kinds of incentives and normative legitimacy as support. In this approach all organizations have political economies: the model bureaucracy has a form of rule and ethos as does a school system "outside of politics." Politics and political economy are endemic to all forms of organizational life, not just the conflictual part that occasionally shows.

REFERENCES

Anderson, Theodore, and Seymour Warkov.
1961 "Organizational Size and Functional Complexity: a Study of Administration in Hospitals." American Sociological Review 26: 23–28.

Bakke, E. Wright.
   1959 "Concept of the Social Organization." Pp. 16–75 in Mason Haire (editor), Modern Organization Theory. New York: John Wiley.
Barnard, Chester F.
   1938 The Functions of the Executive. Cambridge, Mass.: Harvard University Press.
Berle, Adolph A., and Gardiner C. Means.
   1934 The Modern Corporation and Private Property. New York: Macmillan.
Bidwell, Charles E., and Rebecca S. Vreeland.
   1963 "College Education and Moral Orientation." Administrative Science Quarterly 8:166–191.
Blau, Peter M., and W. Richard Scott.
   1962 Formal Organization. San Francisco: Chandler Publishing Co.
Buchanan, James A.
   1964 "What Should Economists Do?" Southern Economic Journal 30: 213–222.
Burks, Richard V.
   1961 The Dynamics of Communism in Eastern Europe. Princeton, N.J.: Princeton University Press.
Carlson, Richard O.
   1962 Executive Succession and Organizational Change: Place Bound and Career Bound Superintendents of Schools. Chicago: Midwest Administration Center.
Chandler, Alfred Dupont, Jr.
   1962 Strategy and Structures: Chapter in the History of the Industrial Enterprise. Cambridge, Mass.: MIT Press.
Chazeau, Melvin G., and Alfred E. Kahn.
   Integration and Competition in the Petroleum Industry. New Haven, Conn.: Yale University Press.
Crecine, John P.
   1966 A Computer Simulation Model of Municipal Resource Allocation. Unpublished Doctoral Dissertation, Carnegie-Mellon University, Pittsburgh, Pa.
Crozier, Michel.
   1963 The Bureaucratic Phenomenon. Chicago: The University of Chicago Press.
Duverger, Maurice.
   1954 Political Parties. New York: John Wiley.
Edelstein, J. David.
   1967 "An Organizational Theory of Union Democracy." American Sociological Review 32:19–31.

Emerson, Richard M.
   1962   "Power-Dependence Relation." American Sociological Review 27:
          41–55.
Etzioni, Amitai.
   1958   "Administration and the Consumer." Administrative Science Quar-
          terly 3:251–264.
   1961   A Comparative Analysis of Complex Organizations. New York:
          Free Press of Glencoe.
Galbraith, John K.
   1967   The New Industrial State. Boston: Houghton Mifflin.
Georgopoulos, Basil S., and Floyd C. Mann.
   1962   The Community General Hospital. New York: Macmillan.
Gordon, C. Wayne, and Nicholas Babchuk.
   1959   "A Typology of Voluntary Associations." American Sociological
          Review 24:22–79.
Grusky, Oscar.
   1963   "Managerial Succession and Organizational Effectiveness." Ameri-
          can Journal of Sociology 64:21–31.
Guest, Robert H.
   1962   Organizational Change: The Effect of Successful Leadership.
          Homewood, Ill.: Irwin-Dorsey.
Gynther, Reginald S.
   1967   "Accounting Concepts and Behavioral Hypotheses." Accounting
          Review 42:274–290.
Hanson, Norwood R.
   1958   Patterns of Discovery: An Inquiry into the Conceptual Founda-
          tions of Science. Cambridge, England: Cambridge University Press.
Huntington, Samuel.
   1966   "The Political Modernization of Traditional Monarchies." Daedalus
          95:763–788.
Hurst, James Willard.
   1964   Law and Economic Growth: The Legal History of the Lumber
          Industry in Wisconsin, 1836 to 1915. Cambridge, Mass.: Belknap
          Press.
Levenson, Bernard.
   1964   "Bureaucratic Succession." Pp. 362–376 in A. Etzioni, editor,
          Complex Organizations. New York: Holt, Rinehart, and Winston.
Long, Norton A.
   1962   The Polity. Chicago: Rand McNally.
Lorsch, Jay W., and Paul R. Lawrence.
   1968   Environmental Factors and Organizational Integration. Paper read
          at American Sociological Meeting. Boston, Massachusetts.

Mann, Floyd C., and L. R. Hoffman.
 1960 Automation and the Worker: A Study of Social Change in the Power Plants. New York: Holt, Rinehart and Winston.
Mansfield, Edwin.
 1968 Industrial Research and Technological Innovation: An Econometric Analysis. New York: W. W. Norton
March, James G. (editor).
 1965 Handbook of Organizations. Chicago: Rand McNally.
Messenger, Sheldon.
 1955 "Organizational Transformation: A Case Study of a Declining Social Movement." American Sociological Review 70:3–10.
Palamountain, J. C., Jr.
 1955 The Politics of Distribution. Cambridge, Mass.: Harvard University Press.
Pondy, Louis.
 1964 "Budgeting and Inter-Group Conflict in Organizations." Pittsburgh Business Review 34:1–3.
 1969 "Effects of Size, Complexity, and Ownership on Administrative Intensity." Administrative Science Quarterly 14:47–61.
Rushing, William.
 1967 "The Effects of Industry Size and Division of Labor on Administration." Administrative Science Quarterly 12:273–295.
Sapolsky, Harvey.
 1966 Decentralization and Control: Problems in the Organization of Department Stores. Unpublished dissertation, Harvard University, Cambridge, Mass.
Sayles, Leonard R.
 1958 Behavior of Industrial Work Groups. New York: John Wiley.
Stinchcombe, Arthur.
 1960 "The Sociology of Organization and the Theory of the Firm." Pacific Sociological Review 3:75–82.
Street, David, Robert D. Vinter, and Charles Perrow.
 1966 Organization for Treatment. New York: The Free Press.
Tannenbaum, Arnold S.
 1962 "Control in Organizations: Individual Adjustment and Organizational Performance." Administrative Science Quarterly 7:236–257.
Terryberry, Shirley.
 1968 The Evolution of Organizational Environments." Administrative Science Quarterly 12:590–613.
Thompson, James D., and Fred L. Bates.
 1957 "Technology, Organization and Administration." Administrative Science Quarterly 2:325–342.
Thompson, James D., and Robert W. Hawkes.
 1962 "Disaster, Community Organization, and Administrative Process."

Pp. 268–300 in Man and Society in Disaster, edited by George Baker and Dwight Chapman. New York: Basic Books.

Thompson, James D., and William J. McEwen.
1958 "Organizational Goals and Environment: Goal Setting as an Interaction Process." American Sociological Review 23:23–31.

Thompson, Victor A.
1966 Review of Handbook of Organizations. American Sociological Review 31:415–416.

Warriner, Charles K.
1965a "The Problem of Organizational Purpose." The Sociological Quarterly 6:139–146.
1965b "Four Types of Voluntary Associations." Sociological Inquiry 35: 138–148.

Wildavsky, Aaron.
1964 Politics of the Budgetary Process. Boston: Little, Brown.

Williamson, Oliver E.
1964 The Economics of Discretionary Behavior: Managerial Objectives in a Theory of the Firm. New York: Prentice-Hall.

Wilson, James Q.
1961 "An Economy of Patronage." Journal of Political Economy 69: 369–380.
1966 "Innovation in Organizations: Notes Towards a Theory." Pp. 193–217 in Approaches to Organization Design, edited by James D. Thompson. Pittsburgh: University of Pittsburgh Press.

Wilson, James Q., and Peter B. Clark.
1961 "Incentive Systems: A Theory of Organizations." Administrative Science Quarterly 6:129–166.

Wood, James R.
"Protestant Enforcement of Racial Integration Policy: A Sociological Study in the Political Economy of Organization." Unpublished dissertation, Vanderbilt University, Nashville, Tenn.

Zald, Mayer N.
1962 Organizational Control Structures in Five Correctional Institutions. American Journal of Sociology 68:335–345.
1965 "Who Shall Rule? A Political Analysis of Succession in a Large Welfare Organization." Pacific Sociological Review 8:52–60.
1968 Organizational Change: The Political Economy Approach. Paper delivered at Meeting of Southern Sociological Society, Atlanta, Georgia.
1970 Organizational Change: The Political Economy of the YMCA. Chicago: University of Chicago Press (forthcoming).

Zald, Mayer N., and Robert Ash.
1966 "Social Movement Organizations: Growth, Decay, and Change." Social Forces 44:327–341.

The Political-Economy Approach in Perspective

F. L. BATES

Professor Zald's paper is primarily a plea for us to focus our attention on certain critical aspects of organization that have been more or less neglected in the past. It does not so much present a detailed and logically consistent theory of organization as it presents a very general framework which points to the need for theories.

To place the political-economy approach in perspective, it is perhaps fair to say that it represents a blending of two approaches—one with ancient roots in sociology and the other with roots in social sciences. On the one hand it draws much of its perspective from the "institutional approach" to studying society. On the other it draws heavily on "social-system" theory. It makes the general claim that all organizations (which are forms of social systems) no matter what their mission, have a political and an economic aspect. This means, in effect, that the political and economic institutions of society really exist as parts of organizations and groups and are themselves made up of segments of such organizations. Thus business firms, ordinarily thought of as "economic" organizations, contain a part of the political institution of society and therefore contain an internal political order. Likewise government bureaus, which are thought of as "political organizations," contain part of the economic systems of the society and as a consequence, have an internal economy.

It is tempting to extend Professor Zald's reasoning in this respect and to make the claim that all organizations contain not only parts of the political and economic institutions of society, but also segments of *all other* social institutions which compose society's structure. Thus, they may contain part of the "educational or socialization" institution, part of the "religious" institution, and so forth. The difficulty with this expanded view is that we are more likely to agree that all organizations, no matter what their missions, contain political and economic subsystems than we are to agree that some other institutional systems, which are traditionally posited by sociologists, are similarly found in all organizations.

The political-economy approach, in addition to drawing on sociological perspectives, draws heavily on the fields of political science and economics. This represents both an opportunity and a potentially overwhelming difficulty. It obviously allows the importation of economics and political-science theories and methods into the organizational-study field, and this will no doubt prove advantageous. It just as obviously leads to the possibility that the political-economy approach will become a kind of "superman" field because of the tremendous complexity of both economic and political-science perspectives and problems.

In reading Dr. Zald's paper, a number of thoughts occurred to me concerning theoretical matters which may or may not prove to be problems in applying the political-economy approach to the study of organizations. In Professor Zald's discussion of polity are two interesting assumptions concerning power as it relates to organizations. If these assumptions could be clarified and related to the definition of power in a concise manner, the implicit theory of power which underlies most sociological treatments of organizations would become explicit and usable in research.

The two assumptions are: (1) Quite similar organizations may have varying amounts of power contained within their boundaries. This assumption implies that two organizations of the same size, which produce the same product and utilize the same technology, may differ in the amount of power utilized within their boundaries. One of the two may use more power behavior in the production of the organization's product or in the maintenance of the organization as a functioning system than does the other. (2) Organizations with the same amount of power contained within them may distribute that power differently. This means that organizations having the same offices and the same division of labor among work groups may have a different distribution of power among these offices and work groups.

A number of propositions are utilized to explain the variations in both the amount of internal power contained within an organization and its distribution. Some of the more important are the following: (a)

Organizations vary in the amount of power they have over groups and organizations in their environment; (b) Members of an organization who obtain control over the organization's environment and, therefore, are able to affect the organization's success in dealing with its environment will obtain more power inside their organization than those who have no power external to the system; (c) For this reason the amount and distribution of power within an organization is profoundly affected by the relationship of the organization to its environment.

The first question I would like to raise is whether we can defend these assumptions and propositions, given the definitions of power commonly employed by sociologists. The second is whether we can create an intellectual "accounting system" that will permit us to make these propositions more precise and explicit.

The concept of power has been defined in a great variety of ways by social scientists. In the past few years, as sociologists, political scientists, and now economists have turned their attention to power and its many ramifications in society, the variety of definitions has increased. Despite this tendency to proliferate definitions, there are certain schools of thought concerning the nature of power. Many sociologists define power as the ability on the part of one person to determine or control the behavior of another. This definition implies that acts performed by ego in accordance with ego's goals or purposes produce or determine behavior in alter. It separates from the total effect ego may have on alter in interaction with him (or indirectly on him through interaction with others) those effects which are deliberately sought, or which are produced through certain kinds of behavior which is called "power behavior." Unless some concept of "deliberate control" or "intentional determination" of alter's actions by ego is implied in the definition of power, all interaction between ego and alter becomes power behavior, and power becomes a veiled synonym for behavior itself.

This definition of power defines it positively in terms of ego's goals or objectives, saying, in effect, that ego has power over alter if ego can, according to his objectives or desires, shape alter's behavior as a means of obtaining his own objectives. Zald, in his paper, defines power in an almost opposite fashion. He says, "Power is defined as the ability of a person or group to affect another person's or group's ability to achieve its goals." In other words, ego has power over alter if ego is able, not to effect his own goal-achievement, but to affect alter's goal-achievement. This is a much more inclusive definition of power, since it defines as power anything that ego does which either positively or negatively, directly or indirectly, affects alter's goal-achievement. It leaves moot the question of whether or not ego's goal-achievement is effected. Presumably the actions of ego could, as in the first definition, be directed toward achieving his own goals. Thus Zald's definition represents the first type of power plus an additional increment of nongoal-directed power behavior on the part of ego.

It is clear that both definitions contain the notion of goal-achievement through social behavior and that they both involve the idea that ego possesses power in relation to alter when he is able to affect alter in some way. One definition, however, measures power in relation to ego's ability to produce behavior in alter, and the other measures it in terms of ego's ability to limit alter's goal-achievement.

The Zald definition sees power as setting conditions or limits on goal-achievement to which alter must adapt. It does not necessarily imply control over, nor determination of alter's behavior by ego, but, instead, it implies the limiting of it. Anything that ego can do that affects or "limits" alter's goal-achievement becomes power that ego has over alter, whether or not the effect is intentional on the part of ego. If the question of ego's intentions is left undefined, then the power of ego with respect to alter is a "veiled synonym" for the "total effect that ego has on an alter" and becomes identical to "interaction between ego and alter." Under such a definition, power cannot be used as a term in the explanation of organizational behavior, or as a variable with respect to it, because it becomes identical with organizational behavior. This statement is based on the following reasoning: Since ego and alter are part of the same system, and since all parts of a system affect each other, then all things that ego does will affect alter in varying degrees. Since it is difficult, if not impossible, to conceive of anything affecting alter which does not have some effect on alter's goal-achievement, then anything that ego does will constitute power over alter. It can be argued from this basic reasoning that despite this, some things ego does will have a large effect on alter's goal-achievement and, therefore, represent a large amount of power—while others will have a small effect and therefore constitute little power. This, however, does not change the fact that given this definition power is an assessment of causative potency. As such, it is a disguise for the notion of causation itself.

On this basis it seems desirable to limit the definition of the power concept so that it applies only to certain sorts of organizational behavior or to abandon it altogether. Power as a concept must obviously be limited to one class of causative influence with respect to organizational behavior if it is going to be valuable as an independent variable in explaining such behavior. If, on the other hand, we wish to use power as a dependent variable and attempt to explain its origin in a system of independent variables, one of which is the behavior of actors in the system, we must similarly distinguish power as a phenomenon from all of behavior as a phenomenon.

These arguments lead me to prefer the notion of power which sees it as "the ability of one actor deliberately to control or determine the actions of another." This means that ego must be able through his actions to elicit a desired response-behavior in alter, before he is said to have power over alter.

In most discussions of power it is difficult to avoid confusion between the phenomenon we mean to point to and designate as power and what can be called the source of power.

One school of thought, for example, does not restrict power as a phenomenon to some form of effect that one person has on another but also includes control over objects, resources, money, etc., as power. This type of definition confuses the source of power, "control over resources," with the phenomenon of power itself, "control over behavior." Given this point of view, wealth, property, and the control over the disposition and utilization of such "objects" in an organization is a source of power, rather than power itself.

Since we wish to treat power as a dependent variable as well as an independent variable in organization, it is necessary to distinguish between power and its sources. The sources of power are the independent variables through which we attempt to explain variations in power itself. Such variables as mentioned above seem, on the surface at least, to be almost "naturals" as independent variables with respect to power as a variable phenomenon.

To separate conceptually the notion of power from the concept of its "sources" makes possible the study of the interplay of political and economic factors in organizations suggested by Zald. Economic factors such as the ownership and control over organizational property and over the disposition of rewards in the system can be viewed as sources of power, and thereby we can examine the influence of the "economic phenomenon" on the phenomenon of power and vice versa. Without a conceptual separation of the notion of power from its sources, it is difficult for me to conceive of how the political-economy approach suggested by Zald can be utilized.

For the various reasons suggested above it seems desirable to be conservative in our concept of power and to use a restricted definition rather than an all-inclusive one. The definition "power consists of the ability of ego deliberately to shape or control the behavior of alter" seems more desirable on this account than more inclusive ones.

The definition given above also has some advantages in that it lends itself to a kind of "logical bookkeeping system" for thinking about power, which will allow us to deal with the assumptions and propositions listed at the beginning of this discussion. Such a system allows us to think about the limits of power and about its distribution in more or less precise theoretical terms. It will probably be of little value to us empirically because of our present inability to measure power effectively.

Let me begin by stating that what will follow is not an attempt to represent power as a "zero sum" game. At first it will appear to be so, but as the reasoning is developed it should become apparent that this is not the case.

If power is defined as being deliberate and purposeful control over the behavior of actors in a social system, there are upper and lower limits to the amount of power that can be generated in any given social system. The theoretical upper limit to power in an organization is set by the amount of behavior which takes place in the system. The amount of internal power cannot exceed "total control of all behavior." The lower limit is obviously zero where no behavior in the system is attributable to the control of alter by ego. In real organizations the actual amount of power will always fall somewhere between these limits.

If we were to call the upper limit of power in an organization the "power potential" of the organization, it is apparent that power potential is a function of organizational size. The more behavior and, therefore, the larger the organization, the greater the possibilities for power within the organization. Large organizations can and usually will contain more power than small ones.

Zald distinguishes between the internal and external polity of an organization. This points to a need to distinguish between the amount of power *in* an organization and the amount of power *of* an organization. The power *in* an organization refers to the power contained and utilized inside the boundaries of an organization to produce behavior within the organization. The power *of* an organization refers to the amount of power exercised by members of the organization over persons representing other organizations and groups in the environment, in other words, external power. Such external power is exercised in the community or society and forms the basis of "community power structure" rather than organizational power structure.

Zald and others have implied that external power may add to internal power in an organization. At first glance this claim seems to be erroneous. It can be reasoned as follows: Internal power consists of actions performed between and among members of the organization and takes place within the boundaries of the organization. It constitutes a relationship among members of an organization such that ego can and does control alter's behavior. Both ego and alter are members of the same organization. External power constitutes a relationship between a member of an organization and someone in another organization or group outside its boundaries. Power obtained by ego as a member of an organization over an alter outside must, therefore, be exercised over that particular alter. As a consequence, external power cannot be brought back into the organization and utilized as power over alters within the system. It is by definition power over an external alter.

It is possible, however, to accept Zald's view that external power adds to or increases internal power if we add an additional concept. The power that ego obtains externally in relationships he has in the organization's environment becomes for him a *source of internal power*. Rather than being added to his ability to control others inside the organization, it becomes a *power resource* that he can use in obtaining control over people inside the organization. Since it adds those elements which he can use to control others to the resources of a person inside the system, it can *indirectly* add to the amount of power that exists inside the system.

External power may, however, simply shift power inside the organization from one person to another. If the control that one person has over others inside the system is simply reduced and added to the ability of another person to control, the amount of power actually used in a system will not increase. It is probably true that external power has a far greater influence on the internal distribution of power than on the total amount of power used by members of the system in generating the behavior that takes place within it.

It is probably true that the major sources of power within a social system are contained within what Zald calls the internal economy of the system. Thus it makes a great deal of sense to approach the study of organizational power structure using what Zald calls the political-economy approach. Ownership and control over the disposition of organizational property and resources (the major element in economy) are likely to be the most important *sources* of power *in* an organization.

It is also likely that external power is obtained from relationships in the economic exchanges that members of the organization conduct with persons in its environment. This means the external economy may be viewed as the source of power in the external polity of the organization.

All of this adds up to say that making the distinction between polity and economy on the one hand and external and internal systems on the other promises to lead to fruitful understandings of organizational structure and functioning. It is critical, however, to the use of this approach to (1) use a conservative and restrictive definition of power that allows us to distinguish it from all behavior or all causation, and (2) distinguish carefully between the phenomenon we call power and those factors which produce it which can be regarded as its "sources." If these two things are not done, then polity and economy dissolve into an indistinguishable mass and along with other aspects of organization become simply organizational behavior in general.

7

Toward a Theory
of
Internal Resource-Allocation

LOUIS R. PONDY

Both economics and political science have recognized that all social systems face the problem of allocating scarce resources. Economists, e.g., Cohen and Cyert (1965:3–5), argue that society must answer four main questions regarding resource-allocation: what goods and services to produce; how to produce them; for whom to produce them; and what proportion of resources to devote to future growth as opposed to current consumption. And Lasswell (1936) has congently described politics as being concerned with "who gets what, when, how." However, the two disciplines have tended to focus their study on different mechanisms for allocating resources. Economics has been primarily concerned with market mechanisms operating through a price system: the market interaction of business firms maximizing profit and consumers maximizing utility is assumed to resolve the four questions posed by Cohen and Cyert. On the other hand, political science has focused on power processes, as manifested in political parties and representative governments: through voting mechanisms and coalition-formation, resources are assumed to be allocated among various interest groups. Economics has devoted considerable effort to assessing the social efficiency of market mechanisms and price systems as means of allocating scarce societal resources. However, considerably less attention has been devoted to the social efficiency of *political* mechanisms (e.g., alternative voting rules) for resource-allocation. There are exceptions to the latter assertion, of course, but most of the rigorous analyses of political efficiency have been carried out by economists or quantitatively oriented sociologists (Bower, 1965a, 1965b; Buchanan and Tullock, 1962; Coleman, 1966; Downs, 1957; see also the collection of papers and bibliographies in Tullock, 1966a, 1967a, 1967b, 1968).

Though the two disciplines focus on different allocation mechanisms, traditionally they have been concerned only with resource-allocation *among* the autonomous subunits (individual consumers, business firms, interest groups) in society at large, with society being treated by economics as an "economy of markets" and by political science as a "polity of power centers." Only recently have the social sciences begun to direct substantial attention toward understanding the process of resource-allocation *within* the constituent institutions of society—business firms, government agencies, universities, hospitals, labor unions, and so forth. Their success in this effort rests in large measure on the developments over the last three decades in the theory of organizational decision-making (Barnard, 1938; Simon, 1945; for a recent survey of such theories, see Feldman and Kanter, 1965). Although sociologists have devoted considerably more attention to studying the structure and behavior of formal organizations than other social scientists, they have tended not to focus on the resource-allocation problem. In part this is due to their using theoretical frameworks other than that of organizational decision-making (Downs, 1967:1).

Two related factors account for the growing interest in resource-allocation within large formal organizations. First, as Boulding (1953) and Presthus (1962) point out, large-scale organizations and concentration of power in them are relatively recent phenomena in American society. As documentation of the current concentration, consider that in 1964, 700 industrial corporations (out of 1.5 million) controlled nearly 50 percent of industrial assets, and the 360 largest colleges and universities (out of roughly 2000) enrolled, employed, or controlled 80 percent of the students, staff, and assets in American higher education. In 1968 the federal budget accounted for roughly 20 percent of GNP, with the Defense Department alone accounting for about 10 percent. There is reason to suspect that such large, powerful organizations may not be sensitive to the dictates of the market or the political process. To the extent that the social sciences regard the proper use of society's resources as an important problem, the allocation of resources within large organizations through administrative mechanisms becomes an important subproblem.

Second, market mechanisms as a means of resource-allocation throughout the economy have grown progressively less effective. This is due partly to the growing dominance of large organizations referred to above, but market imperfections may be created by other factors than oligopolistic concentration. Barriers to entry (e.g., patent-protection, high initial investment cost), for example, may permit firms to earn excess profits through restriction of output and/or raising prices above competitive levels without fear of competition from new firms. But the reduced effectiveness of markets as social-control mechanisms is also due to the growth of *nonmarket* organizations—foundations, government agencies, public universities and hospitals, labor unions— which are insulated to a great degree from the rigors of price competition in output markets and sometimes even in input markets (Downs, 1967: 29–30). Society has not yet developed effective social-control mechanisms for guaranteeing that these nonmarket organizations allocate their resources efficiently, relative to the aggregate preferences of society's members. Finally, market mechanisms have become less efficient resource-allocation devices because of the growing divergence between private and social benefits and costs (Cohen and Cyert, 1965:296– 297). As population becomes denser and more urbanized, and as the division of labor becomes progressively finer, it becomes increasingly likely that the self-interested actions of one social unit will impose external costs on another social unit or deprive it of external benefits. The imposition of water pollution on, and the failure to provide flood protection for, downstream areas are examples of such externalities which exist because markets fail to equate private and social benefit-cost ratios. In part, the growth of large organizations can be interpreted as an attempt to internalize such externalities. (For cross-cultural evidence on the correlation between division of labor and average size of organizations, see Gibbs and Browning, 1966.) Furthermore, the emergence of nonmarket organizations, especially government agencies, is in part a response to the need for regulation of actions subject to large external costs and benefits. (Downs, 1967:32–34; Buchanan and Tullock, 1962:43–62).

In summary, the growing interest in internal resource-allocation is seen as due to (a) the emergence of giant organizations which control large blocks of societal resources, and (b) the reduced effectiveness of market mechanisms as a means of guaranteeing that formal organizations efficiently allocate societal resources.

It should be emphasized, however, that the latter point does not imply that free market mechanisms operating through a price system are being or should be replaced wholly by administrative mechanisms for resource-allocation.

However, because of market imperfections and the existence of externalities, it is probably rational for society to supplement market mechanisms with certain administrative or nonmarket mechanisms of resource-allocation. We say "probably" rational because relatively little is known of the social efficiency of administrative decision-making, especially in nonmarket organizations (Downs, 1967:253–260), despite Presthus's (1962:287–316) claims of social inefficiency. Indeed, it is an unfortunate fact that little is known with any degree of certainty about the process of internal resource-allocation, let alone about its social efficiency.

The prime purpose of this paper, therefore, is to review and extend current efforts to develop a general theory of internal resource-allocation, which is capable of explaining and predicting how resources are allocated in a wide variety of organizational types, ranging from a business firm operating in purely competitive input and output markets to nonmarket organizations characterized by diffused control of resources, goal conflict among organizational subunits, flexibility in the choice of domain and technology, and nonzero costs of information-processing. In doing so, we shall rely heavily on the work of Cyert and March (1963), Williamson (1964, 1967a, 1967b), Downs (1967), Buchanan and Tullock (1962), Thompson (1967), Perrow (1967), Tullock (1966b), Arrow (1964), Wildavsky (1964), Olson (1965), and others. Following their lead, we shall proceed primarily by successive relaxation of the assumptions underlying the classical theory of the firm. Of special interest will be the gradual introduction of "political" mechanisms into the allocation process as these assumptions are relaxed.

Where appropriate, we shall cite empirical results which tend to support or disconfirm hypotheses derived from the various models, but shall also indicate the derived hypotheses for which no evidence exits.

Where possible we shall indicate in very general terms how the resulting theory might be used to establish public policies governing the formation, management, or regulation of formal organizations.

ASSUMPTIONS UNDERLYING CLASSICAL THEORY OF THE FIRM

Why should we begin our analysis with the assumptions underlying the classical theory of the firm? First, the assumptions are clear and unambiguous so that the process of deriving testable conclusions from them is a tractable problem.[1] Second, the assumptions embody the notion of an intendedly rational pursuit of self-interest, which, as we shall argue, provides the most reasonable basis for a theory of viable organizations. Third, the implications of and deductions from the assumptions have been traced out in great detail. Fourth, empirical hypotheses isomorphic to these deductions have been widely tested and found to be substantially confirmed. Therefore, any general theory of internal resource-allocation which also is based on the rational self-interest axiom must include the classical theory of the firm as a special case. To proceed in the development of a general theory by relaxing the assumptions of the classical theory of the firm does not, however, reduce our obligation to test the deductions of the general theory under conditions different from those prescribed by the special theory.

Nevertheless, the consistency of the general theory with classical theory of the firm will enhance our confidence in it as an explanation of resource-allocation and as a basis for prediction and control, over

1. Economists will recognize the ambiguities of the assumption of profit maximization under uncertain and nonstatic conditions. Other central assumptions of economic theory are nearly as ambiguous. However, relative to the other social sciences, economics does achieve more precision in the statement of its theories.

and above any confidence deriving solely from empirical confirmation of hypotheses not germane to the classical theory.

Although the assumptions were meant to apply specifically to business firms, they can be phrased in terms of organizations in general. They are: (1) The domain of the organization is given. By domain we mean the general class of goods produced or services rendered by the organization (Thompson, 1967:25–26), e.g., steel and steel products, health services, undergraduate education. (2) The technology of the organization is given. By technology we mean the techniques used in transforming inputs into outputs. It is represented as a production function which describes the various combinations of outputs from a set of inputs. (3) The process ,of securing, transmitting, and assimilating information on alternative courses of action and their consequences is costless. (4) The goals of the organization are given and are shared by all members of the organization. (This and the previous assumption allow us to treat the organization as a single decision-maker, since we can ignore any problems arising out of communicating information from one member to another, and any other difficulties of consensus-formation, conflict-resolution, enforcement of rules, or distribution of discretionary resources). (5) Resources are generated by selling (exchanging) the goods and services of the organization in output markets. Some or all of these resources are used to purchase factors of production (i.e., exchanged for other resources) in input markets. In a barter economy, the outputs are directly exchanged for inputs, but in a money economy input and output markets can be divorced because of the existence of money as a generalized resource or carrier of value. It is assumed that market prices exist which specify the rate of exchange between money resources and real resources (goods, services, and factors of production). (6) The organization, acting as a single decision-maker, chooses alternative courses of action (i.e., allocates resources to alternative activities) in order to maximize its goals, subject only to the constraints of the production function, the organization's markets and domain, and the availability of resources. (7) The organization is also assumed to maximize profits (i.e., excess of revenues over costs).

Under certain conditions, this last assumption follows from the more fundamental goal of survival; if the organization is operating in purely competitive input and output markets and it has no other source of resources than the sale of its outputs, its operational goal (i.e., its criterion for allocating resources) *must* be to maximize profits or else it will fail to survive. In long-run equilibrium, under conditions of free entry of competitive organizations into the domain, revenues will equal costs and profits will be zero. Thus under conditions of pure competition, the goal of profit-maximization is seen to be derivable from the more fundamental goal of survival.

If market conditions and technology are such as to make nonnegative profits impossible, the organization will eventually cease to exist and resources will gravitate to other organizations in the domain or to other domains until equilibrium is restored.

On the other hand, if imperfections exist in either input or output markets, positive profits may exist without competitive organizations entering the domain. Because of this possibility, the operational goal of profit-maximization no longer necessarily follows from the fundamental goal of survival. Thus it is necessary under conditions of market imperfections to introduce the goal of profit-maximization as an *explicit* assumption, as classical theory of the firm in fact does. To be precise, however, profits represent returns to the owners of the firm, who provided risk capital in expectation of yields in excess of those from alternative nonrisky investments. If instead we think of the excess of revenues over costs as *discretionary resources,* then we open up the possibility that these resources may be allocated to profit, as defined above, *or to other purposes.* What other purposes? They might, for example, be used to support a *revenue*-maximization goal, subject to a minimum profit-constraint (Baumol, 1959). The managers might, after all, derive more utility from operating a large business than a small, but more profitable, one, so long as survival is not endangered. Or, the discretionary resources might be used to hire additional staff and provide special management emoluments and superfluities over and above those specified by the market (Williamson, 1964). These two alternative criteria for allocating discretionary resources are the most prominent recent revisions to the classical theory of the firm which still retain the single decision-maker assumption. They are important because they have implications different from those of the profit-maximizing assumption regarding reallocation of the firm's resources in response to shifts in demand and changes in the rate or type of taxation. However, they also begin to relax some of the assumptions of classical theory, especially those related to the sharing of goals and the costlessness of information. Either they must assume that owners and managers have identical goals different from profit-maximization, or that owners value profit-maximization but are unable or unwilling to enforce their preferences on management without incurring costs in excess of the potential gain in profits.

In any case, the existence of market imperfections introduces the possibility of discretionary resources and gives us the first hint that the internal structure and processes of organizations may affect the pattern of resource-allocation in ways not completely dictated by external markets. Furthermore, the concept of discretionary resources provides us with a means of generalizing the profit-maximizing assumption to a nonbusiness-firm analog, to wit, that organizations seek to allocate their resources in such a way as to maximize discretionary resources. In the case of shared goals and zero information costs, this assumption is perfectly consistent with the axiom of rational, self-interested behavior when applied to the members of the organization.

The Special Case of Nonmarket Organizations

We have already pointed out that in a money economy input markets are divorced from output markets; that is, outputs are not directly exchanged for inputs, as in a barter economy. The organization's environment can be fragmented still further. Some organizations derive part or all of their revenues from sources other than the direct recipients or beneficiaries of the output of the organization. Downs (1967) includes the absence of an output market as one of his defining characteristics of bureaus. In the extreme case, none of the revenues of the organization arises out of voluntary quid pro quo transactions between the organization and recipients of the outputs, as for example in charities, unless one wishes to treat a charity as selling "satisfaction" to its donors (Tullock, 1966b). Universities and hospitals, among others, represent intermediate cases in which some but not all resources are derived from nonmarket sources. It is a well-known fact that students provide only a fraction of the operating revenues to universities, typically one fourth to one half.[2] The remainder comes from endowment income and gifts or grants from private individuals, foundations, business firms, and government agencies, none of whom are the direct recipients of the educational output, except in isolated cases such as classified research for the Defense Department. However, as Levy (1968) points out, unclassified research is properly termed a collective or public good which benefits others besides those who might directly support (purchase) it. An increasingly important characteristic of hospitals is the presence of "third party" payers (e.g., health insurance companies). Thus patients of the hospital do not bear the full marginal cost of health care. In the case of governments, it is true that the citizens are both the source of tax revenues and the beneficiaries of government services, but only in rare cases is it true that the act of paying taxes results in the "purchase" of some *specific* government service through a voluntary quid pro quo transaction.

This separation of revenue sources from output markets has two tremendously important implications: (1) It deprives the organization of a direct way of evaluating its output activities relative to the costs of the inputs used to produce them. As in the case of discretionary resources arising out of market imperfections, the personal goals of the organization members themselves may be invoked to rationalize the allocation of resources, thus introducing the possibility of social inefficiencies (Downs, 1967). (2) If the organization is assumed to maximize its discretionary resources, a certain proportion of its current resources will be devoted to promotional activities designed to increase the flow of nonmarket resources. This diversion of resources to promotional activities will be enhanced if the revenue sources do not derive at least indirect intrinsic benefit from the output, or are ignorant of the benefits. We are quick to point out, however, that these two enhancing factors hinge on the assumption that information-processing is costly (Tullock, 1966b).

---

2. In the case of large state universities which are heavily supported by federal funds (e.g., the University of California), tuition accounts for only about 5 percent of current funds revenue. On the other hand, in small private colleges, tuition may account for 70 percent to 80 percent or more of current funds revenue.

The foregoing discussion suggests that one important basis for classifying organizations is the degree to which they are nonmarket-oriented, perhaps as measured by the percentage of revenues derived from other than voluntary quid pro quo transactions between the organization and recipients of its noncollective outputs of goods and services.

Resource-Allocation in Closed Systems

Even in a pure nonmarket organization, the amount of resources received from elements in the environment depends on its activities (i.e., how it allocates its current resources internally). Either environmental elements respond to the promotional activities of the organization, or they provide resources to support the outputs which the organization delivers to others.

Suppose, however, that the resources the organization receives from the environment are *completely independent* of the activities carried out by the organization. (Assume for the sake of argument that the organization cannot generate new resources internally through its own efforts.) In no way can the organization increase or decrease its future flow of generalized resources (i.e., money or purchasing power). Also assume that the organization faces a market on the input side from which it may purchase inputs, and specifically that individual members join or leave the organization according to the inducements offered them by the organization. The Ford Foundation might provide an approximate example of this extreme case.[3]

How are resources likely to be allocated in such an organization? And are the resource-allocation mechanisms likely to be different from those in market-dominated and nonmarket but environmentally dependent organizations? If so, why?

The first thing to realize is that the allocation and use of resources is completely at the discretion of the membership of the organization, without the need to answer to any external elements in the environment and without the possibility of generating new resources either internally or externally. Clearly, promotional costs will go to zero, but what other

---

3. Or Rockefeller University which is said to have an endowment of one million dollars per student.

alternative uses of resources are there? [4] Basically, resources may be used either to support the output activities of the organization or to satisfy the purely *personal* preferences and wants of the members. However, we can easily include satisfaction of the members' own personal wants in the set of output activities. If the set of output activities includes nothing but various means of satisfying members' wants, the organization reduces to a pure case of what Blau and Scott (1962) have called "mutual benefit associations."

But we still need to make explicit our assumptions regarding goal consensus and information-processing costs. For example, assume that all members share the same set of goals, and that information-processing costs are zero. As in the classical theory of the firm, this allows us to treat the organization as a single decision-maker. Its goals can be described by a utility function, the arguments of which are the various alternative output activities. If, in addition, the domain of the organization is assumed to be given, it specifies the relevant output activities, though perhaps not the tradeoffs the organization is willing to make among them (e.g., legal versus medical education, if the domain is graduate professional training). Finally, if the technology is given, this implies a production function which describes the rates at which inputs are transformed into outputs. Under these assumptions, resource-allocation to various output activities takes place so as to maximize the organization's utility function, subject to the budget constraint of limited resources. Resources will be *re*allocated in response to changes in input prices, the production function, the level of available resources, and the goals of the organization. But this is essentially the theory of individual consumer behavior, modified only by the introduction of a production function. The "price" of a particular output activity, however, may vary depending on what combination of inputs is used to produce it.

This "consumer theory of organizations" goes beyond the theory of individual consumer behavior in one very important respect. It provides us with a language for describing how the entry or exit of members of the organization may change the production function and/or the goals

4. However, in the case of the Ford Foundation, the threat of federal taxation of foundations may induce it to allocate resources to promotional activities which are designed to defend its activities and publicize its social responsibility.

of the organization, and therefore the allocation of resources to selected output activities. For example, a potential member with some scarce skill or talent may demand as an inducement to his participation that the organization change its goals. If his command of a special technological skill sufficiently changes the production function so as to allow the organization to achieve its existing goals more effectively, the organization may be willing to make a "policy side-payment" (i.e., change its goals) in return for his participation (Cyert and March, 1963). This, of course, will affect the pattern of resource-allocation. This analysis, however, seems to violate our assumptions in two ways (but it also suggests a direction for generalizing the model): (a) To endow a potential member with a special technological skill violates the assumption that information (e.g., about technology) is costless to the organization; (b) Attributing to him goals different from those of the organization violates the goal-consensus assumption. The second difficulty is easily removed when we realize that goal consensus can be re-established *after* he becomes a part of the organization. The first difficulty is partially removed by pointing out that possession of scarce technological skills does not violate the assumption that information transmission and assimilation *within* the organization is costless. The cost to the organization (the disutility of changing its goals) arises out of incorporating the scarce technological knowledge, but this cost is offset by the increased productivity made possible by the new member.

Thus a consumer theory of organizations allows us to specify in general terms how resource-allocation, under the condition of a fixed resource stream, is affected by input prices, the production function, and the goals of the organization. And we have used it to describe one mechanism by which goals and the production function are modified.

But, as long as we retain the assumptions of goal consensus and free information, our theories remain relatively sterile in that they tell us little more than the classical theories of the firm and of individual consumer behavior, even when we relax the assumption about output markets. When the assumptions about goals and information costs are relaxed, however, we can no longer treat the organization as a single decision-maker. In treating the organization as a set of *multiple* actors (Feldman and Kanter, 1965), we shall be able to introduce more realism into our assumptions and therefore make our theory a richer explanation of internal resource-allocation phenomena. The next three sections trace out the implications of relaxing first the free-information assumption, second the goal-consensus assumption, and finally both assumptions simultaneously. In particular, admitting the possibility of goal conflict among members will help to make clear how "political" behavior affects the allocation of resources.

RELAXATION OF THE FREE-INFORMATION ASSUMPTION

In this section we admit the possibility that the acquisition, transmission, and assimilation of information are costly processes in that they require utilization of resources for their completion. That is, we assume that the process of deciding how to allocate resources is itself a resource-absorbing activity. However, we retain the assumption of goal consensus. All members of the organization are assumed to share the same set of goals because either (a) their compliance has been purchased as part of the employment contract; (b) they have been persuaded to accept the goals of other members through the use of indoctrination, training, or human relations techniques; (c) they have been selectively recruited on the basis of natural goal compatibility; or (d) they have segmented their personal and official goals and have accepted as official goals those prescribed for the organization by society (Feldman and Kanter, 1965). In any case, the assumption of goal consensus excludes the possibility that subunits of the organization will be motivated to increase their share of the organization's resources at the expense of other departments.

The internal allocation of resources under these conditions depends strongly on how ownership and/or control of resources is distributed among the members of the organization. Three ideal types are identified, and each is shown to be associated with some special problem: (1) Polycentered (Perrow, 1967) control of resources, and the problem of co-ordination when "externalities" exist among the subunits; (2) Centralized control of resources, and the problem of cumulative control-losses across hierarchical levels; (3) Atomized control of resources, and the problem of collective action, i.e., specifying the conditions under which a latent group of persons will commit resources to provide the group with a public or collective good.

The Co-ordination Problem

In this section, we shall discuss the conditions under which it is rational for an organization to co-ordinate the activities of two or more component departments. Beginning with the simplest case, consider an organization composed of two departments, D_1 and D_2. Suppose that each department produces some product or renders some service in quantities q_1 and q_2, respectively. Suppose further that the outputs of these two departments are sold in separate markets at prices p_1 and p_2, respectively, and that each department is motivated to maximize its profit. The problem facing each department is how much output to produce in order to achieve its goal of maximum profit. The optimum level of output will be a function of each department's cost structure, as well as of its market price.

Assume, for the sake of argument, that each department's cost is a quadratic function of its own output:

(1a) $\qquad C_1 = c_1 q_1^2$

(1b) $\qquad C_2 = c_2 q_2^2$

and that the respective revenues are given by

(2a) $\qquad R_1 = p_1 q_1$

(2b) $\qquad R_2 = p_2 q_2$

Then the profit for each department is given by

(3a) $\qquad \pi_1 = R_1 - C_1 = p_1 q_1 - c_1 q_1^2$

(3b) $\qquad \pi_2 = R_2 - C_2 = p_2 q_2 - c_2 q_2^2$

The optimum level of output for each department is then derived by differentiating π with respect to q, setting $\dfrac{d\pi}{dq} = 0$, and solving for q^*, whence:

(4a) $\qquad q_1^* = \dfrac{p_1}{2c_1}$

(4b) $\qquad q_2^* = \dfrac{p_2}{2c_2}$

The total profit for the entire organization is then given by

(5) $\qquad \pi^* = \pi_1^* + \pi_2^* = \dfrac{p_1^2}{4c_1} + \dfrac{p_2^2}{4c_2}$

Since the two departments are autonomous, self-contained units, there are no profits to be gained from co-ordinating their decisions on output levels.

Presence of Externalities.—Suppose, however, that they are not autonomous on the production side of the enterprise. In particular, assume that their respective cost functions are as follows:

(6a) $C_1 = c_1 q_1^2 + e_1 q_2$

(6b) $C_2 = c_2 q_2^2 + e_2 q_1$

That is, the cost which D_1 bears is partly a function of D_2's level of output, and vice versa. This may come about for a wide variety of reasons. Each may produce pollutants, noise, etc., which the other can reduce only by incurring some expense. In such a case e_1 and e_2 are positive, and we refer to their presence as "negative externalities" (negative, because one department's activities reduces the other's profits; external, because such profit-reductions are outside the department's control). However, e_1 and e_2 might be negative (i.e., positive externalities exist). For example, useless scrap from D_1's production might be a valuable raw material to D_2.

Since D_1 cannot control the level of q_2, nor D_2, q_1, the optimum levels of output for each separate department are still $q_1^* = \dfrac{p_1}{2c_1}$ and $q_2^* = \dfrac{p_2}{2c_2}$. Suppose, however, that q_1 and q_2 are set jointly to maximize $\pi_1 + \pi_2$. The total profit for the organization is given by

(7) $\pi = \pi_1 + \pi_2 = R_1 + R_2 - C_1 - C_2$

(8) $\pi = p_1 q_1 + p_2 q_2 - c_1 q_1^2 - e_1 q_2 - c_2 q_2^2 - e_2 q_1$

Taking the partial derivatives of π with respect to both q_1 and q_2, and setting them equal to zero, we obtain:

(9a) $\dfrac{\partial \pi}{\partial q_1} = p_1 - 2c_1 q_1 - e_2 = 0$

(9b) $\dfrac{\partial \pi}{\partial q_2} = p_2 - 2c_2 q_2 - e_1 = 0$

And solving for the optimum levels of output,

(10a) $q_1^{**} = \dfrac{p_1 - e_2}{2c_1}$

(10b) $q_2^{**} = \dfrac{p_2 - e_1}{2c_2}$

where ** denotes the *co-ordinated* optimum output levels.

Using the unco-ordinated optima, $\dfrac{p_1}{2c_1}$ and $\dfrac{p_2}{2c_2}$, the departments' respective profits are given by

(11a) $\qquad \pi_1{}^* = \dfrac{p_1{}^2}{4c_1} - \dfrac{e_1 p_2}{2c_2}$

(11b) $\qquad \pi_2{}^* = \dfrac{p_2{}^2}{4c_2} - \dfrac{e_2 p_1}{2c_1}$

for a total profit of

(12) $\qquad \pi^* = \dfrac{p_1{}^2}{4c_1} + \dfrac{p_2{}^2}{4c_2} - \dfrac{e_1 p_2}{2c_2} - \dfrac{e_2 p_1}{2c_1}$

But using the co-ordinated optima given in equations 10a and 10b, the departmental profits are given by

(13a) $\qquad \pi_1{}^{**} = \dfrac{p_1{}^2}{4c_1} - \dfrac{e_1 p_2}{2c_2} - \dfrac{e_2{}^2}{4c_1} + \dfrac{e_1{}^2}{2c_2}$

(13b) $\qquad \pi_2{}^{**} = \dfrac{p_2{}^2}{4c_2} - \dfrac{e_2 p_1}{2c_1} - \dfrac{e_1{}^2}{4c_2} + \dfrac{e_2{}^2}{2c_1}$

for a total profit of

(14) $\qquad \pi^{**} = \dfrac{p_1{}^2}{4c_1} + \dfrac{p_2{}^2}{4c_2} - \dfrac{e_1 p_2}{2c_2} - \dfrac{e_2 p_1}{2c_1} + \dfrac{e_1{}^2}{4c_2} + \dfrac{e_2{}^2}{4c_1}$

Comparing (14) with (12), it can be seen that the total profit resulting from co-ordinating decisions on q_1 and q_2 exceeds the total profit when q_1 and q_2 are set disjointly, by an amount equal to:

(15) $\qquad \Delta\pi = \pi^{**} - \pi^* = \dfrac{e_1{}^2}{4c_2} + \dfrac{e_2{}^2}{4c_1}$

That is, if externalities exist between the two departments, *whether positive or negative,* operating profits will be higher if decisions regarding resource-utilization are made jointly (i.e., if they are co-ordinated) than if they are made separately. With some qualifications, this result is easily generalized to the case of more than two subunits. Generally speaking, the larger the number of subunits that make their resource-allocation decisions jointly, the lower the external costs arising out of autonomously made decisions. In the absence of information-processing costs, therefore, all decisions ought to be made jointly by all subunits in consultation with one another.

As formulated above, however, the potential increase in total profits (or, alternatively, reduction in external costs) does not take account of the cost of co-ordinating the two units. At the very least, the act of co-ordination involves exchanging information about externalities among the subunits. (We are assuming differential access to information; e.g., only department No. 1 knows the value of e_1, and this information must be communicated to department No. 2.) Since we are assuming nonzero information-processing costs, the act of co-ordination is therefore a costly process. If, in fact, the cost of co-ordination exceeds the potential gain in total profits, then it is more rational *not* to co-ordinate the units, but instead to allow them to continue making decisions autonomously.

Other things being equal, the cost of co-ordination will increase as the number of subunits being co-ordinated increases. For example, consider an organization comprising 12 subunits, each of which imposes external costs on the others. Co-ordinating all 12 together is more costly than co-ordinating the decisions within two groups of six units each, which in turn is more costly than co-ordination within three groups of four subunits each, etc. When all 12 subunits allocate their resources autonomously, co-ordination costs are zero, but external costs are at a maximum. As the size of the co-ordination unit increases, the co-ordination costs increase (probably at an increasing rate),[5] but the external costs decrease (probably at a decreasing rate) until external costs reduce to zero under full co-ordination, as in Figure 1.[6]

The assumption that the organization acts rationally (pursues its goals efficiently) implies that it will attempt to minimize the total of external costs and co-ordination costs. Playing a variation on a theme by Buchanan and Tullock (1962), this allows us to derive a proposition about the optimum level in the organization (i.e., the optimum size of

5. For example, if twelve subunits are departmentalized into three groups of four subunits each, we say that the size of the co-ordination unit is four. To say that co-ordination costs increase as the size of the co-ordination unit increases only takes account of co-ordination costs *within* each co-ordination unit. We assume that *no* co-ordination takes place *between* co-ordination units.

6. Under full co-ordination, all decisions are made jointly, and therefore all externalities are internalized, and external costs fall to zero. This analysis ignores another class of costs arising out of biased or distorted information-exchange. The next section treats these control-losses as they relate to the size of an organization.

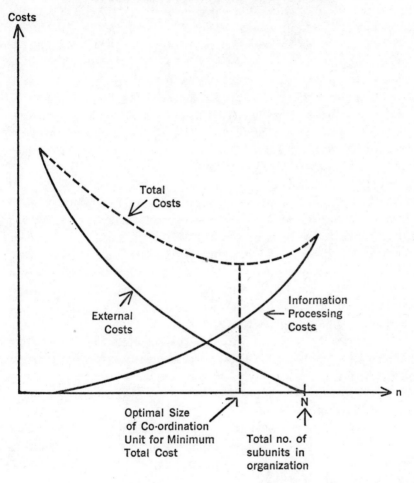

FIGURE 1.

EXTERNAL AND INFORMATION PROCESSING COSTS AS
A FUNCTION OF SIZE OF CO-ORDINATING UNIT

Costs

Total
Costs

External
Costs

Information
Processing
Costs

n

N

Optimal Size
of Co-ordination
Unit for Minimum
Total Cost

Total no. of
subunits in
organization

n = size of Co-ordination unit

the co-ordination unit) at which resource-allocation decisions ought to be made: Assuming that organizations value efficiency, the degree to which resource-allocation decisions are centralized will increase with the magnitude of interdepartmental externalities and decrease with the costs of information-processing.

It will be obvious to some that use of the concept of externalities is just one way of clarifying the concept of interdependence used by many scholars (e.g., Thompson, 1967). Thus, the budgeting function tends to be centralized at the *corporate* level in integrated firms, such as U.S. Steel, which are departmentalized into interdependent functional units (e.g., mining, refining, finishing, marketing), but decentralized at the *divisional* level in multiproduct firms, such as PPG Industries, which are departmentalized along self-contained product lines (e.g., glass, paint, chemicals, plastics).

Furthermore, any factor which increases the cost of information exchange and processing will lead to decentralized or polycentralized control of resources (e.g., geographical dispersion, differential access to information, diversity of perceptual mechanisms, etc.) (Ramstrom, 1967; March and Simon, 1958). To our knowledge, these propositions have not been subjected to rigorous empirical tests, but they are generally consistent with Chandler's (1962) historical analysis of multi-divisionalized industrial enterprises.

The above analysis has assumed that co-ordination takes place through joint consultation among the relevant subunits. But other less direct means of co-ordination are possible under conditions of goal consensus and nonzero information costs, and have received considerable attention from economists.

One line of analysis attempts to derive artificial prices, which take account of the interdepartmental externalities. In our example, for instance, artificial prices of $p_1 - e_2$ and $p_2 - e_1$ for departments 1 and 2, respectively, would lead each department to allocate its resources in a manner optimal for the firm as a whole. As the number of subunits increases, it becomes more efficient to channel information about externalities to some central unit and allow it to derive the optimal set of prices, instead of an all-to-all exchange of information. Under certain conditions of decomposability, it is also possible to define profit centers for control purposes which are autonomous when operating under the appropriate artificial prices. For example, see Arrow (1964), Baumol and Fabian (1964), and Haas (1968).

On the other hand, team theory (J. Marschak, 1959; T. Marschak, 1965) attempts to derive decision rules which describe optimal subunit responses to environmental changes with a minimum exchange of information. Both of these lines of analysis were developed primarily for normative or prescriptive purposes; they are, however, also testable as empirical propositions, but have not been so tested to our knowledge.

The Control-Loss Problem

For the purposes of this section, suppose that the control of resources and the allocation-decision process are completely centralized. Information necessary to make those decisions, however, is typically distributed throughout the organization and must be communicated across hierarchical levels to the central budget officer. Furthermore, decisions regarding the allocation of resources must be communicated back down through the organization, again across successive hierarchical levels. Tullock (1965) has argued that information is unintendedly distorted and biased each time it is passed from one level to another, upward or downward, even in the absence of goal conflict among members. (The distortion and bias are of course greater when goal conflict exists, and may in fact be deliberate.) The more hierarchical levels there are in an organization, the greater the *cumulative* distortion and bias of information; therefore the greater the divergence is between actions at the operational level and goals at the top of the organization. Tullock argues that such cumulative control losses eventually create an internal limitation to the size of the organization. His argument has been refined and extended by Downs (1967) and formulated as a mathematical model by Williamson (1967a). Their analysis allows us to make some rough estimates of the proportion of an organization's resources absorbed as unintended inefficiencies and/or as costs of enforcing control. (It is not, however, designed to predict what activities or subunits will be funded or receive resources.)

Williamson expresses the proportion of any subordinate's activities which contributes to his immediate superior's objectives as a compliance parameter, α. Given certain assumptions about the span of control and other parameters, he estimates α to be in the neighborhood of 0.9 for the General Motors Corporation. For an organization with n hierarchical levels, the total effective compliance at the working level of the organization is therefore $\propto^{n-1}$, since *cumulative* control losses occur across $n-1$ levels. Given this formulation and certain other assumptions (e.g., profit-maximization), Williamson is able to deduce that the optimal size of organizations will: (a) increase with compliance; (b) decrease with labor intensity; (c) increase with the span of control (assuming compliance is independent of the span of control); and (d) decrease as the ratio of wage rates between successive levels increases.

One interesting implication of the Tullock-Williamson model not investigated by them arises out of allowing the compliance parameter, $\propto$, to vary in different parts of the organization. Suppose $\propto$ is higher in one division of the organization than in another, and that neither division's size is limited by falling demand curves or rising supply curves. Then their model implies, other things equal, that the division with the higher compliance will be larger (i.e., *more resources will be allocated to it*), than the division with the lower compliance. Partial confirmation of this hypothesis has been provided by a laboratory experiment conducted by Pondy and Birnberg (1969). To the extent that low compliance is reflected by biased estimates and irrelevant or misleading communication on the part of division managers, Pondy and Birnberg found that larger budgets were allocated to "experimental managers" who exhibited high compliance. This finding is qualified by the fact that when all managers were equally profitable and equally accurate in their estimates of profitability, the larger budget was allocated to the manager who exerted the greater pressure in the form of misleading comments. This deviation from our expectations was greatest when actual profits were high and estimates biased for all managers, and least when actual profits were low and estimates accurate for all managers. Actually, this last result is consistent with our earlier allegations that the effect on resource-allocation of *internal* structure and processes is minimized under purely competitive conditions, i.e., when discretionary profits are near zero and a state of perfect knowledge is approached.

To our knowledge, no other direct evidence exists on the relationship between divisional compliance and the size of divisional budget-allocations. One excellent and potentially fruitful source of data and intermediate results has, however, been generated by Davis, Dempster, and Wildavsky (1966). In their study of incremental budgeting in the federal government, they have estimated the rate of budgetary increase from year to year for 56 nondefense agencies. Williamson (1967b) has attempted to explain the interagency variation in rates of budgetary increases in terms of the political attractiveness of the agency's activities, but the variations might also be explained in terms of variations in agency compliance. For example, OEO and other poverty program agencies have been critized on the grounds of inefficient use of resources and noncompliance with program objectives.

The Collective-Action Problem

In this section we review briefly Olson's (1965) analysis of the conditions under which the individuals or subunits of a latent group are likely to commit their resources to provide some "collective good" for the group as a whole. We assume that the ownership and/or control of resources is atomized or widely dispersed among group members. In a sense, Olson's analysis is concerned with the *converse* of resource-allocation; i.e., resource-mobilization, but from the viewpoint of the elemental subunits it deals with *their* allocation of resources to support collective action. It thus allows us to talk about the conditions under which organizations come into being as collective entities.

The key concept in Olson's analysis is the "collective good," which is defined relative to some group of persons. A good is said to be collective such that, if any person in the group consumes it, it cannot be *feasibly* withheld from others in the group. By contrast, a "private good" can be consumed selectively by some *subset* of group members. Examples of collective goods are the availability of common facilities (e.g., transit facilities, roads, schools); or common conditions (e.g., non-polluted air or streams); group attributes (e.g., prestige); and market characteristics (e.g., price or tariff levels, tax rates, etc.) Private goods are, for example, most consumer goods.

Olson's treatment of collective action embraces collectivities more general than formal organizations, for example the firms in an industry or the citizens of a political unit, but this does not reduce its applicability to the analysis of formal organizations.

The central idea of his essay is that large groups of individuals have no tendency to act *voluntarily* to further their *common* interests, unless the group is able to *enforce* co-ordination (in which case action is not voluntary) or unless the group has an independent source of *selective* incentives (in which case the motivation to serve common interests is supplemented by a motivation to serve personal interests). Small groups are more likely to act jointly to secure common interests, but even that propensity is by no means assured. The reason large groups do not spontaneously act jointly is that each individual perceives his contribution to be so small as not to be noticeable in the over-all effect. Since any given individual, by *himself,* can guarantee the collective good *only* by bearing the entire cost, he will not be motivated to act jointly. This will be true for all individuals in the group. Thus, despite the fact each and every individual rationally might desire the collective good, no spontaneous mechanism exists which will allow them to act in concert. If all other group members act to provide the collective good, he will receive the benefits therefrom even if he does not so act; therefore, he is motivated *not* to act jointly. He incurs the same cost if he acts jointly, independent of whether the others act jointly or not. But every individual member reaches the same conclusion, and thus the collective good is not provided despite the fact that its provision would be rational to the individual if every, or perhaps if even only some, other members could be counted on to *share* the cost of providing it. Therefore, solely on the grounds of voluntary self-interest, large organizations are unstable and would not exist.

Thus Olson questions whether it is rational for the individual worker voluntarily to make contributions to create and support a labor union even when he would enjoy the fruits of a union's efforts to provide higher wages and other collective benefits. Similarly, he asks whether a business firm would rationally contribute to the creation and support of a lobbying group for its industry, even though it would benefit from the formal pressure group's achievements of legislation favorable to the industry without his contribution.

He concludes that as the latent group grows large, the likelihood that its individual members will rationally act to provide some collective good decreases. In very large groups (analogous to purely competitive situations), an individual member's effect on providing the collective good is imperceptible, and the direct benefit to him from his action is less than the cost of his participation.

The fact that large business firms, labor unions, pressure groups, and professional associations do in fact exist requires explanation. Olson argues that they exist only because one or more of the following conditions obtain: (a) Membership is compulsory; e.g., as required by labor legislation legalizing the union shop and closed shop; (b) The organization has a pool of discretionary resources which can be used to offer *individual, selective incentives* to induce participation; (c) Interest in the collective good is so uneven that the most powerful group member will bear the entire cost and provide the collective good to all group members; (d) The organization already exists for some other purpose, and the provision of a particular collective good is merely a "byproduct" activity.

Olson's view of group action is contrasted with more traditional theories of group behavior which assume that groups have some organic, anthropomorphic life of their own, or that individuals possess some group *instinct*. (But the instinctual approach begs the question.) In Olson's view, groups and larger systems exist, to the limited extent that they do, only because individuals *want* them to exist, find self-interested merit in their existence, and work to create them. Groups under limited conditions may spontaneously spring into existence because of individual self-interest, but they do not possess an existence per se of their own. We need to find the rationale of organizational existence in the self-interested behavior of individuals. Olson's methodological individualism is inconsistent with the social-systems approach of most sociologists who argue that subsystems exist because they are functional for the parent system. We argue in contrast that subsystems exist because they fulfill needs of individual members.

One subtle, but essential, idea of Olson's is that even *perfect consensus by itself is insufficient* to guarantee collective action if the group is so large that at least one person by himself is not motivated to provide the entire collective good.

Some other social science works have recognized the difficulty which increasing group size creates for co-ordination of the groups, e.g., Thibaut and Kelley (1959:239), but even they seem to assume that, once norms evolve to ensure consensus, the problem of collective action is solved. But Olson's point is that even perfect consensus is not sufficient for spontaneous joint action. Consensus does not usually generate the necessary individual incentives, especially in large groups.

Only if we assume that each individual "identifies" psychologically with the group—invests himself psychically in the collective welfare—is group or joint action likely to spring forth (Coleman, 1966b). More likely is that the collectivity will be made viable only by providing individual noncollective inducements to participation. Olson's distinction between collective and selective incentives and the role each plays in creating the organizational equilibrium is an important adjunct to the "inducements-contributions balance" model of March and Simon (1958) and the "economy of incentives" model of Barnard (1938).

However, some latent large groups may be collectively mobilized by *federating* them, that is, by coalescing them into a small, manageable number of subgroups, each of which is also small enough to be stable collectively. In this way *hierarchies* may grow up for purposes of collective stability. What is important is not the total number of individuals but the number of *decision centers*, each of which may be made up of several individuals. Thus, not only may the size of a given group be important, but its *structure* may also be important. But this is exactly Olson's point—for very large groups, collective action is possible only with some explicit co-ordination or administrative mechanism which coerces compliance or induces it through the use of selective incentives. Once the organization has been formed by the commitment of resources to collective activity, it then faces the problem of reallocation of those resources within the newly created organization.

RELAXATION OF THE GOAL-CONSENSUS ASSUMPTION

In this section we admit the possibility of goal conflict among the members of the organization, but retain the assumption that information-processing costs are zero. It is not our intent to explain in any detail why goal conflict exists in organizations. (For a full discussion of the sources of goal consensus and diversity, see Downs, 1967:223–246.) We merely accept the fact that the members' personal goals and/or their goals for the organization may not be fully compatible, and seek to trace the implications of this fact for internal resource-allocation.

As in the preceding sections the distribution of ownership or control of resources exerts a strong influence on how resources are allocated to support various activities. If the ownership and control of organizational resources is completely centralized in the hands of one person, discretionary resources will be allocated so as to maximize *his* utility function. This follows from the assumption that information is costless, and therefore that the cost of enforcing his preferences on the rest of the group is zero. This needs to be qualified only to the extent that he might need to modify his goals in order to secure the services of some person who possesses a scarce technological skill, as was described in our analysis of resource-allocation in closed systems.

If the ownership and control of organizational resources are dispersed in a roughly even fashion among the members of the organization, and if the organization is large, the situation reduces to that of pure competition. That is, resources will be allocated to organization activities through some form of exchange system, with each participant attempting to maximize his own self-interest, but with insufficient power to influence the allocation process solely through his own efforts.

The only interesting case, given our assumptions about goals and information, occurs when resource control is polycentered, but not atomized. To be more precise, it is not strictly necessary that resource control be polycentered, so long as the members have other sources of power, such as possession of some scarce skill or talent needed by the organization. The set of members who derive power from one source or another together constitute a minimum coalition for organization viability, and each exercises an effective veto over any collective decision, including resource-allocation decisions.

In making decisions about how resources shall be allocated among the interest groups, the organization as a whole (or, more precisely, the dominant coalition of powerful members) faces a *constitutional* question. That is, what rules and mechanisms should be set up for carrying out the allocation process? These decisions about procedure precede any specific allocation decisions. The rules and mechanisms may include the establishment of committees, the use of formal budgets and long-range plans, the legitimization or definition of different classes of resource-use, etc. Because each coalition member has veto power, agreement on constitutional arrangements will need to be unanimous. The only reason a rule of *less* than unanimity for every decision would be agreed to by the members of the dominant coalition is that unanimity leads to excessive decision-making costs; but if we assume zero costs of information-processing, the dominant coalition members will adopt a rule of unanimity for *all* decisions.

This is analogous to our earlier allegation that co-ordination under goal consensus will be completely centralized in the absence of information-processing costs, with one crucial difference: No superordinate set of goals (joint preference-ordering) exists to guide the allocation of resources. Furthermore, Arrow (1963) has proven that it is impossible to develop a social-welfare function which uniquely and exhaustively maps the set of individual preference-orderings (goals) into a joint preference-ordering and which also satisfies four other conditions of reasonableness (i.e., nondictatorship, nonimposition, independence of irrelevant alternatives, and a positive association of individual preferences with the joint preference-ordering).

Thus, our requirement that resource-allocation decisions be unanimous within the dominant coalition implies a much weaker criterion of optimality than maximizing a superordinate utility function, specifically Pareto optimality. An allocation of resources is said to be Pareto optimal for the organization if any reallocation makes at least one member of the dominant coalition worse off relative to his own goals. Clearly a number of allocation patterns, perhaps an infinite number, will satisfy this weak criterion for any given organization; but it at least excludes from consideration those allocation patterns which are suboptimal in the Pareto sense. To understand how an organization chooses a specific allocation pattern from among those in the Pareto set, we need to examine more closely the internal dynamics of communication, persuasion, and the exercise of personal power (Lieberman, 1965).

Even before we reach that point, however, considerable work needs to be done, and some is being carried out, to design group-decision rules which are in fact Pareto optimal. Merely stating the criterion does not tell us how to go about achieving it. One line of investigation has examined the role which "side-payments," "vote-trading," and "logrolling" play in achieving Pareto optimality (Buchanan and Tullock, 1962:171–199; Coleman, 1966a; Plott, 1967). The essence of the argument is that if each member makes concessions on those issues he values least in order to gain concessions from others on those issues he values most, some or all of the members may be made better off without any member being made worse off.

Despite theoretical interest in the social-choice question, relatively few empirical studies have been carried out on the comparative performance characteristics of different group-decision rules (Lieberman, 1965:1), especially as they apply to resource-allocation decisions (Wheeler, 1967). Birnberg and Pondy (1968), for one, have studied the comparative effects of different voting rules on the allocation-decisions of experimental three-man committees. Restrictive voting rules (e.g., unanimity rule) caused the committees to agree only on budgets with small total payoffs which were evenly divided among the committee members. Less restrictive voting rules (e.g., simple majority) caused the committee to agree on budgets with larger total payoffs, even though the payoffs were less evenly divided among the members. Payoffs to the three committee members across the set of available allocation plans were always partially conflicting. Each committee made 54 relatively *simple* decisions, in that full information on payoffs was available to all members. But no communication was permitted for the purpose of exchanging intentions or making offers of co-operation. In a similar experiment, Bower (1965a, 1965b) studied the comparative effects of a majority and unanimity voting on investment decisions in two types of committees—"teams" (equal division of group payoffs among members) and "foundations" (individual shares of the group payoff dependent on individual performance). Extensive exchange of information and discussion of investment alternatives was permitted among group members. Contrary to common expectations, Bower found that under certain specified conditions (e.g., truncation of the sample to exclude no-choice outcomes), committees operating under the restrictive voting rule of unanimity made *better* decisions, relative to an objective but complex criterion, than those operating under the less restrictive rule of simple majority, and that the relative improvement due to a shift from majority to unanimity rule was greater for foundations than for teams. Bower inferred that the combination of restrictive voting rules and intracommittee conflict intensified the processes of search and analysis, and thus improved the quality of the group decision. If the cost of searching for and analyzing investment alternatives and of exchanging information among committee members were zero, all of those informational activities would be carried out equally under all voting rules. But those activities clearly involved costs in time and effort to the subjects. They would rationally be carried out only if the cost of not doing so were higher. Since the cost of failing to reach agreement is more likely to be incurred under restrictive voting rules and in the presence of intragroup conflict, intensified search and analysis are more likely under those conditions. When full information is already available (as in the experiment by Birnberg and Pondy), or when information costs are zero, the differences among voting rules in aggregate performance (e.g., total group payoff) will be due strictly to their relative effects on the probability of agreement, in which case the less restrictive voting rules will be superior. But even this difference will disappear if we assume that the costs of reaching agreement are also zero. What remains under a condition of free information, as we have already said, is the differential capacity of voting rules to produce Pareto-optimal decisions.

RELAXATION OF BOTH ASSUMPTIONS

By relaxing the free-information and goal-consensus assumptions simultaneously, we make our analysis both more relevant to the real world and less tractable. In part, simultaneous relaxation of the assumptions merely intensifies some of the effects described previously. For example, cumulative control-losses (and therefore limitations to organization size) are greater when goals are inconsistent than when goals are shared (Williamson, 1967a). But relaxing both assumptions also introduces some wholly new phenomena, most of which revolve around problems of enforcement.

Need for Hierarchial Control of Co-ordination

Consider again the problem of co-ordinating two subunits in the presence of interdepartmental externalities. Previously we had assumed that each department was merely maximizing an objective function which bore no relation to the self-interest of the department's managers. Suppose, however, that each department's profits represent discretionary resources which it can use to advance its own special interests. Under these conditions, co-ordination will involve not only (a) an exchange of information about each other's external costs, but also (b) bargaining over how to divide the total increase in profits between the two departments, and (c) enforcement of the jointly set output levels.

Because each department is attempting to maximize its own self-interest, all three of these co-ordinative activities may be exceedingly difficult to implement successfully. Just because the organization as a whole benefits from jointly deciding q_1 and q_2 does not mean that both departments individually benefit from joint decision-making. For example, if $e_1 = 0$ (i.e., D_1 experiences no externalities), but $e_2 > 0$ (i.e., D_1 causes D_2 to experience external diseconomies), then the potential change in D_1's profit is

$$(16a) \qquad \Delta\pi_1 = \pi_1^{**} - \pi_1^* = -\frac{e_2^2}{4c_1},$$

actually a decrease in D_1's profits, due to the fact that D_1 must cut back production from $q_1^* = \dfrac{p_1}{2c_1}$ to $q_1^{**} = \dfrac{p_1 - e_2}{2c_1}$ in order to reduce D_2's external diseconomies. But since D_1 experiences no externalities, D_2 can maintain $q_2^{**} = q_2^*$, and as a result of D_1's output reduction, has a potential profit increase of

$$(16b) \qquad \Delta\pi_2 = \pi_2^{**} - \pi_2 = +\frac{e_2^2}{2c_1}$$

Thus, unless D_2 offers D_1 a side-payment in excess of $\dfrac{e_2^2}{4c_1}$, D_1 will not be motivated to participate voluntarily in the joint determination of q_1 and q_2. Furthermore, the size of the side-payment is indeterminate. It may range anywhere from the minimum of $\dfrac{e_2^2}{4c_1}$ up to the entire $\dfrac{e_2^2}{2c_1}$. Considerable effort may be expended in bargaining between D_1 and D_2 about the appropriate size of the side-payment necessary to induce D_1's co-operation.

Let us return now to the case where *both* e_1 and e_2 are positive. Then the potential departmental gains in profit are given by

(17a) $$\Delta\pi_1 = \frac{e_1^2}{2c_2} - \frac{e_2^2}{4c_1}$$

(17b) $$\Delta\pi_2 = \frac{e_2^2}{2c_1} - \frac{e_1^2}{4c_2}$$

When (18) $\frac{c_2}{2c_1} < \frac{e_1^2}{e_2^2} < \frac{2c_2}{c_1}$, $\Delta\pi_1$ and $\Delta\pi_2$ will both be positive, and side-payments will not be necessary to induce co-operation in joint setting of q_1 and q_2. However, this is not sufficient to remove the necessity for bargaining over a division of the gains from co-operation. In fact, the bargaining may be more difficult because the full range of percentage-splits is available since neither party is hurt by joint decision-making.

So far we have assumed that the two departments will exchange information on externalities without deliberately attempting to bias estimates. In fact, other things being equal, D_1's profit will be higher whenever D_2's output is lower, and *mutatis mutandis*. Since the joint optimum for D_2 is given by

(19) $$q_2{**} = \frac{p_2 - e_1}{2c_2},$$

D_1 is motivated to bias his estimate of e_1 upward, thus increasing his profit at the expense of D_2 (and at the expense of total profit!). Neither party is, in fact, motivated to estimate his external costs accurately. Thus, co-ordination of the two departments also involves attempts to guarantee the accuracy of exchanged information.

But even if the bargaining problem is resolved and accuracy of information-exchange is guaranteed, there still remains the problem of enforcing the jointly set optimum output levels. As in the case of information-exchange, each department will find it in its own self-interest to "welch" on the co-ordinated agreement and to revert to the unco-ordinated output level. This can be seen in a numerical illustration, using the above model. Assume the following parametric values:

$p_1 = p_2 = 24$

$c_1 = 3 \qquad e_1 = 4$

$c_2 = 2 \qquad e_2 = 6$

Then the unco-ordinated and co-ordinated optimum output levels are:

$q_1{}^* = 4 \qquad q_1{}^{**} = 3$

$q_2{}^* = 6 \qquad q_2{}^{**} = 5$

The unco-ordinated and co-ordinated optimum profit levels, and the profit gains are:

$\pi_1{}^* = 24 \qquad \pi_1{}^{**} = 25 \qquad \Delta\pi_1 = +1$

$\pi_2{}^* = 48 \qquad \pi_2{}^{**} = 52 \qquad \Delta\pi_2 = +4$

$\pi^* = 72 \qquad \pi^{**} = 77 \qquad \Delta\pi = +5$

However, what happens when D_1 produces $q_1{}^{**}$, but D_2 produces only $q_2{}^*$ (that is, D_2 welches on his agreement to restrict production)? Or, alternatively when D_2 produces $q_2{}^{**}$, but D_1 produces only $q_1{}^*$? As can be seen, the department that welches gains, at the expense of the other department.

For $q_1{}^{**}$ and $q_2{}^*$, $\qquad \pi_1 = 21 \qquad \Delta\pi_1 = -3$

$\pi_2 = 54 \qquad \Delta\pi_2 = +6$

$\pi = 75 \qquad \Delta\pi = +3$

For $q_1{}^*$ and $q_2{}^{**}$, $\qquad \pi_1 = 28 \qquad \Delta\pi_1 = +4$

$\pi_2 = 46 \qquad \Delta\pi_2 = -2$

$\pi = 74 \qquad \Delta\pi = +2$

These results are summarized in the payoff matrix in Figure 2. Each square of the matrix shows the change in departmental profit from the $(q_1{}^*, q_2{}^*)$ condition (D_1's incremental profit is in the lower left triangle, D_2's in the upper right triangle, of each square), as a function of the two output levels.

This payoff configuration is in the form of the familiar prisoner's dilemma. It is advantageous to a given party to co-operate only if the other party also co-operates. If trust breaks down (that is, if each party suspects that the other will renege on his agreement to co-operate), then the system will revert to the unco-ordinated state, and *both* parties will be worse off relative to the co-ordinated optimum.

In most bureaucratic organizations, relations between officials tend to be impersonal and circumscribed. Under such conditions, interpersonal trust is unlikely to develop. Therefore other mechanisms must be developed to enforce the co-ordinated optima. The most common mechanism is the use of hierarchical authority. Because authority figures control organizational resources and also exercise control over the wel-

FIGURE 2.
DEPARTMENTAL GAINS IN PROFIT AS A FUNCTION OF OUTPUT LEVELS

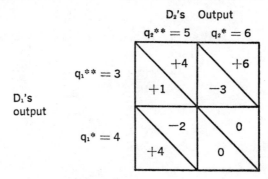

fare of individuals (e.g., promotion, salary level, etc.), they are able to extract departmental compliance with co-ordinated decisions.

Another mechanism that is less likely to require the exercise of personal influence by an authority figure is the adjustment of prices facing each department. For example, the organization could impose an overhead charge to each department—in effect reducing its market price. If D_1 is charged e_2 dollars of overhead for each unit produced, then D_1's effective market price is $p_1 - e_2$. At this price, its unco-ordinated optimum output level is $q_1^* = \dfrac{p_1 - e_2}{2c_1}$, exactly the output level desired under the jointly set output levels!

The difference between these mechanisms of co-ordination and voluntary co-operation between the departments is a subtle, but important, one. Problems of biased communication still exist, of course, but because of the authority figure's control over promotion, etc., welching is much less likely.[7] More important, if artificial pricing mechanisms are

7. Lowe and Shaw (1968) have recently completed an empirical study of the sources of bias in forecasting sales in a large chain of retail outlets. They concluded, as we have, that biases result from the rational self-interest of managers. Specifically, they found that the reward system tends to bias estimates downward (because estimates were used to set sales quotas) and that insecurity of managers and recent company practices and norms tend to bias estimates upward (because estimates were used to make resource-allocation decisions and because in part they reflected managers' perceptions of their superiors' aspirations). Their study, of course, deals with biased exchange of information between superiors and subordinates, whereas our analysis has dealt

used and if the department accepts the modified price, then self-interest mechanisms will lead the department to maintain output at the appropriate level. Bargaining between departments over a division of the gains from co-operation is replaced by bargaining between the authority figure and each department over the effective price. But once D_1 in effect agrees to contribute e_2 dollars to overhead for every unit produced, then his self-interest will cause him to produce q_1** units, and he will not be motivated to deviate from this level. Thus, one of the important implications of self-interested subunit behavior is the emergence of hierarchical control of co-ordination.

We can now summarize the main elements of our analysis of co-ordination: (1) Each department is rational and self-interested. It will agree to participate in joint activities if, and only if, it believes such participation will help to achieve its goals in a more efficient manner. (2) The existence of externalities is a necessary, but not sufficient, condition for co-ordination to take place. (3) If the total potential gains from co-ordination exceed the cost of co-ordination, co-ordination may be agreed to, provided the problem of dividing the gains from co-ordination between the departments is resolved. (4) If co-ordination is on a voluntary basis (exchange of information on externalities, agreement to abide by joint-decision rule), each department is motivated both to overestimate the extent of its externalities and to welch on its output agreement. (5) Co-ordination through hierarchical authority will tend to reduce estimation bias and noncompliance with intentions, primarily because of the authority figure's control over the careers of departmental officials and over other resources required by the departments.

Effects of Ownership-Management Separation

One of the most important recent developments, one related very directly to the political-economy approach to organization behavior

---

primarily with biased exchange between peers. Nevertheless, self-interest as the source of bias remains the essential feature of both situations. The use of deliberate biasing is but one of a whole range of strategies and tactics used by subunits to increase their shares of organization resources. See Pondy (1964) and Wildavsky (1964) for more general discussions of these strategies in industry and government, respectively.

(Zald, 1969), concerns the effect of differing patterns of ownership and control on internal resource-allocation. Although interest in the effects of ownership-management separation began as early as Berle and Means's (1932) classic study of the modern corporation, intensive investigation of the phenomenon has been under way only since the early 1960s. More or less independent treatments of a "managerial" theory of the firm were developed by Marris (1963, 1964), Williamson (1964), and Monsen and Downs (1965).

The basic argument is as follows: Owners (i.e., stockholders) view the firm as a wealth-maximizing institution and therefore have as a goal for the firm the maximization of profits, since this most nearly advances their personal self-interests. As long as the owners are also the key managers or decision-makers, therefore, it is reasonable to assume that the firm will allocate its resources so as to maximize its profits. That is, any particular resource will be used up to that point where its marginal revenue equals its marginal cost. However, with the advent of the modern corporation, the management of the firm was no longer predominantly made up of the owners of the firm, and it was no longer true that profit-maximization was coincident with the personal self-interests of the key decision-makers. On the contrary, professional, nonowner managers, so long as they earn a "satisfactory" profit, are likely to allocate discretionary resources in ways that advance their own personal income, power, prestige, security, and convenience, rather than in ways that increase profitability above the satisfactory level. Thus, other things being equal, we would expect manager-controlled firms to be less profitable than owner-controlled firms. In a recent study of 72 large firms (from Fortune's 500), Monsen, Chiu, and Cooley (1968) demonstrated precisely that.

It is important to specify more precisely what we mean by "control." It is not necessary that the owners be a part of active management for them to exercise effective control over allocation of the firm's resources. If ownership of voting stock is concentrated in the hands of a few stockholders, it is relatively easy and inexpensive for them to remove ineffectual management or to threaten such removal, and thereby exercise control-at-a-distance over management decisions. However, if stock-ownership is dispersed among a large number of stockholders, they become what Olson (1965) has called a latent group, and the exercise of control becomes too costly for any one stockholder relative to the benefits to be derived from increased profitability. It is this latter case that results in *management* control of the firm.

More explicitly than the rest, Williamson (1964) has attempted to specify the nature of the managerial utility function. He hypothesizes that the management goals include not only profitability, but also certain "expense-preferences," that is, preferences per se for certain factor inputs to the production function of the firm. He particularly identifies a preference for "hierarchical expense" or administrative staff, since this is likely to contribute to management power and security. We would thus expect that as owner-control of the firm becomes weaker, the relative size of the administrative staff (i.e., resources devoted to administration) would grow larger. In a recent study of 45 industries, Pondy (1969) did in fact find that administrative intensity increased with the separation of ownership and mangement.

These basic ideas can also be extended to nonprofit organizations. For example, private universities and hospitals are roughly analogous to manager-controlled firms, in that they are relatively free from external control and tend to have self-perpetuating boards of trustees. On the other hand, public universities and hospitals are like owner-controlled firms in that they are subject to external control by boards of trustees typically appointed by state or local government legislative bodies. In a study of universities and hospitals (Pondy, *et al.,* 1969), it was in fact found that, other things equal, administrative intensity is higher in private institutions.

To conclude this section, we should stress that the hypothesized effects of management control on internal resource-allocation depend on two assumptions: (a) The personal goals of nonowner managers differ from the goals of owners or other external control agents; and (b) the inability of owners to enforce their goals on management is due to the high costs of information-processing (e.g., detecting deviations from profit-maximizing behavior) and decision-making. Were the cost of informational activities zero, no enforcement problems would exist, and the separation of ownership and management would have no influence on internal resource-allocation.

SOME PUBLIC POLICY IMPLICATIONS

We argued at the outset that processes of internal resource-allocation become relevant only when an organization is operating in imperfect markets or when markets (usually output markets) are absent altogether. Only under these conditions is the organization able to generate discretionary resources, the allocation of which is affected by internal structure, goals, and processes. Not only does the absence of output markets deprive the organizational decision-makers of external criteria against which to judge alternative uses of resources; it also deprives the clients of the organization of a means of social control over the organization's activities. As we have attempted to show, these dual problems are exacerbated by the high cost of information-processing. If the acquisition, transmission, and assimilation of information are too costly, the external and internal enforcement of efficiency ceases to be a feasible activity. These considerations suggest the following important public policy recommendations: (1) Wherever possible, the creation of nonmarket organizations should be accompanied by the creation of suitable social-control mechanisms. (2) Nonmarket organizations and organizations operating in imperfect markets should be required to make full disclosure of information to relevant publics. Disclosure of financial information by business firms to the investing public is an established tradition (although controversy still persists, as in the recent problems concerning use of information by "insiders"), but disclosure of information to the consuming public (e.g., truth in lending and truth in packaging legislation) is only in the early stages of development.

An illustrative comment about the need for social-control mechanisms appropriate to nonmarket organizations is in order. Governor Nelson Rockefeller recently advocated the creation of some form of national health insurance "as the first line of defense" against soaring costs of health care. Implementation of his program would in fact accomplish just the opposite. Insuring against health expenses merely fragments the output market into direct sources of revenue (the insuring agency) and recipients of health services, who bear no marginal costs in the short run. Thus, the nonmarket character of the health industry is further accentuated. And under these conditions, hospitals and other health-related institutions have little incentive to allocate their resources efficiently. An alternative means of solving the insurance problem, while at the same time providing for some means of social control, is the creation of prepaid health care plans tied to specific group-practice clinics, provided that subscribers are represented on the board of governors of each such plan. The characteristics of such consumer-sponsored health care plans has recently been studied by Schwartz (1968).

With regard to the full-disclosure recommendation, we urge especially that it be applied to charities (Tullock, 1966b), universities, hospitals, and other nonbusiness organizations, as well as to business firms. Only with such full disclosure, can the clients of these organizations make intelligent decisions regarding utilization of organizational services. And intelligent consumer decisions constitute a necessary, if not sufficient, condition for efficient allocation of resources within organizations.

One final comment is in order regarding the implications of internal goal diversity for social efficiency. Our analysis has suggested that goal conflict among members creates problems for the organization, and thus organizations seek to develop a consensus on goals. To the extent that this minimizes the impact of purely *personal* interests, it is probably socially efficient as well as organizationally efficient by, for example, reducing the effects of bias and the costs of bargaining and internal enforcement. However, permitting diversity on organizational goals of a nonpersonal nature may be one way of internalizing social-control mechanisms. That is, organization members whose goals conflict may serve as advocates of interests external to the organization. Thus, policies which encourage or induce internal goal diversity may enhance the social efficiency of internal resource-allocation procedures. Like many of the propositions in this paper, this one, to our knowledge, is empirically untested.

REFERENCES

Arrow, Kenneth J.
　1963　Social Choice and Individual Values. New York: Wiley.
　1964　"Control in Large Organizations." Management Science 10: 397–408.
Barnard, Chester I.
　1938　The Functions of the Executive. Cambridge, Mass.: Harvard University Press.

Baumol, William J.
1959   Business Behavior, Value and Growth. New York: Macmillan.
Baumol, William J., and Tibor Fabian.
1964   "Decomposition, Pricing for Decentralizatin and External Economies." Management Science 11:1–32.
Berle, A. A. Jr., and G. C. Means.
1932   The Modern Corporation and Private Property. New York: Macmillan.
Birnberg, Jacob G., and Louis R. Pondy.
1968   "An Experimental Study of Voting Rules." To be published in the proceedings of the Social Choice Conference, University of Pittsburgh, September 9–12, 1968.
Blau, Peter M., and W. Richard Scott.
1962   Formal Organizations. San Francisco: Chandler.
Boulding, Kenneth E.
1963   The Organizational Revolution. New York: Harper.
Bower, Joseph L.
1965a   "The Role of Conflict in Economic Decision Making Groups." Quarterly Journal of Economics 70:253–277.
1965b   "Group Decision Making: A Report of an Experimental Study." Behavioral Science 10:277–289.
Buchanan, James M., and Gordon Tullock.
1962   The Calculus of Consent. Ann Arbor: The University of Michigan Press.
Chandler, Alfred D.
1962   Strategy and Structure: Chapters in the History of Industrial Enterprise. Cambridge, Mass.; M.I.T. Press.
Cohen, Kalman J., and Richard M. Cyert.
1965   Theory of the Firm: Resource Allocation in a Market Economy. Englewood Cliffs, N.J.: Prentice-Hall.
Coleman, James S.
1966a   "Foundations of a Theory of Collective Decisions." American Journal of Sociology 71:615–627.
1966b   "Individual Interests and Collection Action." Pp. 49–62 in Gordon Tullock (ed.), Papers on Non-Market Decision Making. Charlottesville, Va.: Thomas Jefferson Center for Political Economy.
Cyert, Richard M., and James G. March.
1963   A Behavioral Theory of the Firm. Englewood-Cliffs, N.J.: Prentice-Hall.
Davis, O. A., M. A. H. Dempster, and Aaron Wildavsky.
1966   "On the Process of Budgeting: An Empirical Study of Congressional Appropriations." Pp. 63–132 in Gordon Tullock (ed.), Papers on Non-Market Decision Making. Charlottesville, Va.: Thomas Jefferson Center for Political Economy.

Downs, Anthony.
  1967   Inside Bureaucracy. Boston: Little, Brown.
Feldman, Julian, and Herschel E. Kanter.
  1965   "Organizational Decision Making." In James G. March, Hand-
          book of Organizations:614–649. Chicago: Rand-McNally.
Gibbs, Jack P., and Harley L. Browning.
  1966   "The Division of Labor, Technology, and the Organization of
          Production in Twelve Countries." American Sociological Re-
          view 31:81–92.
Haas, Jerome E.
  1968   "Transfer Pricing in a Decentralized Firm." Management Sci-
          ence 14:310–331.
Lasswell, Harold D.
  1936   Politics: Who Gets What, When, How. New York: McGraw-
          Hill.
Levy, Ferdinand K.
  1968   "Economic Analysis of the Non-profit Institution—The Case of
          the Private University." Public Choice 4:3–18.
Lieberman, Bernhardt.
  1965   "Combining Individual Preferences into a Social Choice." Re-
          search Memo SP-111.2, University of Pittsburgh, Department
          of Sociology.
Lowe, E. A., and R. W. Shaw.
  1968   "An Analysis of Managerial Biasing: Evidence from a Com-
          pany's Budgeting Process." Journal of Management Studies
          5:304–315.
March, James G., and Herbert A. Simon.
  1958   Organizations. New York: Wiley.
Marriss, Robin.
  1963   "A Model of the 'Managerial' Enterprise." Quarterly Journal of
          Economics 77:185–209.
  1964   The Economic Theory of Managerial Capitalism. New York:
          Free Press of Glencoe.
Marschak, Jacob.
  1959   "Efficient and Viable Organizational Forms." Pp. 307–320 in
          Mason Haire (ed.), Modern Organization Theory. New York:
          Wiley.
Marschak, Thomas A.
  1965   "Economic Theories of Organization." Pp. 423–450 in James G.
          March (ed.), Handbook of Organizations. Chicago: Rand
          McNally.
Monsen, R. Joseph, and Anthony Downs.
  1965   "A Theory of Large Managerial Firms." Journal of Political
          Economy 73:221–236.

Monsen, R. J., J. S. Chiu, and D. E. Cooley.
1968   "The Effect of Separation of Ownership and Control on the Performance of the Large Firm." Quarterly Journal of Economics 82:435–451.

Olson, Mancur.
1965   The Logic of Collective Action. Cambridge, Mass.: Harvard University Press.

Perrow, Charles.
1967   "A Framework for the Comparative Analysis of Organizations." American Sociological Review 32:194–208.

Plott, Charles R.
1967   "A Method for Finding 'Acceptable Proposals' in Group Decision Processes." In Gordon Tullock (ed.), Papers on Non-Market Decision Making, 2:45–60. Charlottesville, Va.: Thomas Jefferson Center for Political Economy.

Pondy, Louis R.
1964   "Budgeting and intergroup conflict in organizations." Pittsburgh Business Review 34:1–3.
1969   "The Effects of Size, Complexity, Ownership, and Certain Economic Variables on Administrative Intensity." Administrative Science Quarterly, forthcoming.

Pondy, Louis R., and Jacob G. Birnberg.
1969   "An Experimental Study of the Allocation of Financial Resources within Small Hierarchical Task Groups." Administrative Science Quarterly, forthcoming.

Pondy, L., T. Arroyo, W. Fitzsimmons, B. Lutsk, and D. Tutt.
1969   "Administrative Intensity in Universities and Hospitals." Paper presented at the annual meetings of the Southern Sociological Society, New Orleans, La., April 10–12, 1969.

Presthus, Robert.
1962   The Organizational Society. New York: Knopf.

Ramstrom, Dick.
1967   The Efficiency of Control Strategies: Communication and Decision-Making in Organizations. Stockholm: Almqvist & Wiksell.

Schwartz, Jerome L.
1968   Medical Plans and Health Care. Springfield, Illinois: Charles C Thomas.

Simon, Herbert A.
1945   Administrative Behavior. New York: Macmillan.

Thibaut, John W., and Harold H. Kelley.
1959   The Social Psychology of Groups. New York: Wiley.

Thompson, James D.
1967   Organizations in Action. New York: McGraw-Hill.

Tullock, Gordon
    1965   The Politics of Bureaucracy. Washington: Public Affairs Press.
    1966b   "Information Without Profit." Pp. 141–159 in Gordon Tullock
            (ed.), Papers on Non-Market Decision Making. Charlottesville,
            Va.: Thomas Jefferson Center for Political Economy.

Tullock, Gordon (ed.).
    1966a ⎫
    1967a ⎬ Papers on Non-Market Decision Making, I, II, and III. Char-
    1967b ⎭ lottesville, Va.: Thomas Jefferson Center for Political Economy.
    1968   Public Choice. Charlottesville, Va.: Thomas Jefferson Center
            for Political Economy.

Wheeler, Harvey J.
    1967   "Alternative Voting Rules and Local Expenditure." In Gordon
            Tullock (ed.), Papers on Non-Market Decision Making, 2:61–
            70. Charlottesville, Va.: Thomas Jefferson Center for Political
            Economy.

Wildavsky, Aaron.
    1964   The Politics of the Budgetary Process. Boston: Little, Brown.

Williamson, Oliver E.
    1964   The Economics of Discretionary Behavior: Managerial Objec-
            tives in a Theory of the Firm. New York: Prentice-Hall.
    1967a   "Hierarchical Control and Optimum Firm Size." Journal of
            Political Economy 75:123–138.
    1967b   "A Rational Theory of the Federal Budgeting Process." In
            Gordon Tullock (ed.), Papers on Non-Market Decision Making,
            2:71–89. Charlottesville, Va.: Thomas Jefferson Center for
            Political Economy.

Zald, Mayer N.
    1970   The Political Economy of the YMCA: Structure and Change.
            Forthcoming.

Nonmarket Organizations
and Organizational Co-ordination

WILLIAM H. STARBUCK

Louis Pondy thinks clearly and writes well, and in this instance he has produced an intelligible and insightful summary of the theory of nonmarket resource-allocation. He emphasizes the important points, and on the whole I agree with what he says. However, a few questions should be raised about particular statements in his paper. It would be unprecedented if one academician were to read the work of another and to find no grounds for debate.

The Separation of Revenue Sources from Output Markets

In introducing the idea of a nonmarket organization, Pondy says the "separation of revenue sources from output markets has two tremendously important implications. . . . It deprives the organization of a direct way of evaluating its output activities relative to the costs of the inputs used to produce them. . . . [and] If the organization is assumed to maximize its discretionary resources, a certain proportion of its current resources will be devoted to promotional activities designed to increase the flow of nonmarket resources." I disagree with both conclusions.

Evaluation of output activities is not contingent upon the existence of a price-setting output market. Rather, a price-setting market is a special case which simplifies evaluations for those organizations which accept its judgments. Should the market be purely competitive—involving infinite numbers of infinitesimally small buyers and sellers—and should the market react instantaneously to changes in supply or demand, sellers should accept the market's evaluations of their outputs, because prices will stabilize at the outputs' marginal contributions to social welfare. But very few real markets even approximate pure competition, and most organizations operating in price-setting markets lack persuasive rationales for accepting market prices as output evaluations. For example, electric power companies derive their revenues from output markets, but whether the price of electricity equals the value of electricity is moot. At a minimum, the power companies should debate the equivalence of price and value, and that debate implies a nonmarket standard for value.

The need to evaluate outputs is an implication, not of the separation of revenue sources from output markets, but of the nonexistence of pure competition. The need is shared by nearly all organizations, both those in price-setting markets and those whose revenues are (partially) independent of their outputs. The former are likely to take prices as starting points for their evaluations, and the latter are likely to start from unit costs, but cost-plus pricing is so prevalent that the differences between the two starting points are not obvious. Both types of organizations have the option of establishing evaluation subunits which measure the preferences of individual consumers for their outputs, and then aggregate these preferences across all consumers.

It is in this aggregation of individual consumers that evaluations by market and nonmarket organizations tend to differ. In a market, a buyer who spends twice as much as another buyer exercises twice as much influence in the evaluations of the traded outputs. The preferences of individuals are aggregated according to the rule "one dollar equals one vote," and the preferences of wealthy consumers are weighted much more heavily than the preferences of poor consumers. The economic rationale for accepting this aggregation rule is based on the assumption that wages and interest rates are set by instantaneously equilibrating, purely competitive markets: an individual's income is proportional to his marginal contribution to social welfare, and those who contribute more resources are awarded more say about the distribution of resources.

Casual observation suggests that business organizations—especially the very large ones which control the bulk of resources—accept the dollar-aggregation rule unquestioningly. They rarely ask whether their output markets are sufficiently competitive to make dollar-aggregation socially efficient, and they rarely ask whether their customers' wealths have been determined through pure competition. Their accounting information systems assume the desirability of dollar-aggregation and practically bar the adoption of an alternative rule. They behave as if problems of output valuation have unique answers, and they ordinarily resolve disagreements about the values of outputs by references to higher authority within the organization. Market organizations which attempt to follow an alternative rule do so with difficulty, as witness the case of medical care organizations.

Nonmarket organizations, on the other hand, rarely have rationales for following the dollar-aggregation rule, and they are more successful than market organizations at not following it. Some nonmarket organizations—like most governmental units and voluntary associations—attempt to implement the "one man, one vote" rule. Other nonmarket organizations—like judicial systems and most universities and endowed foundations—attempt to serve principles which are independent of consumer preferences. It is obvious that both types of organizations have difficulties in adhering to principle—they are more sensitive to wealth than their charters say they should be. But they recognize wealth-determined influence as a deviation from principle; they often change policies or punish members that show favoritism toward wealthy clients; they place minimal reliance on their accounting systems, and the accounting systems they do use incorporate a high proportion of non-financial data. Most nonmarket organizations behave as if problems of output valuation do not have unique answers: they tolerate disagreements among members about the values of outputs, and they often resolve such disagreements by negotiation and compromise.

In short, a nonmarket organization will generally value its outputs differently from a market organization, even though the two organizations produce identical outputs, and serve identical consuming groups. The differences in valuation are not strictly due to the separation of revenue sources from output markets, but the separation facilitates evaluations which deviate from the dollar-aggregation norm and thus preserves the principles on which the nonmarket organization was founded.

Promotional activities are also not contingent upon the separation of revenues from output markets—as is made evident by the extensive promotional activities of business firms. Promotional activities are potentially useful whenever an organization's revenues are subject to influence, i.e., not strictly determined by the price and quality of the output itself. Since nearly all nonmarket organizations can influence their revenues, they should consider undertaking promotional activities. But the same proposition applies to market organizations. If an organization has revenues which cannot be influenced—for example, farmers and the Ford Foundation—promotional activities are not worth their cost.

Market and nonmarket organizations probably differ less in the proportion of resources devoted to promotion than in the forms of promotion undertaken. In markets, consumers are rather weakly organized; the preferences of one consumer are not strongly linked to the preferences of another. Market organizations tend to advertise simultaneously to large numbers of consumers, and their advertising techniques do not rely heavily on communication among consumers. Some nonmarket organizations—like the National Foundation—also derive their revenues from weakly organized collectivities, but it is more common for nonmarket organizations to derive their revenues from strongly organized collectivities. For example, the revenues of the National Aeronautics and Space Agency are almost entirely determined by discussions with and among a few individuals in the executive and legislative branches of the government; once persuaded, these individuals undertake to influence others, and of course, the legislators are authorized to speak for the population at large. NASA undoubtedly derives indirect benefits from broad-scale promotion activities, but the promotion activities focused on influential individuals are more decisive.

Of course, many nonmarket organizations are established by other nonmarket organizations, and they inherit the revenue networks of their parents. But when sources of revenues are not already organized into influence networks, many nonmarket organizations try to establish such networks. For instance, private schools group alumni into graduating classes and address fund requests through the class officers; political parties emphasize geographic and ethnic groupings and solicit funds through subgroup leaders; charities enlist neighborhood and work-place representatives who can relay appeals on a personal basis.

It seems plausible that this is a pattern and that the pattern is a direct consequence of the separation of revenue sources from output markets. Anonymous and impersonal promotional modes evoke an expectation of *quid pro quo*—partly because they are a cultural style which is associated with commercial advertising and partially because they do not challenge the legitimacy of self-interested behavior. But nonmarket organizations do not offer *quid pro quo*. When nonmarket organizations engage in anonymous and impersonal promotions, they evoke expectations which they cannot fulfill. Conversely, personal appeals evoke the expectation of social approval—a commodity for which the contributor has few objective referents. The interpersonal context suppresses self-interest, and many nonmarket organizations have institutionalized mechanisms for actually delivering social approval to large contributors: publicity, testimonial dinners, honorary degrees and titles, introductions to famous people, and committee and board memberships.

Co-ordination Costs

Pondy explains his Figure 1 as follows:

Other things being equal, the cost of co-ordination will increase as the number of subunits being co-ordinated increases. For example, consider an organization comprising 12 subunits, each of which imposes external costs on the others. Co-ordinating all 12 together is more costly than co-ordinating the decisions within two groups of six units each, which in turn is more costly than co-ordination within three groups of four subunits each, etc. When all 12 subunits allocate their resources autonomously, co-ordination costs are zero, but external costs are at a maximum. As the size of the co-ordination unit increases, the co-ordination costs increase (probably at an increasing rate), but the external costs decrease (probably at a decreasing rate) until external costs reduce to zero under full co-ordination, as in Figure 1.

The logic of this paragraph is obscure. The opening phrase "other things being equal" means that only the cost of co-ordination and the number of subunits in a co-ordination unit are allowed to change. The kinds of information exchanged, the decision criteria, and the decision processes are among the other things which are equal. Every subunit will make the same decisions under each arrangement of subunits, and hence, external costs will be the same in all cases.

Moreover, it is far from obvious why "the cost of co-ordination will increase as the number of subunits being co-ordinated increases." Suppose each subunit writes the information needed by each other subunit on a piece of paper. "Co-ordinating all 12 together" amounts to exchanging these pieces of paper—264 sorting and shipping operations. "Co-ordinating the decisions within two groups of six" amounts to routing about half of the papers through two clearinghouses and requires 408 sorting and shipping operations; "co-ordination within three groups of four" requires 648 sorting and shipping operations. Clustering the sub-units does offer the possibility of savings in decision time—fewer itera-tions in the planning process—but the savings can only be realized if the clearinghouses forecast the decisions each subunit will make and then alter the co-ordination information before passing it along. The forecasting cost is likely to be large because the decision processes of the subunits must be duplicated at the clearinghouses, and the savings in decision time are likely to be small unless a sudden, drastic change has occurred in the organization's environment. When the environment is stable, each subunit will be able to forecast the other subunits' de-cisions on the basis of "tomorrow will be like today," and the exchange of co-ordinating information will produce only small adjustments of the initial plans.

The last half of Pondy's paragraph—beginning with the clause "when all 12 subunits allocate their resources autonomously"—really discusses a subject different from the first half. It implicitly drops the *ceteris paribus* assumption and lets decision criteria, information exchanges, and decision quality change as "the size of the co-ordination unit in-creases." The crucial assumption is stated in footnote five: "*no* co-ordi-nation takes place *between* co-ordination units."

However, Pondy's logic is still not adequate to convince me that co-ordination costs increase with the size of the co-ordination unit. If sub-units do not exchange co-ordinating information, they must forecast each other's behavior,[1] and the cost of forecasting should be at least equal to the cost of information exchange. As the size of the co-ordination unit increases, the cost of information might increase slightly, but the cost of forecasting should decrease, and the total cost of co-ordination should decrease.

The really effective constraints on centralization are technological and

---

1. Forecasting has no value to the two departments described in Pondy's hypothetical example (his equations 1 to 15). The reason is that the externalities are not interactive—the external cost borne by D_1 as a result of D_2's behavior is independent of D_1's own behavior, and hence D_1's optimum output in the absence of pooled profits is independent of D_2's output. The example would be more realistic, I think, if D_1's cost function had the form

$$C_1 = c_{1q_1}2 + e_1q_1q_2.$$

Then $q_1{}^* = (p_1 - e_1q_2) / 2c_1$, and D_1 would have to forecast q_2 in order to determine $q_1{}^*$.

motivational. Much of the information on which decisions are based is not available for communication. It is acquired through experience and stored in inexplicit form in the minds of decision-makers; it cannot be articulated and transmitted to other people even when its possessor is willing to transmit it. Moreover, most decision-makers derive pleasure from autonomous control of their circumstances, and they value the performance of their subunits more than the performance of the whole organization.[2] They resist centralized injunctions which will reduce their autonomy or which will lower the performance of their subunits. Both of the above phenomena place lower bounds on the achievable level of external costs. To the extent that co-ordination of a larger number of subunits diminishes the importance of each subunit, adds more constraints on the autonomy of each subunit, and demands more precise and detailed information from each subunit, the lower bounds on external costs will increase with the size of the co-ordination unit. Thus, the technological and motivational constraints convert external costs into a U-shaped function of the size of the co-ordination unit.

Of course, the above reasoning abrogates Pondy's proposition about centralization. The total costs would start to increase when the increase in external costs due to adding one more subunit to the co-ordination unit begins to exceed the decrease in co-ordination costs due to adding one more subunit. However, Pondy's proposition is misleading even if one rejects my logic and accepts his. First, the external and information processing costs referred to in the proposition are not the external and information processing costs graphed in Figure 1. Figure 1 shows the aggregate costs for all subunits; one could add a constant amount to the external cost curve or subtract a constant amount from the information processing cost curve, and the optimum size of the co-ordination unit would be unaffected. The optimum co-ordination unit is determined by the *slopes* of the curves in Figure 1—the *changes* in external and information processing costs due to adding one subunit to the co-ordination unit. Since these changes can be attributed to the subunit which is added, they can be thought of as costs per subunit, and Pondy's proposition apparently refers to the external and information processing

2. This statement obviously violates Pondy's assumption that there is goal consensus. It seems that information processing costs alone are inadequate to explain centralization and decentralization problems.

costs per subunit. Second, the proposition is phrased in a way which leads one to think of the subunits as a homogeneous group. If the subunits were all alike, the optimum organization would be either totally centralized or totally decentralized, and there is a question of optimum centralization only because the subunits differ from one another. In particular, consider the case where all but one of the subunits are centralized and one subunit is autonomous. One could raise the externalities or lower the information processing costs *among the already-centralized subunits* without making further centralization desirable. One could also lower the externalities or raise the information processing costs *between the autonomous subunit and the centralized ones* without making further decentralization desirable.

Control Losses and Collective Action

Pondy attempts to discuss centralization-decentralization, control losses, and collective action within the constraint of assumed goal consensus. The constraint is too strong. His discussion of co-ordination would be more convincing if it recognized that divergent subunit goals induce resistance to centralization. His discussion of information bias lacks motivation—for example, he says compliance is the proportion of a subordinate's activities which contributes to his immediate superior's objectives. Under goal consensus, the subordinate and superior have consistent objectives, and it is difficult to see why acts which contribute to one's own goals should be called compliant, or why one devotes effort to noncompliant acts. In his discussion of collective action, Pondy talks about individual differences in the benefits from, and attitudes toward, group action.

There are two points where Pondy's language bewilders me. He says, "One subtle, but essential, idea of Olson's is that even *perfect consensus by itself is insufficient* to guarantee collective action if the group is so large that at least one person by himself is not motivated to provide the entire collective good." Surely Olson did not mean this; it says collective action is impossible for a group of one hundred even when ninety-nine of them are all willing to provide the entire collective good by themselves. Possibly Pondy's statement should read "if the group is so large that no one person by himself is motivated to provide the entire collective good," but even this version excludes the possibility of co-operation by subgroups. Suppose there are two group members each of whom is willing to provide more than half of the collective good; are they forbidden to act co-operatively?

Pondy also says, "Only if we assume that each individual 'identifies' psychologically with the group—invests himself psychically in the collective welfare—is group or joint action likely to spring forth." Why must the interest in collective welfare be unanimous? Is it not sufficient that some (enough) individuals dedicate themselves to the collective welfare?

Of course, both of these points would be explained if Pondy interprets goal consensus as goal identity. Then "at least one person by himself is not motivated to provide the entire collective good" would be equivalent to "every person by himself is not motivated to provide the collective good," and "each individual identifies psychologically with the group" would be the only alternative to "no individual 'identifies' psychologically with the group." If this is what Pondy means, his statements would be unquestionable, but the case he discusses would be so unrealistic as to be irrelevant.

Co-ordination Among Subunits [3]

Pondy's discussion of co-ordination would be stronger if he had distinguished between short-run and long-run phenomena. For example, he says a department "will agree to participate in joint activities if and only if it believes such participation will help to achieve its goals in a more efficient manner." "Believes" is both too ambiguous and too conclusive. In the short run, a department may participate as an experiment

---

3. I have only one minor comment concerning Pondy's section on goal diversity. I would not describe Arrow's assumptions as "conditions of reasonableness." Arrow did not attempt to show that his assumptions conformed to the empirical evidence about human behavior. For example, there is no evidence that human preferences are independent of irrelevant alternatives, and there is substantial evidence that they are not. Arrow also made no use of the similarity of preferences across individuals—socialization. If all individuals have identical preferences, construction of a joint preference-ordering is trivial. Of course in a large, loosely organized society, there is likely to be enough diversity in preferences to make Arrow's theorem relevant; but in problem-solving groups and organizations which have stable memberships over long time periods, individual preferences shift toward mutual consistency. Organization theory needs a theorem which is more conditional and less conclusive than Arrow's.

—thinking that there is a probability of benefit but being prepared for the alternative. In the long run, the department can extrapolate past experience. Similarly, Pondy says "co-ordination may be agreed to, provided the problem of dividing the gains from co-ordination between the departments is resolved." Obviously, each department must believe that the distributive problem can be solved, and in Harnett's laboratory studies of monopolist-monopsonist markets, the subjects negotiated the distribution of joint rewards before negotiating the total amount of joint rewards. However, Walton and McKersie have observed that in field settings integrative bargaining to determine the total joint rewards often precedes distributive bargaining, and personal experience suggests that in situations where the joint rewards are nonmonetary and not easily divisible, it is usually necessary to determine what rewards will be available for division before attempting to divide them. Such problems of sequence are primarily short-run problems; in the long run in a stable situation, past experiences act as patterns.

Pondy's comments about the prisoner's dilemma properties of co-operation also stress short-run phenomena. Rapoport's experiments suggest that co-operation-co-operation is a highly stable equilibrium for prisoner's dilemma games in the long run, and they also suggest that co-operation can be elicited by the strategy "tit-for-tat-plus-one." One implication is that hierarchical control of co-ordination is primarily useful for initially establishing co-operative patterns of behavior and is not necessary for maintaining co-operation. Another implication is that too much hierarchical emphasis on co-operation may interfere with the behaviors which produce mutual co-operation spontaneously.

So far as I know, Pondy is the first person to observe that organizational co-operation poses a prisoner's dilemma problem. The observation is plausible, applicable to organizations generally, and suggestive of hypotheses for empirical test. New and fruitful ideas are not often published, and this one alone justifies a reading of Pondy's paper.

On Contrasts Between Private Firms and Governmental Bureaus

BENJAMIN WALTER

To help make my remarks brief, I'll cheerfully forego any comprehensive critique of Pondy's genuinely imaginative and intellectually compelling paper. What I'd like to do is to make some quick comments on some of the separate points that Pondy raises in his paper.

On the "Social Efficiency" of Political Mechanisms. Rather early in his paper, Pondy gently chides political scientists for scanting any assessment of the "social efficiency of *political* mechanisms for resource-allocation." (The emphasis is Pondy's, not mine.) The accusation is imprecise. Since Aristotle, political scientists have recognized that both polity and market allocate income, power, and prestige. In recent years, many American political scientists have been excoriating the American political system for withholding goods, services, and dignity from certain segments of the population. Though I think the critics' passionate indignation often outruns ascertained fact and mangles logic, I mention them solely to show that our guild has not been completely allergic to handling problems of resource-allocation.

Nonetheless, it is still true that most political scientists feel vaguely uneasy when people begin to talk about "social efficiency." The queasiness does not arise solely because we have all become pious positivists. The main reason is that it is very hard for political scientists to agree on any yardstick for making comparisons about the "social efficiency" (or "justice," if you prefer the more ancient expression) of political mechanisms. The notion of a Pareto optimality is superficially attractive, but we have yet to formulate it in a way that can be easily used to evaluate the tangle of policy alternatives we confront in the real world. Proponents of a Pareto optimum urge us to seek political choices that leave at least one person better off than he was before, without harming anybody else. The trouble is that politics is an endless game of beggaring Peter to pay Paul. Paul may be happier, but Peter grumbles. If we provide services to one group in society, we finance it with resources commandeered from another. Those who receive the services *may* say they are better off; those who bear the costs will certainly say they are worse off. We can tell the malcontents they are being antisocial, but somehow our sermons fail to convince them. In defining optima, economists have an easier time of it than political scientists. If third-party or spillover costs are zero, economists are on firm ground in asserting that any uncoerced trade leaves all the buyers and sellers better off than they were before. In politics, alas, very few choices are voted into public policy by unanimous vote. So long as there is only one dissenter, no policy choice can attain a Pareto optimum.

While I am at it, I disagree with Pondy's contention that national defense is an example of a *pure* public or collective good. It is not indivisible; some benefit more than others. People employed in the missile industry benefit more than the people who produce bayonets. For militant pacifists, national defense is not a merit want at all. Even if the production of national defense consumed no scarce resources at all—a sheer absurdity—it would still be socially harmful, as seen from the ethical perspectives of a pacifist. For one thing, it encourages the formation of a militaristic culture and causes people to become jingoistic and bellicose, which makes pacifists unhappy. And, of course, in the real world, producing guns and battleships consumes resources that could have been used in building homes and hospitals.

Contrasts between Private Firms and Governmental Bureaus. I was mystified by Pondy's attempts to deal with private firms and governmental bureaus simultaneously. There are important differences between them that I feel have been ignored in Pondy's discussion, which is altogether too cryptic.

Take a brief look at the methods used by business firms to seize the inputs it transforms into the resources they need for operation. Firms sell goods and services to consumers: lipstick to women, bombers to the government, symphonies to the classy. They also sell claims on future income to investors: stock dividends, promises of capital appreciation, and fixed-yield bonds. These two flows of income are used to hire employees, buy real estate, and hire consultants.

On the other hand, governmental bureaus get income from taxpayers and redistribute it to other citizens, either as cash or in kind. The important point is that the people who provide the resources are *not* *necessarily* the same people who enjoy the services.

Several consequences flow from this crucial difference between private firms and governmental bureaus.

Those who provide the resources for a private business firm are substantially indifferent to the way it allocates them. When I buy a car or a book, I do so because I suspect the purchase will benefit me right now. If I take a small plunge on the stock market, I do so because I suspect I will be better off in ten years. In neither case do I care whether the firm hires or fires two more executive vice-presidents; nor do I care whether the firm centralizes or decentralizes its staff activities. On the other hand, the politicians and top-level executives who allocate funds to the administrative departments they supervise have been known to "interfere" in the internal operations of the agencies they fund. I don't want to chew the point to tatters, but the bureau's resource dependency on politicians places it squarely in a network of power relations. The dramatis personae include: the bureau, its clients, the congressmen on the appropriations committee handling the agency's budget, and the professors and publicists who comment on the agency's operations. All these actors become part of the bureau's command and bargaining structure. This is not the case with a private business firm.

Where private firms are concerned, consumers and investors evaluate the firm's output and alter their activities accordingly. If the stock doesn't appreciate as quickly as I want it to, I'll tell my broker to get rid of it and buy something else. If the car breaks down too frequently, I'll sell it and buy something else to enrich my mechanic. However, those who evaluate the outputs of governmental agencies are only *incidentally* consumers and investors. The congressmen who pass on the activities of the Department of Housing and Urban Development may not live in big cities. They certainly do not live in public housing. Recognizing this, governmental bureaus hire people to persuade taxpayers or their agents in the legislature that they are acting in the public interest when they provide the bureau with funds to carry on its activities. Lucky bureaus can get specialists in persuasion to work for them at no cost at all; college professors have been known to break a lance or two in behalf of Model Cities and other programs operated by the Housing and Urban Development Department. Unlucky bureaus have their critics; not many noteworthy college professors or newspaper commentators can find many kind things to say about the Defense Department. Private firms, it is true, pay advertising agencies huge sums of money, but their job is to convince consumers they are acting in their own self-interest when they buy the firms' outputs in the economic marketplace.

Most important, a private business firm is under constant pressure to vary its output to suit the changing preferences of its consumers. (To be sure, advertising is sometimes intended to control consumer preferences, so as to decrease the amount of uncertainty in the firm's external environment.) Since the governmental bureau is funded by the legislature, it can afford to be insensitive to the wants of the people who consume its output so long as it satisfies the legislature that it is doing a good job. A beautiful example is Urban Renewal. Many of the people displaced by urban renewal projects are paying higher rents for inferior accommodations. So long as local councils are satisfied that the central business district is appealing to the eye, the ear, and the nose, they think that urban renewal is doing a good job. That is, I am not at all persuaded by Pondy's asseveration that "market mechanisms have become less efficient resource-allocation devices because of the growing divergence between private and social benefits and costs." Political mechanisms for allocating resources can produce the same unhappy result. It seems to me that we have too long trusted in the "Invisible Left Hand" of government.

In conclusion, what I am telling Pondy is that he doesn't have to become a political scientist in order to deal with the firm's internal resource-allocation problems. In the short run, he can afford to ignore decisions made by consumers and investors. In both the long and short runs, his skills as an economist serve him well in analyzing the internal processes of the business firm. But, to deal with the internal resource-allocation problems of *governmental bureaus,* he is simply going to have to become a political scientist. If that seems a large order, it is; but Pondy is grappling with large problems. As always, the punishment fits the crime.

CONFERENCE SUMMARY

MAYER N. ZALD

One of the trends evident in recent scholarly studies of organizations is the breakdown of disciplinary boundaries. Historically, scholars interested in the management of industrial organization, in public administration, in human relations in industry, in Weber's theory of bureaucracy, wrote and thought with little attention to the work being done in neighboring disciplines. These disciplinary boundaries (and blinders) were, I believe, largely a consequence of the academic origins and institutional locations of these scholars; they were not intrinsic to analytic distinctions about the subject matter.

Several intellectual and institutional trends have led, if not to the collapse of these disciplinary walls, to the emergence of large holes in them. First, the spread of empirical approaches to the study of organizations has led the more traditionally normative disciplines (e.g., business management and public administration) to incorporate behavioral science concepts, analytic approaches, and research methodologies into their approach. Second, disciplines which traditionally focused on part of the subject matter have turned their attention to other aspects which others were already studying. For instance, economists have in the past largely been concerned with the environmental context of firms; some have now turned to their internal structure. Sociologists largely have focused on the internal structure of organizations; some have begun to focus on organizational environments. For economists the theory of the firm has appeared to be increasingly inadequate to explain organizational pricing, production, and growth decisions. For sociologists, the scientism of an earlier era has obstructed their pursuit of important theoretical questions.

The theme of this conference—power in organizations—is central to the study of organizations, no matter what the discipline. Social psychologists largely interested in morale have studied the effects of participation or influence in decision-making upon morale and adjustment. Sociologists have been concerned with power both as a dependent and an independent variable. Students of business organizations have examined causes and consequences of management control vis-à-vis owners and centralization and decentralization as aspects of the distribution of power. Political scientists have examined the influence of external constituencies on policy-making and administration in governmental agencies.

Although the panelists in this conference were largely drawn from sociology, their papers represent a variety of methodological and theoretical approaches. At one time sociologists (except for followers of the human relations approach) rarely studied industrial organizations; here two of the papers were based on intense and deep involvements with manufacturing firms. Perrow's information on the perception of power in manufacturing firms was derived from data drawn from questionnaires administered to management in twelve companies. Goldner's study relied largely on depth interviews and observations of the interrelationships of Industrial Relations managers with other members of management in a large company.

The other two empirically based papers differed both in method and setting. Rue Bucher presented a detailed analysis of the political process and structure of the medical school, which grew out of her concerns with social process in professions. A faculty member of the school, she has studied this one organization for more than five years; thus it is a study par excellence in participant-observation. Peter Blau's comparative study of employment security agencies, relied largely on a statistical analysis to explore problems in the centralization and decentralization of bureaucracies and to expose contradictions or incompatibilities in the components of bureaucracy.

The theoretical papers also differed in scope and method. Harvey and Mills extended the work of Cyert and March, relating problems of organizational adaptation and political structure to organizational problem-solving cycles and processes. Pondy utilized findings from his own experimental studies as well as those of others to illuminate problems of resource-allocation within the firm (a topic largely ignored to this date), synthesizing and extending recent modification of the theory of the firm to include internal structural factors. Zald's theoretical framework was designed for use in comparing and contrasting complex organizations of all major types, whether governmental bureaucracies, social-movement organizations, churches, or businesses. Where Pondy's paper was abstract, precise, and focused on a specific problem—that of resource-allocation, Zald's paper was very general, somewhat diffuse, but aimed at encompassing a wide range of organizations and organizational processes.

Several problems and themes appeared in the conference. Although all of the panelists and commentators saw the study of power as a central topic in the study of organizations, they used a range of definitions and measurements of power and politics. For instance, Perrow essentially dealt with *perceptions* of power and power-deprivation. As Bates noted, however, there are both inclusive and limited definitions of the concept of power. He argued for a very limited one and for a clear distinction between the sources of power and the uses of power.

The problem involved in the interpenetration of role and unit differentiation, functional interdependence, and political life was a central theme of all of the empirical studies and of two of the theoretical papers.

Several of the papers also touched upon another aspect of organizational politics, the interaction of the internal life of organizations with the external environment. Here attention was drawn to the extent and fluctuations of societal support, legitimation, and mechanisms of control. However, unfortunately, the conference perpetuated a historic feature of the sociology of organizations: while the theoretical papers discussed the impact of environments, the empirical papers largely dealt with internal matters.

Finally, and related to the above, the conference touched upon a central problem of modern society, the responsiveness of organization to social change, the mechanisms of controlling organizations, and the achievement of social values.

INDEX